This Wide and Universal Theater

THIS *WIDE* AND UNIVERSAL THEATER

Shakespeare in Performance

Then and Now

DAVID BEVINGTON

The University of Chicago Press   CHICAGO & LONDON

David Bevington is the Phyllis Fay Horton Distinguished Service Professor
Emeritus in the Humanities at the University of Chicago. Among his
many publications are, most recently, *English Renaissance Drama: A Norton
Anthology; Shakespeare: Script, Stage, Screen;* and *How to Read a Shakespeare Play.*

The University of Chicago Press, Chicago 60637
The University of Chicago Press, Ltd., London
© 2007 by The University of Chicago
All rights reserved. Published 2007
Printed in the United States of America

16 15 14 13 12 11 10 09 08 07   1 2 3 4 5

ISBN-13: 978-0-226-04478-1 (cloth)
ISBN-10: 0-226-04478-5 (cloth)

Library of Congress Cataloging-in-Publication Data

Bevington, David M.
　　This wide and universal theater : Shakespeare in performance, then and now /
David Bevington.
　　　　p. cm.
　　Includes index.
　　This study examines how Shakespeare's plays have been transformed for the
stage by the demands of theatrical spaces and staging conventions.
　　ISBN-13: 978:0-226-04478-1 (alk. paper)
　　ISBN-10: 0-226-04478-5 (alk. paper)
　　1. Shakespeare, William, 1564–1616 — Stage history. 2. Shakespeare, William,
1564–1616 — Dramatic production—Methodology. I. Title.
　　PR3091.B485 2007
　　792.9′5—dc22

2006036167

♾ The paper used in this publication meets the minimum requirements of the
American National Standard for Information Sciences — Permanence of Paper for
Printed Library Materials, ANSI Z39.48–1992.

In loving memory of my brother Philip (1933–1980)
and Peggy's and my son Philip (1963–1977)

Contents

Figures

Ex Dono Will Iaggard Typographi. ao 1623

Mr. WILLIAM
SHAKESPEARES
COMEDIES,
HISTORIES, &
TRAGEDIES.

Publifhed according to the True Originall Copies.

Martin Droeshout sculpsit London.

L O N D O N
Printed by Ifaac Iaggard, and Ed. Blount. 1623.

1.1. An engraving of William Shakespeare by Martin Droeshout for the 1623 edition of *Mr. William Shakespeare's Comedies, Histories, and Tragedies.* By permission of the Folger Shakespeare Library.

❧ 1 ❧

Actions That a Man Might Play

AN INTRODUCTION

In what sense was Shakespeare a man of the theater? He wrote plays for the acting company to which he belonged and took part in the performance of many of those plays, and yet to succeeding generations of students and readers his reputation has often been primarily that of a great poet, a profound thinker, and a perceptive observer of the human condition (fig. 1.1). He is taught in schools and colleges by English teachers for some of whom the theater is a strange and unfamiliar place. The Romantic poets all but ignored the theatrical dimensions of his accomplishment. Many admirers today of Shakespeare are only sketchily informed about the theatrical conditions for which he wrote. And, although Shakespeare has made a strong recovery in our own day as a writer to be admired in performance, modern audiences and readers are sometimes ill equipped to appreciate how his plays have been transformed by the lively demands of modern theatrical spaces and staging conventions. We see Shakespeare on film or television, or on an array of modern stages, without an awareness of how the scripts he wrote were originally devised for a very remarkable and enabling kind of theatrical world.

The intent of this book is thus threefold: to provide an account of Shakespeare's theater in all its complexity of physical space, casting capacities, and audience expectations; to place Shakespeare's plays in that original theatrical space as a way of suggesting how an awareness of their theatrical dimensions can illuminate numberless dramatic situations inherent in the dialogue; and to juxtapose those insights with more modern instances in film, television, and theatrical performance in order to appreciate some ways in which changed modes of presentation can arise out of, and contribute to, changed perceptions of the text.

One reason that such a comparative study of presentational modes can make special sense today is that modern Shakespeare in production is excitingly closer to that of Shakespeare's own theater than was the theater world of the eighteenth and nineteenth centuries. Or so, at any rate, we like to think, in our desire to make him one of our own. Granted an element of wish-fulfillment in such a desire, we can identify some concrete ways in which the claim is defensible. Theater buildings of the eighteenth and nineteenth centuries were heavily committed to visual realism framed by the proscenium arch. Audiences sat in increasingly large auditoriums, facing the stage at one end of the hall. As in many large opera houses today, a curtain lifted at the start of the play to reveal a handsomely constructed set that visually announced the locale for the ensuing action. Breaks between scenes required the lowering of the curtain so that a series of illusions of varied locales could then be presented. Eighteenth-century sets were comparatively simple ones mounted on painted panels that could be slid in from the wings to create the effect of an interior room or a sylvan scene; nineteenth-century sets were increasingly verisimilar and expensive, requiring longer intervals between scenes in order to move the scenery, but in either case the intent was to provide the spectators with a scenically plausible imitation of a throne room or a castle exterior or a landscape. William Charles Macready, staging the historical plays of *King John* and *Henry VIII* numerous times between 1823 and 1848, gave scrupulous attention to historical accuracy in costuming and set, erecting interiors onstage with carved Gothic tracery in the windows and monumental thrones on raised daises. Charles Kean, not content with the already lavish spectacle called for in the text, added in 1852, at the Princess's Theatre, a scene of King John's capitulation to the barons' demands at Runymede, in order to give a striking visual display of that important historical event which Shakespeare had somehow managed not to mention. Every one of Kean's expensively built locations was copied from a specific medieval castle or ruin of the twelfth and thirteenth centuries.

The trend toward costly elaboration reached its culmination in the productions of Herbert Beerbohm Tree in the years right around 1900. For his *Twelfth Night* at Her Majesty's Theatre in 1901, he created a garden for the mansion of the Countess Olivia replete with trickling fountains, live grass, pathways, and descending steps (fig. 1.2). Not surprisingly, he simplified the scenic structure of the play so that the action

1.2. Herbert Beerbohm Tree as Malvolio, cross-gartered and in yellow stockings, address-ing Maud Jefferies as the Countess Olivia (incorrectly identified as Viola in original cap-tion), in act 3, scene 4, of Tree's 1901 production of *Twelfth Night* at Her Majesty's Theatre. Olivia's terrace and garden featured real grass, fountains, pathways, and a cascade of descending steps. This realistic Italian garden was so difficult to move that the sequence of scenes had to be extensively rearranged. From the *Illustrated London News*, February 16, 1901.

could remain continuously at Olivia's house for extended stretches of action rather than shuttling back and forth between that location and Orsino's house, as in Shakespeare's script. For his *A Midsummer Night's Dream* at Her Majesty's in 1900, Tree provided a carpet of thyme and wildflowers; in 1911, at the renamed His Majesty's Theatre, live rabbits scampered through an enchanted forest. When he staged *Antony and Cleopatra* in 1906 at His Majesty's, Tree dressed some of his actors in the Egyptian garb of the old pharaohs and staged the meeting of the two title figures at the river of Cydnus, complete with all the exotic effects of barge, oarsmen, Cupid-like attendants, waiting-gentlewomen, and other details that Shakespeare's text presents only verbally through Enobarbus's description. This famous encounter was to be filmed later, in 1963, in Joseph L. Mankiewicz's Cecil B. DeMille-like extravaganza based not on Shakespeare's play but on a Hollywood version of the story, starring Richard Burton and Elizabeth Taylor.

When William Poel started his Elizabethan Stage Society in 1901 with an intent of restoring something closer to original Shakespearean staging, then, he was doing something revolutionary. His undertaking was both a historical restoration and a bold break with tradition. By abandoning expensive verisimilitude in favor of simpler sets nearly de-void of scenic representation, Poel revisited what he perceived as the essential idiom of the Shakespeare script, moving rapidly from scene to scene without a shift in sets, relying on the audience's imagination to create the desired illusory effect. At the same time, by doing so he also aligned himself with a movement toward theatrical self-awareness that was to be further developed in the twentieth century by avant-garde playwrights like Samuel Beckett and by experimental directors like Peter Brook. The stage was now capable of being presentational rather than representational, that is, descriptively and persuasively aware of its own artifices of illusion rather than wedded to a literalist notion of showing what the scene appears to call for in representational terms. What seemed so new in this movement was also perceived as a recapit-ulation of the moving spirit of Shakespeare's theatrical world.

At the heart of this discovery was the revelation of a paradox to which a great deal of modern theater is still committed: namely, that the more the theater eschews a literalist kind of realism, the more it invites the imaginative participation of the audience and thereby fosters a more ac-tive involvement of that audience. The result can be an intensifying of experience that increases rather than decreases a sense of what is "real." The traditional proscenium arch theater, when compared with this experimental model, seems inert, relegated to a self-contained illusion of reality separated from the audience by the "fourth wall" of proscenium arch and curtain.

This is not to argue simplistically that Shakespearean staging of the eighteenth and nineteenth centuries lacked a remarkable grandeur of its own. These were the years of many justly famous actors and actresses, such as David Garrick, Peg Woffington, John Philip Kemble, Charlotte Cushman, Samuel Phelps, Isabel Glyn, Helen Faucit, Henry Irving, Madame Vestris, and Ellen Terry, along with Charles Kean, Macready, Tree, and many others. Elaborate verisimilar spectacle was their idiom and their discovery; they were innovators as much as were their successors in the twentieth century. The history of Shakespearean staging is a history in shifting tastes as a cultural response to shifting cultural values. The large theaters of the nineteenth century brought Shakespeare to life for expanding audiences in an age of a rapidly developing middle class. We must not smile condescendingly at the achievement of that age, or minimize its importance to the development of the Shakespearean theater we know today. The argument of this book is rather that modern Shakespearean theater has found its own reasons for returning to a mode of presentation that, in our eyes at least, seems closer to the spirit of the original. In that spirit, we can hope to gain a valuable perspective on contemporary theatrical practices by juxtaposing them with what we know about original Shakespearean staging.

Was it simply a coincidence that Poel's rediscovery of presentational staging coincided more or less precisely with the invention of film? That new medium certainly had the effect of compounding the paradox of illusion in the presenting of Shakespeare to audiences, for, from the start, film seemed ready-made as a means of substituting pictures for words. Silent Shakespeare, as for example in the ten- to fifteen-minute Vitagraph excerpts filmed in Brooklyn and vicinity in the early 1900s by J. Stuart Blackton and William V. Ranous, found an efficient way to evoke the splendors of Shakespeare's most popular plays by interspersing title cards with action sequences filmed when possible out of doors in order to do what a stage production could not. In *Twelfth Night* (1916), Viola (played by Florence Turner) emerged out of the sea toward the beginning of the film by wading ashore on a Long Island beach. Julius Caesar was assassinated in an outdoor scene that was suspiciously reminiscent of the steps of the Carnegie Public Library. A flying Puck in *A Midsummer Night's Dream* (Vitagraph, 1909) zoomed around out of doors on the wings of camera stuntcraft. By means of cutting and splicing, the ghost of Caesar materialized out of thin air at Philippi in act 5 of *Julius Caesar* (1908). The trompe l'oeil effects were, as we look back on them now, laughably amateur: Bottom the Weaver (played by William Ranous) was outfitted with an ass's head that required the actor to pull on a lanyard every time he wanted the ass's mouth to open. Short as they were, these truncated versions were addicted to showing scenes merely described in Shakespeare, including the crowning of Julius Caesar in the play named for him, and, in *As You Like It* (1912), the banishment of Duke Senior, the deathbed farewell of Sir Rowland to his two sons, and Jaques's famous evocation of the Seven Ages of Man, here shown seriatim in picturesque detail. The new medium was muscularly eager to show how it could visually transcend the limitations of theater and written text.

Amateurish as it was, silent film Shakespeare has nevertheless brought into focus a question that is still subject to intense debate: how are Shakespeare's scripts to be performed for today's audiences who are unfamiliar with the stage language of Shakespeare's original theater? The new Globe Theatre on the south bank of the Thames in London (fig. 1.3) gives us valuable glimpses into the stage vocabulary of a theater that employs essentially no scenery, relies for its lighting on the open sky in afternoon performances, and provides standing room for a sizable percentage of the audience on three sides of a large, rectangular stage with pillars supporting a roof and with a gallery backstage over the stage doors, but even here we realize that the spectacle is only approximating what the original must have been like. All-male casting for plays like *Antony and Cleopatra* and *Twelfth Night* (both staged recently in this fashion at the new Globe Theatre, with Mark Rylance as Cleopatra in 1999 and as the Countess Olivia in 2002–2003) can provide some taste of what it must have been like to have no women onstage, even if we must admit that adult actors in the roles of Viola and Olivia are not boy actors and that modern audiences are not Elizabethan audiences. Quite sensibly, the acting company at the new Globe argues that it should not be consigned to doing all its work in Elizabethan costume, and so an occasional production there is set in the 1920s or some other period. Other Elizabethan festival theaters in Stratford, Ontario; Ashland, Oregon; and other locations provide a varied diet of Elizabethan and more modern costuming, along with thrust staging, use of upper acting areas, and the like, discovering in the process how any such repertory theater must engage in a continual negotiation between modern theatrical sensibilities and the demands of Shakespeare's scripts. Academically researched

1.3. The new Shakespeare Globe Theatre, Bankside, London, near the site of the original Globe Theatre erected in 1599. The new theater opened for performances in 1996. Audiences stand in the "yard" around the raised platform stage or sit in the galleries. Spectators are sometimes seated also in the gallery over the rear stage, above the stage doors. By permission of the Shakespeare Globe Trust. Photo by Donald Cooper.

purism can be deadly, and in any case misses the larger point, which is that Shakespeare's texts need to live today by interacting with modern temperament. This present book is an attempt to see how such an interaction can work by examining the evidence as to how Shakespeare's plays fitted into their original theatrical space, and then how modern directors and producers have sought, through the varied idioms of film, television, and an assortment of modern stages, to reposition those plays in an aural and visual environment that will engage the passionate attention of today's spectators.

The visual capabilities of film and television inevitably alter the expectations we bring to a performance of a Shakespeare play. His scripts constantly call our attention to the limited ability of the Elizabethan stage to show the meeting of Antony and Cleopatra, the sea battle of

Actium between Antony and Octavius Caesar, Henry V's great victory over the French at Agincourt in 1415, and so on. The actors on the Globe stage in 1599 could not "cram within this wooden O / The very casques that did affright the air at Agincourt" (*Henry V,* opening chorus). Armies of thousands could only be hinted at by a pitiful handful of extras, outfitted in standard armor that made no attempt to reproduce the military hardware of 1415. Metonymy, or the use of a name to represent a larger entity of which it is a part, was then and remains today essential to the theatrical language of stage illusion. Synecdoche, a figure of speech by which a part stands for the whole, is similarly vital to the theatrical experience. Nowhere is this phenomenon more apparent than when we compare stage productions with filmed versions in which events that have only been named or described as having occurred offstage are brought before the viewer through the magic of the screen.

A screen will generally tell us where we are in a given play or scene by devices that nonscenic theater must convey through other means. *As You Like It,* for example, appears to begin in the garden belonging to Orlando's mean-spirited older brother, Oliver; we know this by costume and gesture, and because Orlando speaks angrily about the way he has been raised among the livestock of Oliver's house with no opportunities for self-improvement. A filmed version, such as the BBC's 1978 television production directed by Basil Coleman and produced by Cedric Messina, can show us Oliver's house and grounds, complete with livestock. Not only can film provide details that Herbert Beerbohm Tree so painstakingly imported into the theater; it is expected to do so. We learn a good deal about where we are, and who the characters are, before they speak a word. Characters are thus placed by film into a ready-made complete visual environment that is rich in information. Conversely, on the Elizabethan stage in 1598, the actors would tell the spectators who and what and where they were. They did so by what they wore, what they carried in their hands, how they gestured toward each other, and above all by what they said. Shakespeare's text adroitly handles the exposition in act 1 of *As You Like It* by having Orlando explain to the family servant, old Adam, how he has been mistreated by being kept at home in the role of a menial. The Elizabethan audience could learn from the dialogue a great deal about this idealistic young man, justifiably rebellious at his ignominious treatment. Awareness of location would arise entirely from such theatrical signals as these, from the actors themselves, rather than from the theatrical building, which neutrally lent itself to whatever spatial characterization the playwright and actors wished to lay upon it.

What was at first a garden could instantly become, as the occupants of Oliver's house exit and Rosalind enters with Celia in scene 2, a place at the court of Duke Frederick, evidently outdoors and suitable for a wrestling match. This quick alteration was achieved on the Elizabethan stage by the appearance of two boy actors, dressed as young women, lamenting the hard lot of Rosalind's banished father and then encountering a clown (Touchstone) and a courtier (Le Beau) who informed them that a wrestling match was about to take place where they were standing. The stage became that locale. In the BBC television production, on the other hand, we are shown a handsome castle (in fact Glamis Castle in Scotland, famous for its associations with *Macbeth*), surrounded by handsome greenswards, box hedges, and places for leisurely gathering; the castle itself is rich in battlements, towers, and arched doorways. We recognize the visual idiom: it is that of *Masterpiece Theatre,* highly "realistic" in detail, visually engrossing, leaving little to the imagination. Interior scenes call upon the visual vocabulary of Renaissance painters like Veronese or Vermeer.

To discern such crucial differences in how a scene is conveyed to an audience is not to arrive at easy judgments as to what works best. Shakespeare wrote for a presentational stage, and so we need to know more about the ways in which his theatrical environment worked for him, but the conclusion need not be that more recent productions should come as close as they can to replicating the effects called for in his scripts. The sumptuous pageantry of much nineteenth-century staging had its own esthetic rationale, and was avidly appreciated by large audiences. Film is so fortified with its own technical virtuosity that one can scarcely imagine an abandonment of it capabilities. Modern theater, too, has techniques of lighting, rapid shifting of scenic effects, and costuming that can be put to magnificent use. Shakespeare does need to be constantly reinterpreted, in theater, film, and television as in critical discourse. Film and television generally need shortened texts to keep overall length within acceptable limits and to give filming its opportunity to do the things it can do so well. At the same time, we need to acknowledge a tradeoff. Verisimilar effects ask less of the audience's active imagination. Film directs the viewer's eye to what the camera or the director wishes that eye to see, not permitting the freedom of choice given to a spectator beholding a staged production.

Not surprisingly, some of the finest modern versions on screen are those that acknowledge, and even revel in, the limits of one medium as compared with another. Laurence Olivier's *Henry V* (1944) begins in a mockup of the Globe Theatre in 1599–1600 in such a way as to show its glories and its limitations: the dramatic occasion is enlivened by actors who are outfitting themselves in Elizabethan costume in preparation for their performance to an enraptured audience sitting or standing around the stage, while at the same time the opening chorus apologizes for the acting company's inability to show that audience the full story of Henry's victory over the French. Fittingly, then, the camera does what the playwright cannot do, taking us by degrees back in historical time to 1415 and to a stirring battle fought in open fields and forests by multitudes of knights on horseback and archers shooting off flights of arrows. The production thus comments on the capabilities and short-comings of its own hybrid medium, part theater and part film. (See chapter 4 for a fuller analysis of Oliver's and Kenneth Branagh's screen versions of *Henry V*.)

Similarly, *Shakespeare in Love* (1998) stages the death of Romeo and Juliet in a mockup of an Elizabethan theater with backstage close-ups that enable us to see how the illusion of death is fabricated. Juliet (Gwyneth Paltrow) thrusts a sword beneath her arm and slowly pulls from her bosom a red ribbon signifying her heart's blood. One might suppose that the exposed crudity of such a device would destroy the poignancy of the moment by inviting laughter, but the very reverse is true. Members of the standing audience are awed and terrified by the moment; some burst into sobs; a long silence ensues. Juliet is dead, and Romeo (Joseph Fiennes) as well, having swallowed a vial of poison only moments too soon. We know that Romeo is being enacted by the Shakespeare of this film, and that he is no more dead than any actor at the conclusion of a tragedy onstage, but the sense of tragic waste is immense — partly because Shakespeare's brief affair with Viola de Lesseps (playing Juliet) is coming to an unhappy end. The exposure of the the-atrical trompe l'oeil effect, by coopting the audience and demanding its imaginative participation in the creation of illusion, intensifies the pleasure of the theatrical experience by somehow making it more "real." As the theater entrepreneur Philip Henslowe keeps saying in this film, when asked by the anxious Shakespeare how their *Romeo and Juliet* can possibly overcome the handicaps lying in its way, "It's a mystery."

We need to begin, then, with a sense of what Shakespeare's theater was like.

There Lies the Scene

ACTORS AND THEATERS IN LATE
ELIZABETHAN ENGLAND

We do not know exactly when Shakespeare came to London, or with what aim in life. At the age of eighteen, in Stratford-upon-Avon, his hometown, he had married Anne Hathaway, a woman eight years his senior. She gave birth to their first child, Susanna, in May 1583 (baptismal date, May 26), less than six months after the hastily arranged marriage. Two more children, the twins Hamnet and Judith, were baptized on February 2, 1585. Thereafter, William Shakespeare disappears from the record for some seven years. What was he doing between the ages of twenty or twenty-one and twenty-eight? A late seventeenth-century theatrical tradition proposes that he taught school or tutored in an aristocratic household. Another assures us that he was apprenticed to a trade, perhaps his father's of tanner and glover, making and selling leather goods along with wool, grain, malt, and farm produce. A wilder conjecture is that the young man had to get out of town because he had run afoul of stringent laws forbidding poaching. Something prompted him to leave his family in Stratford and try his luck in the metropolis.

I

Some time around 1590, Shakespeare began writing for one or more of the acting companies that were striving to gain a foothold in the London area. James Burbage, a former joiner or furniture maker, had banded together with a few other actors under the patronage of the Earl of Leicester to lease a site in Shoreditch, just outside the walls and to the northeast of the old city of London, where they built a theater in 1576. Other spaces in the London vicinity had been hosts to theatrical activity, such as the Red Lion amphitheater, established in 1567, but Burbage's Theatre was seemingly England's first permanent commercial building for the purpose. Perhaps it was known as the Theatre because for the moment there was no other. Locating this building outside London's jurisdiction meant that the players did not need to worry unduly about governmental restrictions; the London authorities were wary of public performances of plays because of potentially unruly crowds, decadent behavior of various sorts, and plague, but in Middlesex County Burbage and his compatriots could rely on Queen Elizabeth's Privy Council and its willingness to tolerate playacting. Plays had their defenders as well as detractors. Those who liked plays cited classical precedent to argue that plays could offer moral edification through example as well as wholesome entertainment for the Queen's subjects and indeed for herself.

Shakespeare arrived in London at a good time. Burbage's company soon encountered vigorous competition, for Londoners seemed generally enthusiastic about the rapidly expanding opportunities for playgoing. A playhouse called the Curtain went up in 1577, close by the Theatre in Shoreditch. England's premier acting company in the 1580s, the Queen's Men, learned to their cost that touring the provinces with a few big plays was no longer the way to succeed as a business; they quickly lost out in the 1590s to new actor groups who performed in fixed theatrical locations in London and who necessarily required a sizable repertory of new plays. Boys' companies, comprised mainly of choristers, became active in the mid 1570s at a hall for Paul's boys and at the first of the Blackfriars halls in 1576, both of these located close to St. Paul's Cathedral in the so-called "liberty" of Blackfriars that was, like the suburbs, largely exempt from the control of the London authorities. ("Liberties" of this sort were originally privileges granted by sovereign power to ecclesiastical institutions exempting them from taxation and other restrictions that would otherwise apply; after the Reformation, the secular owners of such properties continued to enjoy these special rights.)

Rival adult acting companies soon discovered that building south of the Thames River, in Southwark, had advantages like those of Shoreditch, with proximity to the city facilitated by London Bridge and a small army of water taxis. The Rose Theatre, owned and operated by Philip Henslowe, entrepreneur extraordinary and keeper of an invaluable diary (really an account book) in spectacularly untidy spelling, went up in 1587.

Francis Langley built the Swan, to the west of the Rose, in 1595. In 1599 Burbage and his company, the Lord Chamberlain's Men, moved their theater operation from Shoreditch to Southwark, taking the structure with them and renaming it the Globe. In 1600 the Fortune Theatre was erected north of the city outside Cripplegate; financed by Henslowe and his son-in-law, the famous actor Edward Alleyn (fig. 2.1), it thereupon became home for the Admiral's Men. All these theaters and acting companies required new plays. Shakespeare could not have picked a better time to be on the scene.

Inevitably, the formative years of the early 1590s saw rapid shifts in company personnel as they competed for the burgeoning market in drama. Prior to 1588, if he arrived that early, Shakespeare might have found work with the Earl of Leicester's Men; their roster included James Burbage and probably some others with whom Shakespeare later joined forces. After that company disbanded in 1588, the possibilities would have included the Queen's Men (formed in 1583, with Richard Tarlton as its best-known actor (fig. 2.2); the Lord Admiral's Men, the Earl of Sussex's Men, the Earl of Pembroke's Men, and the company sponsored by Ferdinando Stanley, Lord Strange, who became the Earl of Derby in 1593. Shakespeare's early tragedy, *Titus Andronicus,* declares on its 1594 title page that the play was "played by the Right Honorable the Earl of Derby, Earl of Pembroke, and Sussex their Servants." A version of Shakespeare's *3 Henry VI* appeared in print in 1595 under the title *"The True Tragedy of Richard Duke of York,* sundry times acted by the Right Honorable the Earl of Pembroke his Servants." That same company seems to have owned the rights at some point to *The Taming of the Shrew.* Henslowe's *Diary* records a performance of *"Harey the vj"* in 1592, perhaps by a combined Strange-Admiral's company at the Rose. About the performance of other of Shakespeare's early plays, including *The Comedy of Errors, Love's Labor's Lost,* and *The Two Gentlemen of Verona,* nothing is known. At any rate, these turbulent years came to a close in 1593–1594. Plague forced the suspension of acting during the crucial warmer months. Pembroke's company folded. The Earl of Derby died in 1594. The Queen's Men had broken apart and were ripe for reallocation. From the ensuing realignment two companies emerged: the Admiral's, and the new Lord Chamberlain's. Shakespeare threw in his lot with this latter group.

Somehow, Shakespeare managed to acquire the sizable stake he needed to become an actor-sharer of this new company. A traditional conjecture is that he was helped by the Earl of Southampton, a young

2.1. Edward Alleyn (1566–1626), the leading actor of the Admiral's Men in the 1590s and 1600s, was chief rival in the competitive theater market to Richard Burbage, James Burbage's son. Alleyn was son-in-law of the theater entrepreneur Philip Henslowe. By permission of the Trustees of the Dulwich Picture Gallery.

2.2. Richard Tarlton (d. 1588), the famous clown of the Queen's Men in the 1580s, was the author of *Tarlton's Jests* and other works. In this woodcut title-page illustration to Armin's *The History of the Two Maids of More-clacke* (1609), the actor is dancing a jig, with pipe and tabor, inside a decorative capital *T*. Jigs were often performed at the conclusion of a play.

aristocrat to whom Shakespeare had dedicated his two early poems, *Venus and Adonis,* published in 1593, and *The Rape of Lucrece,* 1594. Severe outbreaks of the plague may have given him the free time to have composed these works. Their dedications to Southampton are warmly grateful, especially the second of them. Southampton is also a likely person to whom Shakespeare may have addressed his early sonnets beseeching a young man to marry and sire an heir.

Being an actor-sharer meant that Shakespeare helped to capitalize the new Chamberlain's company and thereby took upon himself his share of both the risks and hopes of financial gain in a competitive free-market enterprise. The Burbage family formed the nucleus of the company. James, the father, had built the Theatre; Cuthbert, one of his sons, was a manager; and Richard, another son, was the lead actor (fig. 2.3). Cuthbert and Richard owned half the shares. Shakespeare and four others—John Heminges, Thomas Pope, Augustine Phillips, and Will Kempe—took single shares at 10 percent each (fig. 2.4). Shakespeare was their principal playwright. He also undertook acting roles, at least down through 1603, when he appears on a casting list for Ben Jonson's

2.3. Richard Burbage (1567–1619) was Shakespeare's long-time leading actor in the Chamberlain's Men, beginning in 1594, and then, from 1603 onward, the King's Men. Burbage took the roles of Hamlet, Othello, King Lear, and many others. By permission of the Trustees of the Dulwich Picture Gallery. Photograph by Matthew Hollow.

2.4. Will Kempe (d. 1603) joined the Chamberlain's Men in 1594–1595, in time to play Peter in *Romeo and Juliet* and Dogberry in *Much Ado about Nothing.* As Shakespeare's chief clown in the mid-1590s, he may also have played Bottom the Weaver in *A Midsummer Night's Dream.* When he left the company in 1599 he seems to have been replaced by Robert Armin as a more philosophical fool. Kempe is on the right, above, dancing a jig to musical accompaniment.

Sejanus. Before that he is listed in Jonson's *Every Man in His Humour* in 1598. Stage tradition credits him with acting the parts of old Adam in *As You Like It* and the Ghost in *Hamlet;* a contemporary poem lauds him for his skill in "Kingly parts." These tantalizing hints need to be regarded with some skepticism.

The Lord Chamberlain's Men were versatile actors. They could not afford to be overly specialized in the types of roles they played. To be sure, clownish parts may well have gone to one or more actors with a special gift for being funny. Richard Tarlton was famous as a comic in the 1580s. In Shakespeare's company, Will Kempe is known to have acted Dogberry, the fatuous constable in *Much Ado about Nothing,* and Peter, the Nurse's foolish servant, in *Romeo and Juliet.* He probably played Bottom the Weaver in *A Midsummer Night's Dream.* Kempe left the company in 1599 to be replaced by Robert Armin, whose special brand of witty folly manifests itself in Touchstone in *As You Like It,* Feste in *Twelfth Night,* the Countess's servant Lavatch in *All's Well That Ends Well,* and the Fool in *King Lear* (fig. 2.5). Women's parts were assigned to boy actors, of whom perhaps two might be at the top of their form at any given time. Richard Burbage took the leading roles. Otherwise, the play texts in the Shakespeare canon offer up a plenitude of important secondary roles that must have been handed around to the company regulars without much opportunity for specialization, particularly since doubling of parts was often necessary. In the early years, Shakespeare appears to have been a regular working member of his troupe, writing plays and acting.

The Lord Chamberlain's Men, renamed the King's Men in 1603 on the accession of James I to the English throne, enjoyed a remarkable degree of loyalty and longevity in its roster. Richard Burbage was Shakespeare's colleague from at least 1594, if not earlier, until Shakespeare's retirement in about 1612–1613, playing Richard III, Hamlet, Othello, Lear, and no doubt many other roles. Burbage stayed on as the company's leading actor until his death in 1619. Of the other original members in 1594, John Heminges remained active well after Shakespeare's retirement and death, becoming coeditor of the great First Folio edition of Shakespeare's plays in 1623. Thomas Pope served in the company until his death in 1603, Augustine Phillips until his death in 1605. Kempe left, as we have noted, in 1599. Henry Condell, who joined the company by 1598, became Heminges's partner in editing the First Folio. Will Sly (fig. 2.6) joined in the mid-1590s and served until he died in 1608. John Lowin (fig. 2.7) and Alexander Cooke joined by 1603 and went on to become

THE

Hiftory of the two Maids of More-clacke,

VVith the life and fimple maner of IOHN
in the Hofpitall.

Played by the Children of the Kings
Maiefties Reuels.

VVritten by ROBERT ARMIN, feruant to the Kings
moft excellent Maieftie.

LONDON,
Printed by *N.O.* for *Thomas Archer,* and is to be fold at his
fhop in Popes-head Pallace, 1609.

2.5. Robert Armin (d. probably in 1610) was Will Kempe's replacement as chief fool of the
Chamberlain's Men from 1599 to 1603 and then the King's Men from 1603 onward. He
seems thus to have been the actor for whom Shakespeare wrote the roles of Touchstone
in *As You Like It,* the Fool in *All's Well That Ends Well,* and the Fool in *King Lear.* He was the
author of *Fool upon Fool* (1600), *The History of the Two Maids of More-clacke* (1609), and other
works. This item is reproduced by permission of the Huntington Library, San Marino,
California (RB 56220).

important actors. Some later prominent members of the King's Men,
such as William Ostler and John Underwood, had begun as boy actors.

The company also employed hired actors for lesser parts. Richard
Cowley took the part of Verges in *Much Ado about Nothing,* in partner-
ship with Kempe's Dogberry. John Sincler or Sinklo is mentioned in
such a way as to suggest that his skinniness lent itself to certain physically distinctive roles. Sincler's name appears in the original roster of
1594, along with that of John Holland and also of George Bryan (who left
the company some time after 1596). The boy actors could not be legally

2.6. Will Sly probably joined the Lord Chamberlain's Men when it was formed in 1594. His name appears in all the actor lists of that company from 1598 to 1605. He remained a member until he died in 1608 and is in the actor list of the Shakespeare First Folio (1623).

2.7. John Lowin (d. 1559 or 1569) joined the King's Men probably in 1603. He may have been the original Henry VIII in 1613. He played Bosola in John Webster's *The Duchess of Malfi* in 1612–1614. By permission of the Folger Shakespeare Library.

apprenticed in the company, since it was not a London guild, but some of them seem to have been apprenticed individually to senior actors who were themselves members of various guilds. Not all the actor-sharers had boy apprentices, and some who did, like Augustine Phillips, were not guild members. Perhaps this was possible outside the city where regulations were less stringent.

All told, the company roster at any given time was likely to include from six to ten actor-sharers, an indeterminate number of hired extras, and perhaps four or five boys at varying stages of professional development. Because their voices would change at adolescence, the boys reached the peak of their skill in portraying women only for a relatively short span of time. Thereafter they often went on to become young adult players, and, in a number of cases, actor-sharers. A dramatist like Shakespeare needed to know at any given point what his resources were in terms of juvenile talent. Both *A Midsummer Night's Dream* and *As You Like It* seem designed for an acting company with two leading boys, one taller than the other. (In *A Midsummer,* for example, Helena characterizes Hermia as "something lower than myself," and flees from her saying "My legs are longer, though, to run away" (3.2.304–43).

The actors seem to have had prodigious memories, like many others in an age when the art of memory was a staple of professional accomplishment. Competition for audiences meant that the companies were constantly in search of new plays. Henslowe's *Diary* records a number of transactions in which advances were given to playwrights, followed by part payment and then full payment (normally six pounds in all) when the play was delivered. It then became the property of the acting company. Most playwrights did not belong to acting companies and thus had to operate as free agents; Shakespeare enjoyed an unusually secure status in this regard, presumably in recognition of his extraordinary talent. The acting company might put on as many as two new plays a week at the height of the season, since many plays did not last more than a few performances. Rehearsals, usually in the morning, had to be very efficient and to rely on fairly standard patterns of blocking with which the members of the repertory company would be thoroughly familiar. No director oversaw their work or had the luxury of weeks of preparation. Directorial "concept" was thus entirely impractical. To be sure, Shakespeare's company was fortunate in that he was presumably at hand, often onstage and able to answer any questions, but essentially the company worked as a team, knowing what they had to do.

II

What sort of acting space did the actors find themselves in? Of special interest are the Theatre in Shoreditch, the Globe in Southwark, and the Curtain (nearby the Theatre), where Shakespeare's company performed in 1597–1598 when the twenty-one-year lease on their Shoreditch property expired. Determining the physical dimensions and properties of these theaters involves a fair amount of inference and guesswork. We do know that when the Chamberlain's Men moved from Shoreditch to Southwark in the cold December of 1598, thereby solving their dispute with the landowner at the first site, they took the building itself with them, furtively dismantling its timbers and transporting them (perhaps sliding them) across the frozen Thames. The logical consequence of this piece of information is that the Globe may have been much like the Theatre, indeed a reincarnation of it, since timbers were all hand-hewn and fitted together in such a way that each timber would have served best if refitted precisely into its former location in the new structure. This does not mean, however, that certain adjustments were impossible; to the contrary, one might well suppose that this burdensome relocation brought with it the opportunity to improve certain features of the stage as the result of years of acting experience in the Theater and the Curtain. The Swan, newly built in 1595, may also have given them ideas. The housing for spectators, comprising most of the building, could have been left much as it was before.

What did these buildings look like? An exterior view of the Globe appears in a number of drawings of London from the south. That of Wenceslaus Hollar in 1647 (fig. 2.8) shows two theatrical buildings with their labels evidently reversed, one misnamed "Beere bayting" (i.e., "Bear-baiting"). A double-peaked roof identifies one building as the second Globe, built in this fashion when the first Globe Theatre burned down in 1613. Both buildings in the Hollar engraving are large and essential circular, or more probably multisided. A flag is flying atop one of them, presumably to advertise that a performance is going on within. Also helpful, though on a much smaller scale, are John Norden's 1600 revision of his "Civitas Londini" map and the Norden "Civitas Londini" map now in the Royal Library in Stockholm.

What a public theater may have looked like from the inside is best seen in a drawing made in about 1596 by Arend van Buchell, accompanying a description of the Swan Theatre in Southwark by a Dutch visi-

2.8. A section of Wenceslaus Hollar's "Long View" of London (1647), showing the south side of the Thames River. The labels on two theatrical buildings, "Beere bayting" (i.e., "Bear-baiting") and "The Globe," appear to be reversed. The Globe in this illustration is the second Globe, erected after the first was burned in 1613. By permission of the Guildhall Library, City of London.

tor named Johannes de Witt (fig. 2.9). The drawing appears to be based on that description and may indeed have been realized by van Buchell himself from a sketch by de Witt. It shows a circular enclosed building, open to the sky but with a roof (the *tectum*) over the stage and also over the spectators' seats, which are arranged in three tiers of galleries. Stairways provide entry (*ingressus*) into these stands offering seats (*sedilia*) in sections variously called *orchestra* and *porticus*. The large rectangular stage, called the *proscaenium* (literally, "that which stands before the scene"), juts out into a ground-level yard labeled *planities sive arena* ("the plain place or arena") and is raised above ground level to a height of per-

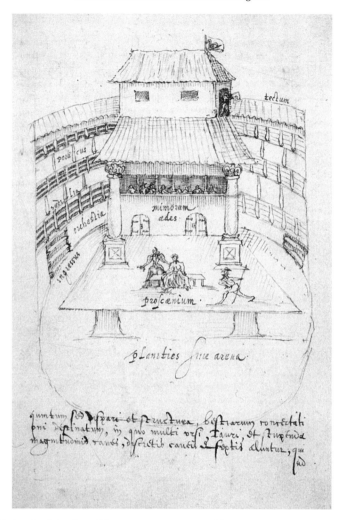

2.9. A sketch of the Swan Theatre, 1596–1598, copied by Arend van Buchell (Arnoldus Buchelius, 1565–1641) from a lost original by a Dutch visitor to London, Johannes de Witt (1566–1622). This is the only depiction of a public amphitheater known to exist from Shakespeare's years in London. By permission of the University Library, Utrecht (MS 842, fol. 132r).

haps five to six feet. No trapdoor is discernible. Two pillars, coming right up through the stage, support the roof over the stage. Above this roof stands a hut; a flag is flying at its peak, and, at a doorway in the hut, a figure appears to be blowing a musical instrument, perhaps to announce the play. Three figures are on the stage, one of them richly costumed and sitting on a bench, with a lady behind and a courtier-like figure offering a bow and a greeting. To the rear of the stage is a partition labeled *mimorum aedes*, i.e., housing for the actors, commonly known in Elizabethan parlance as the "tiring house" or place in back of the stage where the actors attired themselves for performance. Two large hinged doors stand in the tiring-house facade, to either side of a center line. Above these doors, just below the roofline of the structure sheltering a portion of the stage, a gallery is discernible in six bays with figures sitting there as though watching the play as spectators.

A description by another visitor to London in 1599, Thomas Platter, confirms many of the details that are observable in the de Witt drawing, and does so in a way that helpfully generalizes about other theaters as well:

> The playhouses are so constructed that they play on a raised platform, so that everyone has a good view. There are different galleries and places, however, where seating is better and more comfortable and therefore more expensive. For whoever cares to stand below only pays one English penny, but if he wishes to sit, he enters by another door and pays another penny, while if he desires to sit in the most comfortable seats, which are cushioned, where he not only sees well but can also be seen, then he pays yet another English penny at another door. And during the performance food and drink are carried round the audience, so that for what one cares to pay one may also have refreshment.

Platter's description of those who enjoy being seen, like spectators in more recent times in the expensive box seats of theaters or opera houses, would seem to apply well to those figures in the de Witt drawing who are sitting above the stage doors. This may be the space that Ben Jonson refers to as the lords' room "over the stage" at the Globe; it may also have been the musicians' gallery, and at times a place for acting "above," as we shall see. Presumably the actors onstage, surrounded on three sides in any case by the audience, learned to play fully in the round. They would not wish to neglect their wealthiest patrons in the most expensive seats. Other seating locations for the well-to-do were possible near to the stage. The building contract for the Fortune Theatre in 1600 specifies "four convenient divisions for gentlemen's rooms, and other sufficient and convenient divisions for twopenny rooms," together with access stairs, to be fashioned like those of the Globe (see E. K. Chambers, *The Elizabethan Stage*, 1923, 2.436–39).

Various sorts of documentary evidence, including the Fortune Theater contract, suggest that the Globe amphitheater was about seventy feet in diameter in the interior, and that the stage measured approximately forty-three feet across and twenty-seven feet in depth. The playing area was large. A trapdoor, though not visible in the de Witt drawing of the Swan, probably was used, albeit sparingly, at the Globe. Decor was sumptuous. The so-called "heavens" over the stage, on the underside of the stage roof, were particularly impressive, often with emblematic representations of the sun and moon, the planets, and the stars. During Shakespeare's later years at least the hut above the stage roof contained machinery from which ascents and descents through a door in the "heavens" could be managed by means of a winch, pulleys, and ropes. Not all such features were to be found in earlier theaters; the original Rose, for example, erected in 1587, featured a smaller stage that was about thirty-seven and a half feet wide at the back and tapering to only twenty-seven and a half feet in front. De Witt's description accompanying his sketch of the Swan in 1596 estimates that the theater could hold three thousand spectators (probably an exaggerated figure), that flint stone was used in the building construction, and that the wooden columns were painted to resemble marble.

Platter's description is unfortunately more informative about the spectators' auditorium than about the stage, so that we learn nothing from him about the doors or the backstage facade. These are crucial factors when we consider how the plays were actually staged, all the more so in that the demands of many plays put on at the Globe cannot easily be managed with just two doors. Stage directions in plays of the period by Shakespeare's contemporaries sometimes specifically require three doors in use at once: at the start of *Eastward Ho!*, for instance, written by Ben Jonson, George Chapman, and John Marston in 1605, Touchstone and Quicksilver enter simultaneously at *"several doors,"* i.e., separate doors, while "*At the middle door, enter Golding discovering a goldsmith's shop."* In Shakespeare's plays as well, occasions arise when three doors would be wonderfully handy if not indispensable. Most scholars agree that the Globe is likely to have had three ways of entrance onto and exit from the stage, one of them a "discovery space" like that specified in *Eastward Ho!*, located in the middle of the tiring-house wall between the other two doors. Such an entrance could have been covered over by a curtain or other concealing device. "Discoveries" are not uncommon in Globe plays, such as *The Tempest,* where, in act 5, "*Prospero discovers Ferdinand and Miranda, playing at chess*" (5.1.172.1–2). Evidently Prospero pulls back a curtain, revealing his daughter and her beloved at their game. They presumably step forward after a few words of dialogue and the full scene continues on the main stage. This is typical of discoveries; the action is not confined to some inner space.

Theories of an "inner stage," once popular among scholars, are now discredited, owing chiefly to the difficulties that such a space would create in terms of sight lines and hearing. A discovery space or enclosure like that used in *The Tempest,* on the other hand, could be used for many purposes, not simply discovery. The final scene of *Othello* begins, "*Enter Othello, and Desdemona in her bed.*" What this suggests is that Desdemona lies on a bed as it is thrust onstage. Other plays make use of this device: in *2 Henry VI,* for example, the stage direction reads "*Bed put forth*" when Duke Humphrey's murdered body is put on display before members of the court (3.2.146.1). A curtained recess, open at the back into the tiring house, would provide the necessary means.

Similarly, when in the great tavern scene (2.4) of *1 Henry IV* Falstaff retires from the room to evade the sheriff, who has come looking for him after the Gad's Hill robbery, such a curtained recess would be ideal. Falstaff is heard snoring during Prince Hal's awkward interview with the sheriff, whereupon, the sheriff having departed, Peto is ordered by the Prince to "call him [Falstaff] forth." Peto, following the sound of the snoring, discovers Falstaff and reports to Prince Hal, "Falstaff—Fast asleep behind the arras, and snorting like a horse." Ordered next to examine the contents of Falstaff's pockets, Peto "*searcheth his pockets, and findeth certain papers*" revealing the comical fact that Falstaff has consumed inordinate quantities of wine along with a single pennyworth of bread. At the very end of the scene, the Prince and Peto exit by one of the regular doors, while Falstaff, concealed once more by the "arras" or curtain, is presumably able to exit backstage without awkwardly coming into view of the audience. Once again, this is a perfect use of the discovery space.

These doors and the discovery space could become visually identified as leading to specific offstage locations, normally for a particular sequence rather than for the entire play. In *Troilus and Cressida,* when the Greek generals decide to adopt Ulysses' sly advice that they slightingly pass by Achilles in order to impress upon him the idea that reputation is leaving him behind, the stage direction specifies, "*Achilles and Patroclus stand in their tent.*" As though to underscore the spatial arrangement, Ulysses observes aside to his fellow generals, "Achilles stands i'th'entrance of his tent" (3.3.37–38). Earlier too, when Achilles has proudly refused to speak with the generals and has exited abruptly through a stage door, Patroclus informs Agamemnon and the rest that Achilles is

"Within his tent," in response to which Ulysses observes, "We saw him at the opening of his tent" (2.3.76–83). The word "tent" takes on an emblematic signification of Achilles' arrogant unwillingness to go forth to battle. "In his tent," reports Ulysses, Achilles "Lies mocking our designs" (1.3.145–46). Ulysses' subsequent advice to Achilles is to the same point: do not, he urges, "case thy reputation in thy tent" (3.3.188). This does not mean that a stage door was draped in some way to suggest a tent; the action of the play moves too swiftly for that. It does suggest that intermittently, whenever the action is located at the entrance to Achilles' tent, the audience is asked to imagine one stage door fulfilling that function.

When two such "tents" are required in the final act of *Richard III,* on the eve of the battle of Bosworth Field, the two main stage doors presumably take on a similar function, antithetically standing to left and right by way of illustrating the edifying contrasts between the tyrant, Richard III, and his virtuous challenger, the Earl of Richmond. When Richmond and his supporters *"withdraw into the tent"* (5.3.46.1), they need only exit through the door that is, for the duration of this action, understood to be his. When, on the other side of the stage, King Richard repeatedly orders his soldiers, "Up with my tent!" (5.3.7, 14), probably nothing need be done other than to mime the action of tent-raising. The ghosts of Richard's many victims would most plausibly enter between the two doors, turning to one side and then the other as they address first Richard and then Richmond. (This play of 1594 or slightly earlier was acted by the Chamberlain's Men, with Richard Burbage as Richard, and perhaps in the building they called the Theatre, though possibly elsewhere earlier as well.)

These are instances in which the stage doors take on for a limited time a fixed sense of location. Such instances are comparatively uncommon. For the most part, actors quickly came onstage as scene succeeded scene in a fluid and fast-moving sequence. When characters were to meet, they commonly entered *"at several doors"* (*Henry VIII,* 2.1.0.1), meaning more than one door. No scenery was needed to announce to the spectators the location of a scene; the actors themselves did this by their costume, their gestures, and their dialogue. "Well, this is the Forest of Arden," declares Rosalind in *As You Like It* (2.4.13), making a point that is reinforced by the fact that she is now disguised as a young man (*"Enter Rosalind for Ganymede,"* reads the stage direction) and that Celia is dressed for travel; they have made their escape from the envious court, as they earlier planned to do. The audience is asked to fill in the rest of the scene with its imagination.

Costumes take on a special importance in the absence of scenery; so do props, both large and small. When Othello enters prepared to murder his wife Desdemona, he carries a torch or light, which he proceeds to extinguish; the light is both a symbol of the precious life that Othello is about to quench and a conventional way of indicating to the audience that the scene takes place at night. Since public plays were performed in outdoor amphitheaters like the Globe, open to the sky, normally in the afternoon, nighttime had to be suggested by hand props (including torches) and by the actors' gestures suggesting their difficulty in seeing things at night.

A formal scene at court might begin with the bringing on of a throne. In *Henry VIII,* for example, act 1, scene 2 begins with the King entering with Cardinal Wolsey and others; once Henry has taken his place, "*The Cardinal places himself under the King's feet on his right side.*" Soon Queen Katharine arrives and kneels, whereupon the "*King riseth from his place, takes her up, kisses and placeth her by him.*" Two thrones are needed, presumably having been brought on unobtrusively and subsequently removed by stagehands, since they are not needed and indeed would prove inappropriate in many of the play's scenes. Later in the same act, Wolsey himself sits "*under a state,*" that is, in a gorgeously embroidered canopied chair of state, in his own great hall as he entertains his guests. A dining table and chairs are required; much is made of social precedence in the seating arrangements (1.4.1–35). To set the stage for the feast in *Macbeth* to which the Ghost of Banquo makes his spectral appearance, a "*Banquet*" is "*prepared.*" The honored guests are urged by their host to take their places: "You know your own degrees; sit down." When the Ghost enters, it "*sits in Macbeth's place*" (3.4.1–37). The absence of scenery on Shakespeare's stage does not mean the absence of substantial props when needed; to the contrary, the absence of scenery gives a specially marked visual and symbolic importance to these props. They are there only for the scene in question and presumably are quickly removed.

The pillars standing to right and left in the large stage have proved daunting at first to some modern actors in the recreated Globe Theatre of today's London, but in Shakespeare's theater one can imagine how they might prove very useful. Overhearings are a constant stage device in his plays. Benedick and then Beatrice, in *Much Ado about Nothing* (2.3 and 3.1), must hide as they hear themselves talked about by their friends, and must do so in such a way that the audience can perceive their reactions and hear their aside comments. "See you where Benedick hath hid himself?" Don Pedro asks *sotto voce* of his companions as they prepare to lay their trap for Benedick. They see him; Benedick thinks he is unobserved; the audience sees both Benedick and his tormentors (although the sight lines were not always unobstructed for all members of the audience). The pillars offer one easy solution, among other possibilities. (The London Globe production of this play in the summer of 2004 chose to install an arbor against the back wall of the stage, where both Benedick and Beatrice hid themselves.) The pillars are similarly employable when Sir Toby and Sir Andrew and the rest overhear the monologue of Malvolio in *Twelfth Night* and intersperse it with their muffled cries of comic delight and outrage at Malvolio's posturing (2.5), though again the Globe production of 2002–2003 preferred a portable hedge for the purpose. The pillars can be instrumental in more serious stage business, as when Othello conceals himself to overhear Iago and Michael Cassio in a discussion that Othello believes to be about an affair between Cassio and Desdemona but which in fact is about Cassio and his mistress, Bianca (4.1.102–69).

What of the gallery over the stage? Might it have been used for concealment in overhearing scenes, or more generally as a *mise en scène* visually differentiated from the main stage and hence useful as a way of indicating change of location? We have seen that this gallery appears to have served in several capacities, as the "lords' room" for distinguished spectators, as a musicians' gallery, and sometimes for acting. The first use is well attested, not only in the Swan sketch but also in two later drawings. On the title page of William Alabaster's *Roxana*, 1632 (fig. 2.10), appears a dramatic scene in what looks like a public theater, since spectators are standing around the perimeter of the stage. The stage itself, interestingly, is narrower downstage than upstage (matching the description of the Rose Theater), and is bordered on three sides by a small railing about a foot high. Curtains cover the tiring-house wall, as though serving as the arras. And above that wall is a gallery, showing two bays in which sit four spectators who are obviously absorbed in what they are watching onstage.

An engraved frontispiece to Francis Kirkman's *The Wits, or, Sport upon Sport*, 1662 (fig. 2.11), shows a large, flat rectangular stage on which appear various figures from Renaissance drama, including Falstaff and Hostess Quickly, a beggar, and two characters from *The Changeling* by Thomas Middleton and Samuel Rowley. Spectators are ranged along three sides of the stage. Another actor pokes his head out of a curtained entrance in the tiring-house wall, above which is a gallery with six visible bays holding a total of eight spectators. The presence of candelabras and

2.10. From the title page of William Alabaster's *Roxana* (1632), showing a raised platform stage with a low railing that narrows toward the front and curtains backstage that may conceal an inner "discovery space." Spectators are gathered around the stage, while others watch from the gallery above. By permission of the Folger Shakespeare Library.

of footlights (candles) at the front of the stage would seem to suggest an indoor theater.

Such demand for the gallery space in the public amphitheaters might seem to preclude extensive use of that space for acting, especially since the seats there appear to have brought in at least triple the price of general admission for standing in the yard. And indeed theatrical uses of the upper acting area were limited, not only by economic and social considerations but by practicalities of sight lines and audibility. As we shall see in later chapters, characters in Shakespeare's plays appear in the gallery when they are imagined to be in some elevated location, on the battlements of a besieged castle or at a window high above the ground. They converse briefly with persons on the main stage in such a way that the vertical separation takes on dramatic meaning. Although such characters may appear briefly together in this upper acting location, as in Juliet's farewell to Romeo after their marriage night or in Cleopatra's last moments with Antony as he dies in her arms, they ordinarily do not engage there in lengthy or complex scenes. When the action must con-

2.11. The engraved frontispiece to Francis Kirkman's *The Wits, or, Sport upon Sport* (1662) shows the earliest pictorial renditions known to exist of Sir John Falstaff and Hostess Quickly, along with a character from Thomas Middleton and William Rowley's *The Changeling* (1622) and still others. Spectators appear to be standing on three sides of the raised platform stage, with a curtain rear stage and still other spectators in the gallery above. Candelabras and footlights provide stage illumination. By permission of the Folger Shakespeare Library.

tinue, as in both instances just cited, Shakespeare devises means to transfer the scene to the main stage. This is where the preponderance of stage action in Shakespeare's plays takes place. The gallery above and the unseen space below the trapdoor take on symbolic meaning in the cosmic world of the Elizabethan playhouse, with the heavens above and hell beneath, but they do so always in relation to the main stage, the locus of action in this present world.

Perhaps, then, the acting companies sold seats in the gallery for most of their shows, but reserved that location for musicians or actors when necessary. A fair amount of the music in plays for the public theaters was actually performed and sung onstage, and sometimes may have been heard offstage from behind the scenes (as in *1 Henry IV,* 3.1, when the magician Glendower summons musicians who "Hang in the air a thousand leagues from hence," whereupon "*The music plays*"), so that the gallery would usually have been free for paying customers or dramatic action. The actors themselves were often skilled performers or singers; the boys especially had been trained in most instances as choristers. Shakespeare's texts sometimes indicate the need for a particular actor to sing, as when in *Twelfth Night* a servant informs Duke Orsino that his request for a particular song cannot be immediately met: "He is not here, so please Your Lordship, that should sing it." The person to whom this apology pertains, Feste the clown, is summoned and soon arrives to warble "Come away, come away, death," presumably to musical accompaniment, since the stage direction specifies "*Music*" (2.4.1–65). Feste sings other songs as well; he is the chief musical performer for the play. Instrumentalists onstage, or the singers themselves, could provide accompaniment with lute or other stringed instruments. Balthasar in *Much Ado about Nothing,* summoned to perform for Don Pedro and his friends, enters "*with music*" (meaning, with musicians) and apologizes for his bad voice, but sings nonetheless (2.3.36–76). Cassio, in *Othello,* brings onstage a consort of musicians whom he has hired to soften Othello's mood and thereby effect a reconciliation after Cassio's disgrace (3.1). Cloten in *Cymbeline* employs musicians onstage, including a singer, as part of his ineffectual courting of Imogen (2.3).

III

Where did the builders of London's playhouses get their ideas as to what a theater should look like? Staging practices of the ancient classical world were poorly understood. Instead, two distinctly English models seem to have presented themselves to James Burbage and his fellows. One may have been the yard of public inns. The other was the banqueting hall of Tudor mansions and great houses. Traveling actors in the sixteenth century had acted their plays in both sorts of venues, along with similarly designed guildhalls, monastic residences, and schools.

Public inns of the period often featured an enclosed yard for horses and carriages, surrounded by the inn itself in perhaps two or three stories. See figure 2.12 for a picture of London's only surviving galleried inn, the George Inn of Southwark, destroyed by fire in 1676 but rebuilt (with two galleries instead of three) in a configuration not unlike the original.

2.12. The George Inn, Southwark, England. This structure, still standing, has been rebuilt at various times since it was destroyed by fire in 1676, but still preserves the galleries looking on an inner courtyard that could have housed spectators witnessing a play by itinerant players in the courtyard. This hypothesis of the genesis of the Elizabethan playhouse has been subjected to skeptical investigation in recent years. Actual records of such performances are hard to document. By permission of the National Trust Photo Library, Swindon, UK.

From this picture we can perhaps imagine how paying customers of the inn would have been able to watch from their balconies a performance by itinerant players, on a transportable booth stage set up against one side of the inn yard interior. Such a stage might consist simply of a wooden platform on a raised scaffolding and with a curtain at the back to give the actors a dressing area from which to make their entrances. Contemporary pictures of booth stages suggest a height for the platform that would have allowed spectators to gather around it (though, admittedly, archival records of performances in inn yards are scarce). In such a space, the actors would have been able to charge admission to a general public by asking a penny or so at the entrance gate into the yard, enabling such spectators to stand around the stage, while the more affluent guests of the inn would enjoy the show as a perquisite of their stay, having in effect paid the innkeeper for it as part of the charges for their room. If so, the financial arrangement would have been essentially like that in some public amphitheaters of Shakespeare's day, where the acting company got to keep the basic penny charged for admission while the owner of the theater building pocketed a portion (usually half) of the revenues charged for seats and for the lords' room or rooms.

The Tudor banqueting hall provided another possible model. Characteristically, it was a handsome interior rectangular space, high-ceilinged, richly appointed with wood carving and the like. At the upper end of the hall a raised dais accommodated the lord of the manor and his chief guests, while other diners could be ranged in long tables extending from upper to lower end of the hall. Many dining halls at Oxford and Cambridge are laid out in this pattern still today. At the lower end of the hall, a transverse screen, usually richly carved, separated the hall itself from a passageway used by servants in bringing food and drink. The screen might have two or three doorways, and above it stood a gallery, for musicians or whatever. See figure 2.13 for just such a hall screen at the Middle Temple in London, where *Twelfth Night* was staged in February 1602, presumably after having opened at the Globe Theatre. Chandeliers provided lighting, so that performance at night was possible, and indeed customary, since the host was likely to want the show to be part of some feasting occasion. Traveling actors might perform in such a hall, as indeed seems to be the case in *Hamlet,* when visiting players call at the Danish king's castle in hope of employment and are eagerly commissioned by Hamlet to perform a play in the royal presence. Their performance would have been in the hall. Whether such traveling players performed in front of the hall screen is by no means certain, since they may have wished to be closer to the chief guests at the hall's upper end, but at all events the hall itself was bound to become part of the spectacle. And visually the hall screen bore a striking resemblance to the backstage wall of the Swan Theatre, with its two wide doors and facade surmounted with a gallery.

IV

Whatever the influence of this architectural model may have been for the public amphitheaters in London, the great hall certainly com-

2.13. The Middle Temple Hall, where a performance of *Twelfth Night* took place on February 2, 1602. See figure 3.4 for what that performance may have looked like. The Middle Temple is one of the Inns of Court, where students and practitioners of the law lived and studied. Hulton Archive. By permission of Getty Images, Inc.

mended itself as a space for performance by companies of boy actors. Such troupes had long been accustomed to singing and acting for the royal and aristocratic patrons in whose households they found sponsorship and employment. Paul's boys, for example, so called because they performed in an indoor theater space near to St Paul's Cathedral in the 1580s, took a number of John Lyly's plays to the royal court, where they were seen by Queen Elizabeth. We need to consider what the boys' theaters were like, since the adult players as well, especially Shakespeare's company, found themselves increasingly interested in playing indoors as well as outdoors. James Burbage had acquired Blackfriars in 1597. There, a hall of a monastic establishment had been converted some time during the earlier years of Elizabeth's reign into a playing space for the Children of the Royal Chapel and other boys' companies, including the Earl of Oxford's Boys. Burbage converted a similar hall in 1597 into what became known as the second Blackfriars. The Chapel children played there in 1600–1603, after having been forbidden to play during the 1590s because of the satirical thrust of many of their plays. They continued to perform in the second Blackfriars from 1604 to 1608 as the Children of the Queen's Revels, named thus in honor of their patroness, Queen Anne, consort of James I.

The adult King's Men, seeing the advantages of an indoor location during inclement weather or at night, and finding themselves able to attract thereby a more courtly set of spectators just as some puritan-inclining members of the popular theater-going public were turning their backs on the stage, took control of Blackfriars for their own dramatic activities in 1608. The 1622 quarto title page of *Othello* offers the play to the reader "As it hath been divers times acted at the Globe and at the Blackfriars." This advertisement, probably referring to a revival or revivals after 1608, suggests the cachet of indoor performance before a select clientele of socially prominent spectators. *The Two Noble Kinsmen,* on which Shakespeare collaborated with John Fletcher, declares on its 1634 quarto title page that it was "Presented at the Blackfriars by the King's Majesty's Servants," with no mention this time of the Globe. Then, too, Shakespeare's company received a number of much-coveted invitations to perform his plays at court, in surroundings like those of a great hall. *King Lear,* according to its 1608 title page, was "played before the King's Majesty at Whitehall upon St. Stephen's night [December 26, 1608] in the Christmas holidays, by His Majesty's Servants playing usually at the Globe on the Bankside." *Measure for Measure* went to court on St. Stephen's Day in 1604. All in all, Shakespeare and his company had plenty of reasons to think about indoor alternatives and supplements to their Globe performances. Especially during the winter months after 1608, the second Blackfriars was the company's regular playhouse. Shakespeare's late plays show an increasing interest in indoor performance, as we will see in later chapters.

The second Blackfriars displayed its ancestry by its physical resemblance to the indoor hall on which it appears to have been modeled (fig. 2.14). A partition wall with two ornately decorated doors and between them a middle door used for discoveries (as we have seen, for example, at the beginning of *Eastward Ho!*), reminiscent of the screen at the lower end of a great hall, stood at the back of the stage. This wall was surmounted by a handsomely decorated gallery. The stage itself was probably raised from the floor to facilitate sight lines and provide space for a trapdoor, but not to the height of the public stage. Spectators sat facing the front of the stage and in boxes along both sides, as in a modern

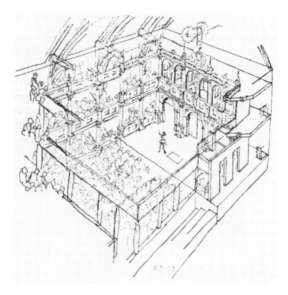

2.14. A reconstruction of the second Blackfriars Theatre, in a drawing by Richard Southern. This indoor theatrical space, built in the Blackfriars precinct between St. Paul's Cathedral and the River Thames, features a rectangular stage, three doors in front of the tiring house or actors' dressing area, and a gallery above the doors. Construction of the second Blackfriars was completed in 1597, using the same building that had served for the first Blackfriars.

opera house or auditorium. Machinery, concealed overhead, made possible descents and ascents. The dimensions of the hall, like those of its monastic pre-Reformation days, were approximately forty-six by a hundred feet. Chandeliers provided lighting. Music was normally played before the show and between the acts, as was generally not the case in the public amphitheaters. Audience capacity was far smaller than that of the public theaters, where perhaps two thousand spectators could be accommodated (though no doubt audiences were often substantially smaller than that); Blackfriars and Paul's, and later the Whitefriars built in 1606 immediately to the west of the old city of London, could hold perhaps six hundred. The price of admission was generally sixpence, six times that of general admission in the public theaters. All of these differences made for a smaller, more affluent, and more socially well connected clientele. Plays put on in these precincts were bound to shape themselves to courtly and sophisticated tastes. That influence on Shakespeare's late work, as his company started performing indoors in the inclement months, is discernible in what he wrote.

ℒ 3 ℒ

A Local Habitation and a Name

STAGE BUSINESS IN THE COMEDIES

From the start of his career, Shakespeare fitted his plays to the playing conditions that were thrust upon him. As a practicing dramatist he had little other choice. His solutions are many, and they are inventive. We do not know what theater buildings he wrote for at first, and would have to guess at the physical capabilities and limitations of those buildings even if we could identify them, but the generic pattern already described in the previous chapter is enough to get us started. Such an exploration will also enable us to compare Elizabethan techniques of staging Shakespeare's plays with more recent interpretations onstage and in film. We will also want to examine ways in which physical space takes on thematic significance in addition to its geographical and locational functions. The physical theater, in Shakespeare's day and ever since then, shows itself capable of conveying multiple possibilities of philosophical, social, psychological, and political meaning.

I

The Taming of the Shrew (c. 1590–1593), acted possibly by the Earl of Pembroke's Men prior to 1594 and passed on to the Lord Chamberlain's company in that year, illustrates how deftly Shakespeare learned to combine neoclassical dramaturgy with more native English theatrical traditions. The play combines two plots, one derived from an Italian neoclassical comedy by Ludovico Ariosto, *I Suppositi* (or *Supposes,* as it was called by its English translator, George Gascoigne), the other taken from ballad and folk tradition. Then, too, Shakespeare provides an induction or frame story in which a whimsical aristocrat plays a trick on a beggar by inducing him to believe that he has suffered amnesia and is himself a lord awakening after years in a comatose sleep. A "pleasant comedy" is provided for this beggar's entertainment. "The Taming of the Shrew" follows at this point and is thus really a play-within-a-play. It is put on by strolling players who have arrived in timely fashion at the lord's great house to "offer service to Your Lordship" (Induction 1, line 77), that is, to act a play for him and his honored guests, just like the players who show up opportunely at the Danish royal castle in *Hamlet*.

This induction poses an interesting challenge on the Elizabethan stage. Thoroughly English in spirit, it makes use of theatrical space in a way that is inventively original rather than neoclassical in its stagecraft. The beggar is Christopher Sly, of Burton-heath or Burton-on-the-heath near Shakespeare's own town of Stratford-upon-Avon. Sly speaks of Marian Hacket, the fat wife of Wincot, another town near Stratford. Christopher Sly is a tinker from the English countryside, a drinker of beer and eater of salted beef. He enters *"aloft"* in the second scene of the induction, with attendants, where he is joined by one of the lord's pages dressed up as his wife, in order that they may sit over the stage to witness a play called "The Taming of the Shrew." This scene is, for Shakespeare, an unusually long and busy sequence to be acted aloft, perhaps in the gallery above the tiring-house doors. At the end of the first scene of the main play itself these comic chorus figures *"above"* speak briefly and then sit once again to "mark" the action below. They are not heard from subsequently, although a much-changed version called *The Taming of a Shrew* (not by Shakespeare) does bring Sly back at the very end, determined to tame his wife just as Petruchio has done in the main action. Whether we have lost some Sly episodes from Shakespeare's text or whether, as seems more likely, Shakespeare preferred to have this choric business fade into the background rather than upstage the play itself, is unclear. In any case, the induction is remarkably metatheatrical. It calls attention to its own theatrical artifice by offering the main body of *Taming* as a kind of play-within-a-play, thereby introducing leitmotifs of dreaming and illusion that will take concrete shape in the many disguisings and deceptions of the main action.

The Italianate half of what Sly and his companions watch is thoroughly neoclassical, with character types drawn from that tradition. A jealously watchful father (Baptista) guards over his marriageable daughter (Bianca), but to no purpose. He is outwitted by a clever young man

(Lucentio), who, to gain secret admittance to the daughter, disguises himself by changing places and costumes with his servant (Tranio). The servant, as in Ariosto's *I Suppositi* and indeed in the comic tradition that reaches back to Ariosto's own classical sources in Terence's *Eunuchus* and Plautus's *Captivi*, is resourceful and witty. He plays the part of his master with such skill that his offer to become Bianca's wooer throws the other candidates off their stride. Equally typical of this familiar neoclassical plot are the outwitted rival wooers of Bianca, including an old man or *pantaloon* (Gremio) and a hapless innocent (Hortensio). All is finally resolved when the identities are revealed, thereby bringing to an end all the "supposes" or misconceptions that have been so exploited for comic effect. Lucentio turns out to be well born and the son of a wealthy father, so that his marriage to Bianca can take place amicably. Traces of Italianate neoclassical staging are everywhere apparent. Old Gremio is called a *"pantaloon"* in a stage direction (1.1.47.2). The characters' names are Italian, including their disguise names (Litio, and Cambio, meaning "exchange"). The characters refer frequently to classical stories, to Ovid's *The Art of Love* (*Ars Amatoria*, at 4.2.8) or to the fabled chastity of "Roman Lucrece" (2.1.293). As in Shakespeare's other early plays, the text is amply supplied with references to the Latin texts he presumably read in school. The *mise en scène* for this Italianate portion of the play demands no more scenic effects than the house of Baptista Minola and the street lying before it. The unities of time, place, and action are preserved, as in Shakespeare's Italianate source.

Conversely, the aggressive wooing of Katharina or Kate by Petruchio is decidedly English in flavor, despite the nominal Italian setting, and thus calls for staging methods that are natively familiar to English audiences. Petruchio addresses Katharina as an English lady, "Kate of Kate Hall" (2.1.188), and puns on the English form of her name ("dainties are all Kates," i.e., "cates," delicacies). She is referred to far more often as Kate, or Katharine, than as Katharina. Most of Petruchio's servants are unabashedly English, with names like Curtis, Nathaniel, Nicholas, Philip, Joseph, Gabriel, Peter, Walter, Adam, Ralph, and Gregory. The humor is broadly physical: Petruchio beats his servants and throws meat, cups, serving plates, and even the table at them (4.1). His wooing of Kate is no less abrupt, and she is capable of violence as well; at one point, her frustrated music teacher (Hortensio, disguised as Litio) emerges onstage with *"his head broke,"* i.e., beaten bloody and sticking through his musical instrument as if he were "on a pillory, looking through the lute" (2.1.141–56).

In an English ballad that Shakespeare may have known, a henpecked Scottish farmer tames his shrewish wife by whipping her and wrapping her in the hide of an old horse so that he can claim that he is only whipping one of his farm animals. Petruchio does not go quite that far, but his course of correction for Kate's shrewishness is pretty abrasive even so. The effect in the theater is to contrast the more sedate and conventional stage gestures of Italianate neoclassical comedy with a rip-roaring English farcical action. The fluid Elizabethan public theater stage, devoid of scenic effects, provides for quick changes of understood location as the play moves from Baptista's house in Padua to Petruchio's country estate, sufficiently far away to require an exhausting journey on horseback. Similarly, the scene moves effortlessly from interior to exterior.

Costuming reinforces the contrast. The more Italianate characters are dressed so much in accordance with their conventional types that when the young master and clever servant (Lucentio and Tranio) change "colored hat and cloak" their subterfuge is entirely successful (1.1.208–32), whereas in the more raucous and English wife-taming plot Petruchio shows up for his own wedding in a getup that is so wildly grotesque that it takes Biondello some twenty-seven colorful prose lines to describe the particulars (3.2.43–70). The English whimsy lends to this plot a vitality that is quite different in texture from the ingenious formulas of the "trick-to-catch-the-old-one" plot taken from Ariosto. Large stage props are recruited to a similar purpose, as we move from Petruchio's comic violence in overturning his table and throwing meat at the servants to the elaborate feast of the final scene that begins with serving-men *"bringing in a banquet."* Tables are brought onstage so that the guests may "sit to chat as well as eat" and drink (5.2.11) as the newly married men place bets on their wives' obedience. Part of the play's astonishing theatrical energy stems from the juxtaposition of these two modes of dramatic presentation.

Two changes are immediately apparent in modern filming of this play: the induction is usually gone, while instead we are shown scenes that are only verbally described in Shakespeare's text. Film, after all, produces its own illusions; it has no need for elaborate framing devices, and would have trouble in attempting to show that the main action of *Taming* is seen through the eyes of an onstage audience, since the film itself acts as the controller of point of view. One exception that proves the rule is the *Animated Tales* version, available on DVD, which manages to keep the induction while reducing the whole play to under thirty minutes (!). Another is the clever adaptation called *Kiss Me Kate,* filmed in

1953 on the basis of the immensely successful stage musical of 1948. Here the framing device is the center of attention, as a matinee idol and his former wife (Fred Graham and Lilli Vanessi, played in the film by Howard Keel and Kathryn Grayson) rehearse for a production of *Taming* only to discover that they are reenacting their stage roles in their own private lives. Lilli, like Kate, hates men, and comes around to her acceptance of domesticity only after Fred has given her a good spanking. The Lucentio-Bianca plot too has its real-life counterpart. *Kiss Me Kate* serves most of all as a vehicle for some marvelous songs by Cole Porter: "I Come to Wive It Wealthily in Padua," "I Hate Men," and, perhaps most memorably, "Brush Up Your Shakespeare." The film adaptation of *Taming* called *10 Things I Hate about You* (1999), set in a Seattle high school, pursues a similar motif of life imitating art when the stridently feminist Kat (Julia Stiles) works out a thoroughly postmodern accommodation with Patrick Verona (Heath Ledger), but does so in a way that employs no framing action: this high-school romance is simply a retelling of the *Taming* story through a modern analogy. In other film treatments as well, the frame plot is gone without a trace.

Taking its place in film treatments of *Taming* are scenes only imagined in Shakespeare's text: lavish interiors in the households of Baptista and Petruchio, the journey on horseback to Petruchio's country estate, and especially the wedding of Petruchio and Katharine. Sam Taylor's 1929 *Taming*, with Mary Pickford and Douglas Fairbanks Sr., spared no expense in providing lavish interiors in Venetian Gothic of carved marble, with expensive and fashionable costumes to match. Franco Zeffirelli, known subsequently for visual opulence in his films of *Romeo and Juliet* (1968) and *Hamlet* (1990), employed four huge soundstages in Rome in which to construct a Padua that was colorfully alive with fruit stands, carts, winding streets, and picturesque buildings. This 1967 film won Oscar nominations for its costumes and art direction. Jonathan Miller's 1981 BBC version for television followed Miller's usual pattern of invoking the sumptuous interiors of Dutch and Italian Renaissance painters like Vermeer and Veronese. The journey on horseback, in Zeffirelli's film, visually subjects Elizabeth Taylor as Kate to a muddy discomfiture that the Shakespeare text only imagines. She must also flee her aggressive wooer (Richard Burton) in a frenetic chase ending with the two of them falling through a roof into a pile of wool and feathers. The disrupted wedding ceremony is a prominent feature of the Pickford-Fairbanks encounter in 1929 and then of Taylor and Burton in 1967; in both, we see Petruchio, dressed in colorfully inappropriate costume (though not as outlandishly as described for us by Biondello in Shakespeare's text), heap insults on the astonished priest, throw wine sops in the sexton's face, and then (as Grumio describes the moment) kiss Kate's lips "with such a clamorous smack / That at the parting all the church did echo" (3.2; see fig. 3.1).

Sam Taylor's choice of Pickford and Fairbanks for his major players in 1929, and Zeffirelli's of Taylor and Burton in 1967, points up another distinctive feature of film: its penchant for celebrity casting. Pickford was "America's sweetheart," Fairbanks the undaunted hero of action films like *The Mark of Zorro* and *The Thief of Bagdad,* and their tempestuous marriage was the stock-in-trade of gossip columns. Taylor and Burton inherited this notorious celebrity. Both films flourished, in good part as a result. Both films devote their main interest to the sparring couple, with a substantial cutting of the text in the Bianca-Lucentio plot.

Modern stage versions have sometimes adopted similar tactics, as in the Alfred Lunt–Lynn Fontaine pairing of a famous theatrical husband-wife team at the Broadway Theatre in New York in 1935. Meryl Streep and Raul Julia starred as the combative couple in Wilford Leach's New York Delacorte Theatre production in 1978 not as a married couple but as celebrated icons in a feminist debate, Streep as an incisively intelligent modern woman and Julia as a self-professed expert in macho Latino mores. Not surprisingly, then, the battle of the sexes onstage has taken a wide range of positions, from the good-natured playful mutuality of Peter O'Toole and Peggy Ashcroft (Royal Shakespeare Company, 1960, directed by John Barton) to another RSC production of 1978 (directed by Michael Bogdanov) in which smoldering female wrath stood up bravely but unavailingly against fatuous male complacency, and, at its most extreme, to Charles Marowitz's bleak adaptation at the Open Theatre in London, 1975, in which Petruchio's relentless brainwashing ultimately reduced Kate to being an automaton deprived of her sanity.

The induction has undergone a varied career in recent stage productions, attesting to its metatheatrical stageworthiness. Sometimes it is dispensed with, as in Chicago Shakespeare Theatre's 2003 production; at other times it has been extended throughout the play. In Barry Jackson's production at the Court Theatre, London, in 1928, Christopher Sly and the Lord remained on hand from start to finish, sitting in one of the boxes dressed in modern clothes; similar effects were created by Ben Iden Payne at Stratford-upon-Avon in 1935 and Tyrone Guthrie at the Old Vic in 1939. Much earlier, in 1844 at the Haymarket Theatre in London, the director Ben Webster seated Sly with his playacting "wife"

3.1. Richard Burton as Petruchio and Elizabeth Taylor as Kate, in Franco Zeffirelli's 1967 film of *The Taming of the Shrew*. The event as narrated in Shakespeare's play takes place offstage, but here, Petruchio boisterously kisses Kate at their wedding, captured in its full glory in this film. Royal Films International/RGA. Courtesy Ronald Grant Archive.

to stage left and the Lord with his servants to stage right throughout, on the main platform, where they were served drinks during the intervals. A more intriguing option (as at the Great Lakes Shakespeare Festival production in Lakewood, Ohio, in 1977) has been to have Sly decide to join the action on the main stage, taking small parts in the concluding action, such as the Pedant who is enlisted to pose as Lucentio's father Vincentio of Pisa, or the real Vincentio himself.

II

A Midsummer Night's Dream (c. 1595) is justly famous for its metatheatrical calling attention to its own theatrical devices. Bottom and his fellow thespians, though laughably inept in their amateur dramatic art, are professional craftsmen as weaver, carpenter, bellows-mender, tinker, joiner (i.e., furniture maker, not a house-builder), and tailor. Shakespeare and many of his fellows came from just such artisanal backgrounds: James Burbage had been a joiner; his son Richard belonged to the carpenters' guild, and John Heminges to the grocers' guild. Shakespeare's father was a tanner and glover. Perhaps Shakespeare's audience would have recognized an in-group joke. The artisans' attempt at dramatic entertainment is certainly a joke, but at whose expense? Even if many of the Chamberlain's Men came from backgrounds like those of Bottom and his fellows, they had become expert professional actors, eager to succeed by reforming some of the inanities of older English drama in the 1570s and 1580s and thereby appealing to audiences with literary taste. What exactly was it they wanted to reform?

"Pyramus and Thisbe," the artisans' show, is daringly close to the larger play that surrounds it. The stories are alike: lovers, thwarted by parental obtuseness and venality, elope into the woods, where they encounter terrors. The lovers of *A Midsummer* emerge from their nightmare to a new amity, whereas Pyramus and Thisbe die in a moment of misperception and tragic mistiming, as in *Romeo and Juliet,* but in both stories the lovers think they are prepared to die for love. In a theater with an unadorned stage, both dramatizations must find ways to create the illusions of nighttime, the separation of the lovers by space and distance, and the intervention into their lives of threatening circumstances. The artisans of Athens, uninstructed in their new calling as actors and playwrights, rely heavily upon a prologue, strange costuming effects that can turn a man into a wall, properties such as dog and lantern and thornbush used to identify one of their number as the man in the moon, animal outfits, stage beards in a dizzying array of colors (orange-tawny, purple-in-grain, French-crown-color), strings for their beards, new ribbons for their "pumps" or slippers, clean linen, a Bergomask dance, and an epilogue (which is politely declined). Shakespeare's play too ends with an epilogue, and elsewhere (as in *Romeo and Juliet*) he is not averse to writing prologues. Like Bottom and company, his actors create their dramatic illusions with the help of costumes and properties. In *A Midsummer* as in "Pyramus and Thisbe," artisans-turned-performers put on their play before an audience that expects to be entertained with diverting illusions. The props of *A Midsummer* are not unlike those of "Pyramus and Thisbe": the love juice squeezed on various pairs of eyes, a broom for Puck in the final scene, and of course the ass's head affixed on Bottom's shoulders. Costumes, props, and gestures are used to transform, disguise, and mislead, as in "Pyramus and Thisbe."

The difference is that the perpetrators of "Pyramus and Thisbe" do not realize how imagination can work to provide those things that cannot be brought into a theater. They think they must literally bring in moonshine in some way, perhaps through a casement in the great chamber window if the moon happens to shine on the night of their performance, or else by means of an actor festooned with moonlike props.

Conversely, they insist on outfitting the lion with a man's face peeking through its neck so that the spectators will understand literally that they are in no physical danger. One purpose of ending *A Midsummer* with their bad play, then, is to underscore by contrast just what it is that Shakespeare, assisted by Oberon and Puck, has achieved. He has shown his audience a forest near Athens without bringing on a single tree. His actors have mimed their anxieties in such a place by their talk of "Dark night, that from the eye his function takes" (3.2.177) and by their complaints of discomfiture. "Never so weary, never so in woe, / Bedabbled with the dew and torn with briers," sobs Hermia as she staggers onstage from her ordeal and falls immediately asleep (3.2.442–43). Puck talks of leading the frightened artisans "Through bog, through bush, through brake, through brier" (3.1.102). Briers are a constant menace, as when "briers and thorns at their apparel snatch" (3.2.29). Effects such as these are conveyed not by physical properties but by dialogue and gesture.

Similarly the dramatist creates for his artisan actors a rehearsal space in the forest, with a "green plot" for their stage and a "hawthorne brake" for their "tiring-house," all presumably without the use of any stage structure (3.1.3–4). Bottom's transformation into an ass is accomplished not only by his ass's head but by his conversation about thistle tops, honey bags, and a peck of "good dry oats," none of which need be brought onstage. Titania's talk meanwhile is of "apricots and dewberries," of "purple grapes, green figs, and mulberries" (3.1.161–62). The magic of the fairy kingdom is further invoked by dancing and by singing about spotted snakes, newts, blindworms, and weaving spiders. Titania describes at some length the unseasonably bad weather that has come about, she insists, because of the continuing marital spat between her and Oberon (2.1.81–117). Oberon and Puck declare themselves invisible (see 2.1.186) and are immediately so in the theater because the audience understands that they are "invisible" and thus able to walk among the mortal lovers without being "seen." Titania's bower, where she sleeps with Bottom, is a place connotatively rich in magical and amorous associations, but without any suggestion of a physical stage contrivance. So too whenever the four young human lovers lie down to sleep: they occupy a forest that we are invited to picture in our minds. Contrastingly, the world of Duke Theseus is one of "solemnities" and "pomp" at court (1.1.11–19) or of hunting horns and baying hounds as he and his entourage intrude upon the magic of the forest. We hear the horns in the theater ("*Wind horns,*" reads the stage direction at 4.1.137), but we do not see the hounds, and probably would have not heard sound effects of their baying in the original production; a stage direction calls for "*Shout within*" but does not specify the sound of dogs. A great deal is conveyed by the stage magic of the imagination.

These contrasts give added point to Theseus's meditation on the "shaping fantasies" of the poet that "Are of imagination all compact" with those of the lunatic and the lover. His wry dismissal of all three as various kinds of lunacy grows, despite his own skepticism, into a vigorous defense of poetic imagination, as it "bodies forth / The forms of things unknown" and "gives to airy nothing / A local habitation and a name" (5.1.3–22). This is precisely what *A Midsummer* manages to do. It gives name and substance to fairy magic, and to characters like Puck, Oberon, Titania, and Bottom who become immortal in art. Are we to "believe" in the fairies we see in this play? Of course we are supposed to believe, in the same way that we "believe" the actors capable of making themselves "invisible" in the theater. We invest the fiction with particularity and credibility in an imaginative conspiracy with the dramatist and the acting company. How could one not "believe" in Puck? He is more real than we, despite his being a fictional presentation designed for an actor who will leave the theater after the play is over and then return the next day for another performance. Puck will endure long after we are dead and forgotten. The stage magic of *A Midsummer* is that it puts us continually in mind of this paradox, teasing us out of thought (in Keats's words) as doth eternity. The ineptitude of "Pyramus and Thisbe" is a reminder of how *A Midsummer* teaches us to believe in, and be transformed by, the self-effacing contrivances of dramatic art. As Theseus says, "The best in this kind are but shadows, and the worst are no worse, if imagination mend them" (5.1.210–11). In these words one is tempted to hear Shakespeare's own plea, that we as audience "mend" the necessary shortcomings of dramatic performance with our imaginations.

Post-Shakespearean productions, both onstage and in film, have often yielded to the temptation to show us viscerally what Shakespeare's theater invokes through suggestion. As early as 1692, at the Queen's Theatre, in a retitled version by Thomas Betterton called *The Fairy Queen* and with enchanting music by Henry Purcell, the play was transformed into an operatic extravaganza. A woodland scene in act 2 consisted of grottos, arches, and flower-adorned paths. In act 3 two great dragons fashioned themselves into a bridge overarching a river in which could be seen, at a distance, two swans transforming themselves into dancing fairies. In act 5, Juno entered a Chinese garden in a machine drawn by peacocks, while monkeys descended from the trees. David Garrick continued the musical tradition at the Theatre Royal, Drury Lane, in 1755, attributing the play, in a new prologue, to "Signor Shakespearelli." Garrick increased the twenty-eight songs of the 1692 production, based on lyrics by John Dryden, Edmund Waller, John Milton, and Shakespeare, to thirty-three songs in 1763. Frederic Reynolds, at the Theatre Royal in Covent Garden in 1816, adopted a musical score by the eighteenth-century English composer Thomas Arne. Felix Mendelssohn's well-known incidental music for the play was performed first in part in 1826 and then in its entirety in Potsdam, near Berlin, in 1843, for a stage production by Ludwig Tieck. This work was much admired by Hector Berlioz, who went on to compose a musical score based on *Romeo and Juliet*. In an 1840 production of *Midsummer* at Covent Garden, as the night in the forest drew to its close, the staging revealed a moon that sank gradually in the sky of the stage's back wall until its fading rays disappeared from the tops of the trees. Act 5 brought staircases and a hall of statues into view, with Parisian lanterns held by the fairies. The moon was a prominent feature of Samuel Phelps's production at the Sadler's Wells Theatre in 1853, shining first in the forest and then on Theseus's handsome palace in act 5. Charles Kean's set at the Princess's Theatre in 1856 conjured up the marble temples and theater of Bacchus in ancient Athens. Herbert Beerbohm Tree, as we have seen in chapter 1, brought this sumptuous tradition to a climax in 1900 at Her Majesty's Theatre and then in 1911 at His Majesty's with carpets of thyme and wildflowers, flickering lights held by gossamer-winged fairies, and scampering live rabbits.

We should not minimize the splendor and creativity of extravagant productions like these. Theater artists like Garrick and Kean explored new means, unavailable in Shakespeare's day, to visualize what the forest of *Midsummer* could be imagined to be like. These productions were not interested in the verisimilar; they recognized that fairies are creatures of the imagination. Nor has this stage tradition of ornate spectacle lost its appeal in the twentieth and early twenty-first centuries. Tyrone Guthrie's lavish production at the Old Vic in London, 1937–38, with Vivien Leigh as Titania, Robert Helpmann as Oberon, and Ralph Richardson as Bottom, devoted a lot of its energy to ballet sequences. Michael Benthall's production at Stratford-upon-Avon in 1949 outfitted the fairies in gauze dresses. A German-text version at Weimar in 1995 featured a rotating stage that successively brought into view every imaginable monstrosity of an enchanted forest. Titania's bower can seem like an inviting target for technical ingenuity, as at Court Theatre, Chicago, in 2001, when Titania and her lover were swung aloft in a contrivance that hung in suspension above the action for some time.

Film has been especially receptive to the attractions of visualized impossibilities. From the very start, a silent Vitagraph film of 1909 focused intently, in its eight short minutes, on a flying Puck and an ass head for Bottom the Weaver which the actor, William Ranous, operated by yanking a lanyard each time he wanted the ass's mouth to open. Max Reinhart's 1935 Hollywood color film, produced at a then-mammoth cost of $1,500,000, made considerable advances in the technology of filming with its aerial stuntcraft by Puck (Mickey Rooney), its opening Masque of Night (choreographed by Nijinsky's sister, Bronislava) in which fairy ballerinas emerge out of a mist-draped enchanted woods, and its artful moving of the camera through an impressive forest of tall ferns, twisted vines, massive tree trunks, sunken ponds, and an occasional grassy clearing. Reinhart had made use of real trees in his Berlin stage production of 1905. The acting of this film is spotty, but the cinematography is at times stunning. Producer Jonathan Miller and director Elijah Moshinsky, in their generally boring televised rendition of the play for the BBC in 1981, owe an avowed debt to Reinhart in their use of a glimmering moon, trees heavy with vines, a giant muddy pool, hooting owls, chirping crickets, and the like. Michael Hoffman's 1999 film, with Kevin Kline as Bottom and Michelle Pfeiffer as Titania, shows what can go wrong with the filming of magic: it puts together contrived special effects and "realistic" forest scenery in ways that seem at once lifeless and grotesque.

Yet even though spectacle and elaborate contrivances are still very much a part of the tradition of staging or filming *A Midsummer*, often with highly satisfying results, a concurrent trend in the modern theater has been to mount a spirited attack on lavishly detailed sets and gossamer outfits. Peter Brook's production for the RSC in 1970 marked a turning point because of the brilliance of its concept and the enormous influence it has enjoyed. Brook turned his acting space into an intensely self-aware theatrical locus in the form of a three-sided white box filled with trapeze artists and other circus denizens engaged in what were plainly a series of performances. Bottom the Weaver, outfitted with the button nose, wide red mouth, and oversized shoes of the circus clown, affirmed his manhood as the lover of Queen Titania by being carried aloft by his fellow workers, one of whom thrust between Bottom's legs a clenched fist raised in a gesture of phallic triumph (fig. 3.2). The fairies

3.2. David Waller as Bottom raised up on the shoulders of his fellow artisans, in Peter Brook's 1970 production of *A Midsummer Night's Dream*. Photograph by David Farrell.

were adult actors. The four young lovers were aggressively physical toward one another in a way that the stage had seldom seen before but that has become something of a sine qua non of *Midsummer* performances since that time.

Peter Hall, directing a highly regarded production for the RSC that was then filmed less successfully in 1969, declared war on "fairies in little white tutus, skipping through gossamer forests." He insisted that the forest was a place of terror for the four young lovers, as indeed it was. Youthful dress codes of the late 1960s, with miniskirts and Nehru jackets, underscored the relevance of this production to an era of sexual revolution and mounting opposition to the Vietnam War. Use of handheld cameras created a grainy impression of documentary urgency. The revolutionary intent was both bracing and unmistakable. At the Guthrie Theater in Minneapolis in 1985, Liviu Ciulei staged the play as a brooding dark comedy about sexual warfare and defiance of paternalistic authority. Numerous productions have seen Puck and Oberon as denizens of a drug culture, dispensing their hallucinogenic "little western flower" with predictably crazy results, as for example in a Young Shakespeare Company version taken on tour to the United States in 1990.

In all these productions, *Midsummer* has been interpreted as about theater and its strange ability to create illusion, with Puck and Oberon walking among the mortals in the assurance that they are "invisible" by theatrical consent of the audience. The theater itself becomes a central emblem of the ambiguous interrelationship connecting fantasy, dream, and social comment. By giving audiences today a wide choice between a sumptuously decorous splendor and iconoclastic, hard-edged metatheater, modern productions explore the seemingly infinite possibilities of interpretation.

III

The forest of Arden in *As You Like It* (1598–1600) is another place of the imagination, another fictional construction that must compel assent if it is to work as a transforming theatrical experience. How does Shakespeare go about creating this very special forest on his Elizabethan stage and in our imaginations? To begin with, we should dispel from our minds any notion that this "forest" is like any real forest we may have seen or read about. It is not even a forest in our normal sense of being covered by a dense growth of trees. There are trees, to be sure, on which Orlando pins his love verse to Rosalind. The malcontent Jaques is reported to have spied a herd of deer as he "lay along / Under an oak whose antique root peeps out / Upon the brook that brawls along this wood" (2.1.30–32). Later, Orlando's older brother Oliver describes how he lay sleeping "Under an old oak, whose boughs were mossed with age / And high top bald with dry antiquity" while a "green and gilded snake" wreathed itself around his neck and "A lioness, with udders all drawn dry, / Lay couching, head on ground, with catlike watch," waiting for Oliver to awaken (4.3.105–17). Yet the nearly comic impossibility of such a tall tale should put us on our guard against taking the story as a plausible representation of the natural world. This "forest" is for the most part a place of shepherds and shepherdesses. Old Corin is employed by a "churlish" landowner who has put "his cote [cottage], his flocks, and bounds of feed" or pasturelands up for sale (2.4.79). This forest is a "desert place" (line 68), a thinly inhabited countryside away from the crowded civilization of court and city.

Indeed, it is several places all at once. Its name conjures up both an ancient royal preserve not far from Stratford-upon-Avon, and the Forest of Ardennes in France, where the source plot for Shakespeare's play, Thomas Lodge's *Rosalynde,* is situated. The name of Arden is also that of Shakespeare's mother's family: she was Mary Arden when she married John Shakespeare. It is a place remembered from childhood and from the reading of stories about Robin Hood and his merry men — who do in fact turn up by name in Shakespeare's play. We are told in the very first scene that the banished Duke lives in the Forest of Arden, "and a many merry men with him; and there they live like the old Robin Hood of England" (1.1.110–12). This forest is a place of the imagination.

How is this place to be figured forth in the theater? The BBC 1978 television production of this play, produced by Cedric Messina and directed by Basil Coleman, makes what some critics have considered to be exactly the wrong choice. In its usual and often successful style elsewhere of highly finished and "realistic" productions, it shows us in act 1 a handsome castle (Glamis Castle in Scotland) with greenswards and attractive landscaping where the wrestling match takes place, whereupon we switch to an actual forest, shot outdoors, with the Duke and his "merry men" sitting around uncomfortably under real trees, swatting midges away from their faces and behaving as though they would rather be back home. They look out of place. So do the old shepherd Corin (David L. Meredith), the lovesick young shepherd Silvius (Maynard Williams), and the rest. Despite some nuanced acting by Helen Mirren as Rosalind, Tony Church as Duke Senior, and Richard Pasco as Jaques, this production founders on a scenic literalism that does what television and film normally do for us: it tells us where we are in the story by putting entire landscapes or interiors in front of our eyes even before the characters have said a word. We "read" the scene first in terms of its visual setting. In this case, the attempt is misguided because it takes away the magic of an imagined landscape where all sorts of things can and do happen that would be absurd in an actual rural location. Paul Czinner's 1936 black-and-white film falls into the same trap. In a studio forest festooned with trees, a mushroom-shaped thatched cottage, a duck pond, and livestock in abundance, Rosalind (Elisabeth Bergner) and Celia (Sophie Stewart) simper and effervesce as though on a picnic excursion from a young ladies' seminary. A tenderly youthful Laurence Olivier as Orlando is unable to rescue this film from its saccharine premise that the play is a good old-fashioned love story set in a picturesque countryside.

Shakespeare conjures up for us a landscape that never existed and never could exist. His actors are in the theater, creating scenes out of their costumes, voices, and gestures. We understand where we are when they tell or demonstrate where they are. A theater of this sort gives the dramatist and his company full license to design a world that is more complex and multifaceted than that in which we ordinarily live.

How then does *As You Like It* go about to create its forest? First, descriptive dialogue invites us as audience to picture in our minds all that the actors talk about: mossy old trees, flowing brooks, pastures, sheep-cotes, and wild animals that can be as vividly strange in our thoughts as the drawings of Maurice Sendak. Then the dramatist introduces various story lines, all of them literary in origin, so much so that we realize we are being asked to recapture a literary landscape going back to Virgil and his eclogues, and before Virgil to the writers of ancient Greek pastoral, Bion and Theocritus. Moreover, the various landscapes of the mind that we thus encounter are of such a different texture that they invite a kind of debate about their respective merits and limitations. Arden refuses to stand still and be one place only.

The shepherds and shepherdesses in *As You Like It,* especially Silvius and Phoebe, are denizens of the Virgilian world of the literary pastoral. Their names are characteristic of that tradition, like those of Tityrus, Cuddie, Thenot, Thomalin, Hobbinoll, Colin Clout, and others who people the eclogues of Edmund Spenser, Sannazaro, Mantuanus, Philip Sidney, and other pastoralists. Corin's name has a familiar ring as well, though he, in Shakespeare's play, serves to define by realistic contrast what the pastoral tradition is not. Corin argues with Touchstone that shepherds' hands are greasy and smeared in tar from handling their ewes and performing surgery on them, so much so that shepherds never kiss hands as courtiers do (3.2.46–61). Corin works hard for his living, likes his "spare" life, and is indeed proud to be a "true laborer" who can "earn that I eat, get that I wear" (lines 19, 71–72). Silvius and Phoebe, conversely, do what shepherds and shepherdesses do in literary pastoral, that is, sit beside brooks or on hillsides singing in honor of Pan to the sound of pipes and timbrels. The young swains of pastoral tradition especially are inclined to sit "in secret shade alone" and "make of love his piteous moan" (Spenser, *The Shepherd's Calendar,* December, 1–6). In this the young lovers of pastoral also resemble those of the "complaint" tradition and the sonnet sequence, inspired by Francesco Petrarch, in which young men suffer from sleepless despair at the hands of their beauteous but hard-hearted mistresses. Silvius and Phoebe are thoroughly representative of this familiar type.

Still another literary genre that Shakespeare imports into his theatrical forest is that of satire. The malcontent Jaques is oddly out of place in Arden, but then it is his profession to be at odds with everything. As the devotee and practitioner of satire, he has the knack of stirring things up and questioning everyone's comfortable assumptions. "Most invectively," we are told, "he pierceth through / The body of the country, city, court" (2.1.58–59). He laughs even at the presumably virtuous motives of those who have left the wealth and ease of the court "A stubborn will to please" (2.5.35–54). He scorns wooing and matrimony. Most of all, he warms to the defense of satire as a socially necessary weapon against complacency and greed. In a sharply engaged colloquy with the banished Duke, he defends the satirist's right to be independent and unhindered as a social critic. "I must have liberty / Withal, as large a charter as the wind, / To blow on whom I please," he insists (2.7.47–49). No potential target of his righteous anger is to be spared. The Duke may wonder out loud if Jaques and other satirists are in fact motivated by a malicious desire to get back at their enemies and enhance their own power as social critics, but Jaques will have none of this. Unrepentant to the end, he decides in his usually perverse way to embrace a hermit's life when the others return to a reconstituted court.

The pros and cons of satire were much in the air in early 1599, when *As You Like It* may have been the opener for the new Globe Theatre on the Bankside. The Chamberlain's Men had just produced Ben Jonson's *Every Man in His Humour* in 1598, with Shakespeare in the cast. Jonson's view of comedy was that it should "sport with human folly, not with crimes" (Prologue to *Every Man In,* in Jonson's 1616 folio edition of his works). Sporting with human folly is just what Jaques does so adroitly.

Jonson's *Every Man out of His Humour,* in 1599, also a Chamberlain's production, was even more acerbic in its depiction of fops, country simpletons, would-be poets, cuckolded city husbands and their randy wives, grasping old misers, and the like. Then, too, nondramatic verse satire had become so scabrous and vitriolic in the final years of the decade that it brought down the wrath of Queen Elizabeth's ministers on the authors, with the result that a number of satirical books were burned in public in 1599. Shakespeare's presentation in the debate about satire is characteristically fair-minded and generous, representing both sides justly and accurately.

Jaques's famous Seven Ages of Man speech, often recited as a set piece of proverbial wisdom, is far more interesting when seen in its forest context. Jaques's wry view in that brilliant piece of satire is that life is a relentless and essentially meaningless saga of growth and then decay as the human animal careens through childhood and romantic courtship toward maturity, old age, and finally "second childishness and mere oblivion." Yet Jaques delivers this oration to men who have been exiled for their perseverance in goodness and who have learned to embrace privation as healthy for the soul. They are accordingly ready to practice human charity. The Duke astutely sees the need for such charity in the very circumstances of their present straitened existence:

> Thou see'st we are not all alone unhappy.
> This wide and universal theater
> Presents more woeful pageants than the scene
> Wherein we play in.   (2.7.135–38)

The Duke's language is richly theatrical: life itself is a play or pageant in which we play our parts. Jaques takes this theatrical metaphor in the direction of seeing human life as comically stereotypical, but the Duke's observation has been prompted by something more complex and unexpected. A starving man (Orlando) has shown up in their forest camp, sword in hand and threatening to kill them if necessary for food. The Duke's response is to urge that he sit with them and partake freely of what food they have. Orlando is melted by their generosity and goes at once to bring along his old servant, Adam, so deprived of nourishment that he is near death. To the Duke, as to Orlando and Adam, the theme of the Seven Ages need not be interpreted mordantly. The injustices that so often inform the "woeful pageants" in the drama called life can provide opportunities for humans to seek comfort in a companionship of suffering. Once again the magical forest of *As You Like It* has fostered a debate, showing what the nonscenic Elizabethan theater can do so very well.

The immediacy of the debate about satire in this scene may have seemed all the more vivid if, as seems likely, Robert Armin, newly arrived in the Chamberlain's company to replace the departed Will Kempe as chief clown, played the part of Touchstone. This wise fool, a new type in Shakespeare's comedies, operates in tandem with Jaques. Both see the absurdity of life, but to Touchstone the absurdity is less mordant and more funny. His stage presence continually unhinges and deflates. Invited by Corin to reflect on the attractions of a shepherd's life, Touchstone sees at once what is so comically self-contradictory in our feelings of city vs. country:

> Truly, shepherd, in respect of itself, it is a good life; but in respect that it is a shepherd's life, it is naught. In respect that it is solitary, I like it very well; but in respect that it is private, it is a very vile life. Now, in respect it is in the fields, it pleaseth me well; but in respect it is not in the court, it is tedious. As it is a spare life, look you, it fits my humor well; but as there is no more plenty in it, it goes much against my stomach. (3.2.13–21)

This cheerful view of the absurd informs everything that Touchstone surveys. He marries with Audrey, it seems, in order to laugh at his own desires: "I press in here, sir, amongst the rest of the country copulatives, to swear and to forswear, according as marriage binds and blood breaks," he tells the Duke (5.4.55–57). His lampoon of the seven "causes" of dueling, ending in the Lie Circumstantial and the Lie Direct, delights us as it delights the Duke with its good-natured amusement at how gentlemen "quarrel in print, by the book" and then extricate themselves from the quarrel with an "if"; "much virtue in if" (5.4.68–102). Touchstone is an essential part of the forest scene in *As You Like It* because he is so adept at keeping its rival and contradictory claims in perennial comic debate. And sadly, these elements of debate are often cut from modern productions as too wordy or cerebral. Czinner's 1936 film, for example, excises Touchstone's mock lecture on the Seven Degrees of Lying. So did an otherwise superbly funny performance by the Creation acting company in Headington Hill Park, Oxford, in the summer of 2005.

Even more essential to the destabilizing of the forest's mythology is Rosalind. She it is who punctures the false emotions of the Silvius-Phoebe relationship and all that this signifies in pastoral and Petrarchan tradition. She is blunt enough to Silvius: "I see love hath made thee a tame snake" (4.3.70–71). Her advice to Phoebe is more caustic:

"Down on your knees, / And thank heaven, fasting, for a good man's love! . . . I must tell you friendly in your ear, / Sell when you can. You are not for all markets" (3.5.57–60). The counseling she offers Orlando is more loving, of course, but it too trades in demystification. He must learn from her to abandon the cliches of Petrarchan sonneteering that have led him to idealize the woman (Rosalind) he has met only once and who is for him a disembodied goddess, a dream. He must be taught that human beings do not really die for love; the romantic tales of Hero and Leander or Troilus and Cressida "are all lies" (4.1.101), the stuff of literary convention. Rosalind prefers the real world, where wives are apt to be, as Rosalind confesses to Orlando that she will be, "more jealous of thee than a Barbary cock-pigeon over his hen, more clamorous than a parrot against rain, more newfangled than an ape, more giddy in my desires than a monkey" (4.1.142–46). When she says this, to be sure, she is disguised as a young man, Ganymede, pretending for the moment to be Orlando's Rosalind; the theatrical fiction, the impersonating of a sexual identity, facilitates their conversation in a way that would be more difficult if Orlando's shyness about women were aggravated by an awareness of sexual difference. Sexual identity is performance here, a fact that would have been borne home to Shakespeare's audience by their knowledge that Rosalind/Ganymede is being played by a boy actor. Through this performance we are enabled to see how Shakespeare's Forest of Arden is above all else a place of imagination, a theatrical space, a dialectic.

Stage productions, especially from the eighteenth into the early twentieth century, have often mounted lavishly realistic settings as background for a romanticized narrative line. An adaptation by Charles Johnson at Drury Lane in 1723 chose to rename the play *Love in a Forest,* taking care to excise Touchstone, Audrey, and the country folk from the script. William Charles Macready, at Drury Lane in 1842, commissioned painted sets by Clarkson Stanfield to enhance a vividly enacted wrestling match in an arena of ropes and staves, followed by pastoral vignettes to the accompaniment of distant sheep bells. At the Lyceum Theatre in 1890, Augustin Daly began his production with scene 3 so that the forest could fill the stage from the very start. In 1885, at the St. James's Theatre, what appeared to be real water rippled "among the sedges" of a brook before disappearing into a grassy marge, all so enticingly presented, in the view of the *Athenaeum,* that it "renders easier the task of the imagination and enhances the pleasure of the spectator." In a production at Stratford-upon-Avon in 1879, Audrey was presented with a turnip from the garden of Anne Hathaway's cottage. A production at His Majesty's Theatre in 1907 made use of "moss-grown logs, two thousand pots of fern, large clumps of bamboo, and leaves by the cartload from the previous autumn" (J. C. Trewin, *Shakespeare on the English Stage, 1900–1964*, p. 47). Frank Benson's very popular production at Stratford-upon-Avon from 1910 to 1919 hung ivy on the walls and strewed the stage ankle-deep with leaves. Even as late as 1974, Dorothy Tutin starred as Rosalind in a version directed by David Jones for the RSC in which huge trees were a dominating element.

However much these elaborate productions were artistically satisfying in their own terms, more recent experiments have discovered the revisionary excitement of mounting this play on a presentational, non-scenic stage. A notable instance was Cheek by Jowl's 1991–1995 production, directed by Declan Donnellan and taken on world tour. Above a plain wooden floor, green banners hung from the flies to signify a sylvan landscape. The all-male cast, accoutered at first in black trousers and white shirts, later in working clothes for the Duke's followers and unpadded long dresses for the female roles, occupied the stage throughout, coming forward from an outer circle when involved in stage action. Some played bits of jazz, especially in the carnivalesque finale. Color-blind casting selected Adrian Lester for the role of Rosalind. Tall, dark-complected, visibly masculine and at the same time energized by the homoerotic resonances of his role as a supposed woman playing a young man who is courting the attractively male Orlando (Patrick Toomey), this Rosalind was the brilliant embodiment of theatrical ambiguity (fig. 3.3). The production chose every means possible to call attention to its own artifice.

Other productions too have chosen to be iconoclastic and anti-illusionary, as in Adrian Noble's 1985 production for the RSC that was pointedly devoid of trees. Clifford Williams employed an all-male cast as early at 1967 (revived in 1974) for the National Theatre, in front of a modernist set fashioned out of Plexiglas tubes and sheets of metal screen. Stephen Pimlott, directing a production in 1996 for the RSC, made use of sheet metal boxes and pillars in aluminum and steel to suggest a thoroughly synthetic forest. At the new Globe in 1998, a solitary tree, bare except for a few apples, was the only concession to realism on an otherwise uncluttered Elizabethan stage, enabling cast members to pursue their gleeful mockeries of the literary conventions out of which Shakespeare has constructed his supple text. Christine Edzard's 1992 film boldly sets the play in a drab urban jungle of homeless waifs and

3.3. Adrian Lester as Rosalind and Patrick Toomey as Orlando, in Cheek by Jowl's production of *As You Like It*, 1991–1995. By permission of the photographer, John Haynes, and Cheek by Jowl.

drug addicts rummaging for something to eat in garbage bins. The images are compellingly iconoclastic and laden with implied social commentary, while at the same time so overdetermined in concept that the play's joie de vivre is given little chance to shine (see Michael Hattaway, ed., *AYLI*, The New Cambridge Shakespeare, 2000).

IV

The very name of Illyria in *Twelfth Night* (1600–1602) suggests that we are in another world of the theatrical imagination. Historically, Illyria is an ancient region in the Balkans along the Adriatic coast, at one time a Roman province. In Shakespeare's rendition it is a place where anything can happen, where mistaken identities abound, and where the denizens are often persuaded that everyone must be mad, including themselves. "Are all the people mad?" asks Sebastian when he is accosted physically by Sir Andrew (who has mistaken Sebastian for his look-alike twin). When he is then invited home by a beautiful countess (Olivia) whom he has never met before but who speaks to him with fond familiarity, Sebastian begins to doubt his own sanity. "Or I am mad, or else this is a dream," he concludes (4.1.26, 60). This bit of stage business is in effect a replay of the scene in *The Comedy of Errors* in which Antipholus of Syracuse is mistaken by an attractive lady for his look-alike twin and is invited into her house. Malvolio is declared mad when he dons cross-gartering and yellow stockings and is locked up in a dark cell; the apostle of sobriety in this play exchanges places with the fool. "I am as well in my wits, Fool, as thou art," he protests to Feste (4.2.88). Olivia confesses privately that falling unexpectedly in love has made her as insane as her allegedly mad steward: "I am as mad as he, / If sad and merry madness equal be" (3.4.14–15). Her violent mood swings convince her that she is deprived of her senses. Love is a kind of madness, and both are akin to dramatic poetry, as Theseus points out in *A Midsummer:* "The lunatic, the lover, and the poet / Are of imagination all compact." The name "Illyria" begins to resonate with the connotations of "delirium." Repeatedly, *Twelfth Night* intently reminds us that we are in the theater, watching a theatrical illusion. As Fabian observes of the plot to discomfit Malvolio, "If this were played upon a stage now, I could condemn it as an improbable fiction" (3.4.129–30).

Viola is, like Rosalind, a young woman played by a boy actor who assumes the disguise of young man. In this case, the shipwrecked Viola does so in order that she may take service in the court of a duke. Once again sexual difference is performative, and once again it serves the purpose of enabling the seeming young male (here renamed "Cesario") to coax the man with whom she falls in love into mature self-knowledge. Orsino is, like Orlando in *As You Like It,* infatuated with a dream. His love-madness takes the form of enervation, moody listlessness, and self-absorption. He talks endlessly of his love-sickness but does little to cure it with effective wooing. His teacher in all these matters is a young person whose role-playing allows him/her to see what wooing and marriage are really all about. Being Tiresias-like in his/her knowledge of what men are like and what women want, Viola/Cesario succeeds brilliantly in capturing Olivia's love without wishing to do so, and simultaneously becomes the best "male" companion that Orsino has ever known. To this seeming young man Orsino is now able to pour out his heart. Once the education of Orsino has completed its course, Viola need only doff her male garb to become the woman that Orsino has yearned for all along without his being aware of the fact.

A stage trick—the removing of a costume and hence of a persona or disguise—unravels all the complications of *Twelfth Night,* as it does in *As You Like It,* where Rosalind's assumption of her "true" identity instantly restores a daughter to her father, a young woman to her lover, and a reformed Phoebe to Silvius. Magic and madness in *Twelfth Night* operate through a similar staging device. Presto-change-o, and suddenly Viola and Sebastian are reunited as brother and sister, Orsino finds an intelligent young woman who adores him, and Olivia steps out of mourning into the full commitment of marriage with Sebastian. Even Toby and Maria are prepared to spend their lives together as merrymakers who know a good joke when they see one. Malvolio is left out of this final resolution, but that is because, like Jaques, he is a perennial and even willful outsider.

Along with Viola, no character in *Twelfth Night* better captures the spirit of theatrical inversion and mad magic than does Feste, the clown and fool. As the opposite to Malvolio in every way, Feste conjures up a world of holiday, of Saturnalia, of inverted norms, while Malvolio (until he is tricked into wearing festive gear and an unaccustomed smile) is the apostle of sobriety. The play thus belongs to Feste. Its very title, *Twelfth Night,* celebrates the twelfth day of the prolonged Christmas holiday in which actors put on their shows in aristocratic households or at the Inns of Court. The first performance of the play on record took place on Candlemas Day, February 2, 1602, at the Middle Temple as part of midwinter festivities (fig. 3.4), where it was compared by a young barrister, John Manningham, to *The Comedy of Errors,* to Plautus's *Menaechmi* (Twins), and especially to the Italian *Inganni.* Two Italian comedies with similar titles, by Niccolò Secchi and Curzio Gonzaga, provided indirect source material for Shakespeare, though he turned mainly to a short story by Barnabe Riche in *Riche His Farewell to Military Profession* (1583). Midwinter inversions were known to Shakespeare also in religious celebra-

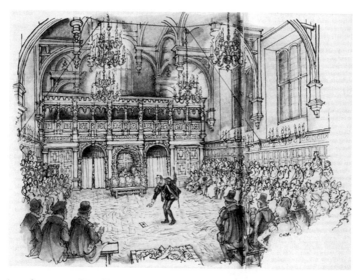

3.4. A performance of *Twelfth Night* in the hall of the Middle Temple, February 2, 1602, as reconstructed in a drawing by C. Walter Hodges. Malvolio finds the letter in Olivia's garden while Sir Toby and Sir Andrew and Fabian watch gleefully from the shrubbery (2.5.81 ff.). Reprinted with the permission of Cambridge University Press.

tions during the Christmas season, especially in mock ceremonials on the Feast of Innocents, December 28, elevating a humble choirboy to be bishop for a day while the lower clergy made braying noises and other infantile blasphemies of the religious service. Christmas was, for worshipers in late medieval and early modern times in Europe, a time to ponder the paradoxes of the Beatitudes that the first shall be last and the meek inherit the earth, and that the mighty tyrant Herod must suffer ignominious defeat at the birth of a babe in a ruined manger in Bethlehem.

Feste embodies the inversions of midwinter Saturnalia, and hence of theatrical illusion. He mocks his mistress, the Countess Olivia, for her ritual mourning of a dead brother in such a way as to suggest that she would do far better to embrace life in all its turmoil of passions. In saying this, Feste is an ally of Viola, for the burden of Viola's homily to Olivia is that "what is yours to bestow is not yours to reserve" (1.5.184), that is, beauty such as Olivia's should be put to use and not hidden from the world. Feste expresses this idea in song:

> What is love? 'Tis not hereafter;
> Present mirth hath present laughter.
> What's to come is still unsure.

In delay there lies no plenty.
Then come and kiss me, sweet and twenty;
Youth's a stuff will not endure.   (2.3.47–52)

Sir Toby is of a similar mind. His rebuke of Malvolio takes aim at those who wish to deny innocently hedonistic pleasure to others: "Dost thou think, because thou art virtuous, there shall be no more cakes and ale?" (2.3.114–15). The joy-seekers of this play band together to defend their ways against those killjoys who feel themselves called upon to become moral guardians of public behavior.

The application of this danger alarm to the Puritans, who were becoming increasingly strident around the time of this play with their stern disapproval of church ales, maypoles, and other familiar customs of communal celebration, gains added point in *Twelfth Night* when Malvolio is called "a kind of Puritan." Having made this charge, Maria immediately takes it back in part, to the extent that Malvolio does not belong to a particular religious group. He is instead a "time-pleaser" and "affectioned ass," too well persuaded of himself (2.3.139–51). Yet to the extent that Malvolio behaves like some Puritans, dressing in black and censoring what he takes to be loose behavior while at the same time hypocritically lusting for power and pleasure, he begins to anticipate Molière's Tartuffe of later date and must be stopped before he becomes too powerful. The hour is late; what's to come is still unsure, and in delay there lies no plenty. With some urgency, *Twelfth Night* confronts the gaunt specter of Puritan opposition to the stage, which had grown in vociferousness during the 1590s and was now resonating with a dull roar. Negotiations between the new King James I and the Puritan wing of the church were to come to an unsatisfactory impasse at the Hampton Court conference of January 1604, some two or four years later than this play. The unusual way in which Shakespeare draws attention to a contemporary controversy suggests that artistic freedom is at stake and that Shakespeare's special brand of stage magic needs to shore up its defenses.

Stage tradition, as in the case of *As You Like It,* has often concerned itself more with the picturesque and verisimilar than with the idea of a magical theatrical space where anything can happen. Henry Irving, at the Lyceum Theatre in 1884, envisaged Illyria as though it were sixteenth-century Venice. Orsino resided in a Palladian mansion. A road led up to Olivia's villa, which was complete with courtyard, terrace, adjoining cloister, and a commanding view of the seacoast. The art of landscape gardening, as one contemporary reviewer noted, had "reached a very high pitch of excellence." Irving was heard to complain that Shakespeare was financial ruin, and he had every reason to know. At the Lyceum Theatre in 1894, Augustin Daly vied with Irving in the department of spectacular effects by launching his production with a magnificent storm. A chorus of happy villagers greeted the cessation of the storm by singing "Come unto these yellow sands" from *The Tempest.* By staging the landing ashore of the shipwrecked Viola and the Captain, rather than beginning with the lovesick Orsino and then with Viola already safely on land, as in Shakespeare's text, Daly found a way to bring his leading lady, Ada Rehan, on at the very start. So elaborate were the sets that Daly chose to run together a sequence of scenes in Duke Orsino's palace before making the cumbersome and time-consuming shift to another long composite sequence at Olivia's villa. The production was a great success.

Herbert Beerbohm Tree did no less well in 1901 at Her Majesty's Theatre. Once again a costly and impressive mansion for Olivia meant that the action continued at her house for a more continuous length of time than is called for in Shakespeare's text. A terrace ran the full length of the backstage wall, from which stone steps descended into a formal garden with live grass, gravel pathways, and flowing fountains (see fig. 1.2 in chapter 1). Directors have often clung to Elizabethan costuming in their productions of this play, as did John Barton at Stratford-upon-Avon in 1969. Outdoor performances, as at the Shakespeare Festival in Ashland, Oregon, or in Regent's Park, London, can enhance an atmosphere of romantic escape amid great natural beauty. Trevor Nunn's well-cast and intelligent film of 1996, with Imogen Stubbs as Viola, Helena Bonham Carter as the Countess Olivia, Ben Kingsley as Feste, Toby Stephens as Orsino, and Nigel Hawthorne as Malvolio, is enhanced by verisimilar scenic effects. Saint Michael's Mount, dramatically situated on the Cornish coast amid picturesque fishing villages and precipitous seacoast cliffs, is enchantingly beautiful as the location of Orsino's mansion in this film, and so is the nearby country dwelling of Olivia (shot at Lanhydrock House and Prideaux House, also in Cornwall), with its spacious lawns and well-tended flower borders. Breathtaking as these effects can be, the splendor of this scenic beauty pulls the film toward the conventions of realism and away from a place of imagination and the improbable. The BBC's *Twelfth Night,* produced by Cedric Messina and directed by John Gorrie in 1980, similarly uses the camera to introduce us to the handsome English country estate of the Countess Olivia, where, in Messina's words, we can savor the play as "the *Upstairs, Downstairs* of the Shakespearean canon." Yakov Fried's 1955 Soviet color film version (in Russian, with subtitles) is a triumph of spectacle, with sweeping vistas of the coast line, hunting scenes, white marble palaces, and sumptuous interiors of Olivia's estate.

Reacting to long-standing conventions of realism, some innovative directors have sought to rediscover Shakespeare's script in a more presentational style. William Poel, actor-manager of the Elizabethan Stage Society, staged *Twelfth Night* on a bare platform as early as 1895, in a conscious revival of what he took to be Elizabethan stage practice. In 1897 he produced the play in the Hall of the Middle Temple in London—where it had been performed in February 1602 (see fig. 3.4 above)—with nothing more elaborate for scenic effects than a table and chair. This event was replicated in 2002 in a four-hundredth-year anniversary celebration of the first Middle Temple performance by an all-male cast of the new Globe company, starring Mark Rylance as an astonishing Countess Olivia. Spectators were ranged on three sides and in the gallery over the hall screen. The actors, entering and exiting by way of this handsome facade at the lower end of the hall, performed in the round, in Elizabethan costume.

Harley Granville-Barker followed up on Poel's pace-setting experimentation with a swift-moving ensemble production at the Savoy Theatre in 1912. Barry Jackson employed a thrust stage at the Birmingham Repertory Theatre in 1916. Jessica Tandy doubled as Viola and her twin brother Sebastian in Tyrone Guthrie's 1937 production at the Old Vic, with Laurence Olivier as Sir Toby and Alec Guinness as Sir Andrew. John Barton, in his production for the RSC at Stratford-upon-Avon in 1969, downplayed scenic effects in order to focus on the versatile performances of Judi Dench as Viola/Cesario, Charles Thomas as Orsino, and Emrys James as Feste. A rock musical version called *Your Own Thing* appeared in 1968. Many recent productions have discovered that the metatheatrical delights of twinning and sexual ambiguity in *Twelfth Night* need no elaborate scenic effects to capture an audience's attention. Like Shakespeare's other great romantic comedies, *Twelfth Night* has a lot to say about the theater of imagination.

V

Let us take a briefer look at six other comedies not yet discussed in this chapter that further illustrate how stage magic enables Shakespeare to transform his theatrical environment into a world of playful illusion.

Mistaken identities, often brought about by the donning of a disguise, are an essential part of the comic confusion in Shakespearean comedy. *The Comedy of Errors* (c. 1589–1594) tells of identical twin brothers and their identical twin servants in the city of Ephesus, where Antipholus of Syracuse has come in search of his long-lost sibling. This farce of mistaken identity, derived from two plays by the Latin dramatist Plautus (*Menaechmi*, or Twins, and *Amphitruo*), seems to posit a theatrical milieu that is recognizably neoclassical in its unity of space. Three locations seem to be visible, one for the house of Antipholus of Ephesus, one for the Courtesan (*"Enter Antipholus [and] Dromio of Ephesus from the Courtesan's,"* 4.1.13.1), and one for the priory or abbey (*"Exeunt to the priory,"* *"Exit one to the Abbess,"* 5.1.37.1–2, 282.1). Whether these unusual stage directions mean that three doorways were to be identified with these three locations throughout, in the style of neoclassical staging, is uncertain, but remains an intriguing possibility. The action of the play observes the classical unity of time, being carefully limited to a single day. The play was thus well designed for performance at the Christmas Revels of December 28, 1594, at Gray's Inn, one of the Inns of Court, with its high-ceilinged Gothic interior and its handsome hall screen at the lower end of the room surmounted with a gallery (see fig. 2.13). Though it must have been performed in a public theater as well, the play shows Shakespeare's apprenticeship to neoclassical stagecraft with unusual clarity. Never again did he deploy such a carefully restricted neoclassical space.

At the same time, the comedy of mistaken identity seems authentically Shakespearean, and has lent itself to much inventiveness on the modern stage and screen. One popular stunt has been to assign the two Antipholuses to a single actor and the two Dromios to another, as in the BBC televised version of 1983–1984 and at the new Globe Theatre in London in 1998. Film can manage this sleight-of-hand easily, whereas stage versions have required considerable ingenuity, since both sets of twins come face to face with their opposite numbers in act 5 (as in *Twelfth Night*). Almost certainly the device was not employed in the play's original run. In 1864, at Stratford-upon-Avon, real twins, Charles and Henry Webb, took the parts of the two Dromios. Other stunt performances have included that at New York's Vivian Beaumont Theater in 1987 (having originated at Chicago's Goodman Theatre in 1983–1984), starring the Flying Karamazov Brothers and the Kamikaze Ground Crew, with baton whirlers and tightrope-walkers ready to deflate any pretense of seriousness and to drive to tears the poor author, William

Shakespeare, who appeared disconsolately onstage from time to time. *The Boys from Syracuse* (1938), by George Abbott and with music by Richard Rogers and Lorenz Hart, cheerfully took the art of adaptation still further by fashioning the play into a popular musical comedy.

In *Love's Labor's Lost* (c. 1588–1597), four young aristocrats at the court of Navarre disguise themselves as Russian visitors to impress their ladies and are trounced in the game of wits by the ladies themselves, who see through the men's disguises. Kenneth Branagh adroitly captures this moment in his film version of 2000 by updating the scene to pre–World War II Oxford or Cambridge, where elegant young aristocratic gentle-

3.5. Alessandro Nivola (King of Navarre), Alicia Silverstone (Princess of France), Matthew Lillard (Longaville), Carmen Ejogo (Maria), Adrian Lester (Dumaine), Emily Mortimer (Katharine), Kenneth Branagh (Berowne), and Natasha McElhone (Rosaline) in Branagh's film version of *Love's Labor's Lost* (2000).

men reenact their discomfiture at the hands of the ladies with a song and dance number called "Let's Face the Music and Dance" (fig. 3.5). A similar comic business recurs in *Much Ado about Nothing* (1598–1599), when Benedick disguises himself as a foreigner and dances with Beatrice, thinking his appearance sufficiently deceptive that he can tell Beatrice what he hears of her reputation for shrewishness, only to be outmaneuvered by Beatrice's awareness of who he really is and her taking the opportunity to tell him what she has heard people say about him. He is hurt by this, since he believes her to be speaking the truth, whereas she has sized up his game. Again, Branagh exploits the dramatic potential of this

3.6. Al Pacino as Shylock in Michael Radford's *The Merchant of Venice* (2004).

complex deception in his hugely successful 1993 film. Onstage, the play has shown its comic universality in a wide range of updated settings: British Raj India (John Barton, Stratford-upon-Avon, 1976), the American Southwest frontier (John Houseman and Jack Landau, Stratford, Connecticut, 1957), early Victorian England (Douglas Seale, Stratford-upon-Avon, 1958), Mafiosa Sicily (Franco Zeffirelli, National Theatre, 1965), small-town mid-America of the Teddy Roosevelt era (A. J. Antoon, Delacorte Theatre, New York, 1972), and many more.

In a similar vein of comic mix-up and disguise, Bassanio in *The Merchant of Venice* (c. 1596–1597) is outwitted by Portia, disguised as a young lawyer, when she asks as her fee for saving the life of Antonio a ring that she sees on Bassanio's finger. It is of course his wedding ring from her that he vowed never to part with. She, knowing perfectly well the honesty of his motives in giving up the ring, takes pleasure in tormenting him about the matter until she has made her point about marital fidelity and the cleverness of wives. Nerissa plays the same trick on Gratiano. (Joan Plowright, as Portia in the 1974 televised version of Jonathan Miller's 1969 production with Laurence Olivier as Shylock, is quite wonderful in her teasing of Jeremy Brett as Bassanio. Equally fine are Al Pacino, Jeremy Irons, Joseph Fiennes, and Lynn Collins in the 2004 film directed by Michael Radford; see fig. 3.6.) In *The Merry Wives of Windsor* (1597–1601), outlandishly improbable fairy disguises enable Mistress Quickly, Pistol, and the others to punish Falstaff for his would-be philandering. Julia's disguise as Sebastian in *The Two Gentlemen of Verona* (c. 1590–1594), is essential to the process by which she uncovers the intended infidelity of her wooer, Proteus, and brings him back into self-possession. All of these disguises positively revel in theatrical magic. It is through the theater's contrivances of costuming that the characters are put to the test and are saved from their worst selves, often with young women as the agents who engineer those illusions.

Similarly, these comedies create their sense of place by the speeches of costumed actors and by props rather than by constructed sets. *The Merry Wives* abounds in references to domestic objects that are so appropriate to this comedy about bourgeois village life: cups, "press, coffer, chest, trunk, well, vault," "birding pieces" or hunting guns that are discharged up the chimney at hunt's end to get rid of unwanted loaded shot, foul linen, buck baskets carried by means of cowlstaffs on servants' shoulders, a muffler, "thrummed hat," kerchief, and gown suited for "the fat woman of Brentford," and still more (see 4.2.54–71). Most of these items are brought onstage. A hilarious production by Bill Alexander at Stratford-upon-Avon in 1985 updated this domestic particularity to the 1950s and the start of the second Elizabethan age by introducing two suburban wives as they sat under hairdryers in a Windsor hairdressing shop, comparing the identical love letters they had received from Falstaff (see fig. 3.7). The forest in *The Two Gentlemen* can be presented in the theater not by trees but by outlaws and by Valentine's talk of "shadowy desert" and "unfrequented woods" (5.4.2–3) to which (as in *A Midsummer* and *As You Like It*) the various exiles repair. Nineteenth-century productions generally opted for colorful scenic effects, as in Charles Kean's staging of *The Two Gentlemen* in 1846 at New York's Park Theatre, but more recent stagings have generally taken a more theatrically self-aware approach by updating the *mise en scène* to the Italian Riviera (Robin Phillips, Stratford, Ontario, 1975) or the polite-society Edwardian England of teacups and croquet (Mark Rylance, the New Globe, 1997). Belmont differs from Venice in *The Merchant of Venice* in the theater not so much scenically as by its being a place of caskets and riddling inscriptions, quiet nighttime conversations about the stars, soft music, song (as when Bassanio contemplates his casket choice, 3.2.63–72), and a pervasive feminine presence; Venice, by contrast, is dominated by men in social and judicial conflict. The never-never-land of Navarre in *Love's Labor's Lost* anticipates *As You Like It* in being a pastoral landscape where earthy peasants like Costard and Jaquenetta are improbably clustered together with a school pedant, a curate, the aptly named Constable Dull, and a fantastical Spanish braggart soldier, Don

3.7. Janet Dale as Mistress Page and Lindsay Duncan as Mistress Ford sit under hairdryers as they exchange information about the identical love letters they have received from Falstaff (2.1), in Bill Alexander's 1985 production of *The Merry Wives of Windsor* at Stratford-upon-Avon. Photo credit: Joe Cocks Studio Collection. Copyright Shakespeare Birthplace Trust.

Armado, as was brilliantly demonstrated in Chicago Shakespeare Theatre's production of 2003. A thrust stage, relatively free of scenic effects and wide open to the spectators' imagination, provides a liberating atmosphere in which such experimental stagings can take place. In all these productions, as in the original performances in Shakespeare's own theater, physical space and properties reinforce visually and reinterpret the multiple significances of his texts.

ℒ4ℒ

Thus Play I in One
Person Many People

PERFORMING THE HISTORIES

A witness to Shakespeare's history plays of the 1590s might have sur-
mised that the siege was a predominant mode of warfare in the thirteenth through fifteenth centuries about which Shakespeare extensively
wrote. Such a spectator might also have concluded that the history of
that period was dominated by nearly continuous military conflict, especially in the fifteenth century. This spectator would be essentially right
on both scores. Shakespeare's nine history plays concluding with *Henry V*
in 1599 all stage military confrontations, more often than not as the
climax of the play's dramatic action. (A number of tragedies involve
warfare as well, notably *Julius Caesar, King Lear, Macbeth, Antony and Cleopatra,* and *Coriolanus,* along with the mixed-genre *Troilus and Cressida.*)
Siege warfare is a staple of the dramatic presentation of war in Shakespeare's theater, especially when the fighting is in France. His accounts
of sieges draw largely upon Holinshed's historical chronicles, where
for example he could read how Richard II was cornered by Henry Bolingbroke in Flint Castle in 1399, how Henry V stormed Harfleur in 1415,
and how Joan of Arc raised the English siege of Orleans in 1429. Siege
warfare continued well into the seventeenth century: the parliamentary
forces built a defense work of ditches and bulwarks around all of London by 1642 at the start of England's civil war, though it was never chal-
lenged by the Royalists, while Bertolt Brecht, in his *Mother Courage,*
tells of siege warfare in middle Europe during the so-called Thirty Years'
War of the seventeenth century. The earlier conflict that had pit-
ted England against France from the reign of Edward III in the second

half of the fourteenth century down through Henry Tudor's defeat of Richard III at Bosworth Field in 1485 became widely known as the Hundred Years' War.

At the same time, some crucially important battles were fought in open battlefield, among them Shrewsbury in 1404, Agincourt in 1415, St. Albans in 1455, Wakefield and Mortimer's Cross in 1461, York soon afterward, Coventry and Barnet and Tewkesbury following in succession, and then Bosworth Field in 1485. Shakespeare found himself called upon to dramatize two types of warfare, that of the siege and that of the open battlefield. He and his fellow dramatists devised correspondingly different stage techniques for these situations, enabling him to follow the spirit of his chronicle sources (though he also felt free to compress time, change dates, decide who was present at a military engagement and who was not, alter ages of the participants, highlight certain achievements and not others, etc.). These differences of siege and open battlefield are sharply etched in Shakespeare's scripts. They are, as we shall see, strikingly different from the conventions of stage fighting with which modern audiences are familiar.

I

The military siege is essential to the conduct of war in *The First Part of King Henry VI,* probably Shakespeare's first history play and one with which he gained considerable fame early in his career. Thomas Nashe remarked in his *Pierce Penniless,* 1592, that it would "have joyed brave Talbot (the terror of the French) to think that after he had lain two hundred years in his tomb, he should triumph again upon the stage." Nashe must be referring to Shakespeare's play, for it gives a central role to Lord Talbot as the brave English general who does indeed terrify the French until he is betrayed by quarreling politicians at home and denied the support needed to win at Bordeaux. Shakespeare did much, indeed, to invent the new and immensely popular genre of the English history play. An anonymous dramatization of *The Famous Victories of Henry V* in the late 1580s had told the story of Prince Hal's rise to manhood and his stunning victory at Agincourt, and Christopher Marlowe's *Tamburlaine* had shown how the English stage could accommodate a series of military conquests, but Shakespeare helped put this all together in terms of English history while at the same time investing it with thematic seriousness.

The English siege of Orleans in *1 Henry VI* offers a classic demonstration of how such an operation was carried off in the Elizabethan theater. We learn in scene 2 that the English have surrounded the city for some time, while the Dauphin Charles and his band of followers, resolved to "raise the siege" by beating off the besieging forces, are encamped "near Orleans" so that they can harass the English. They attempt to do so but are beaten back "*with great loss*," meaning, presumably, that a number of stage "deaths" of French soldiers occur onstage during a brief foray enacted by perhaps four to six extras. The French conclude glumly from this that the English are not to be driven off; as Charles puts it, "Rather with their teeth / The walls they'll tear down than forsake the siege" (1.2.6–40).

When Joan of Arc arrives to put courage into the French, they resolve to try again. A short time later, a French Master Gunner and his Boy, commenting to one another on how "Orleans is besieged" and how the English have won the "suburbs" or surrounding territory (1.4.1–2), place their cannon in such a way that the Boy, entering "*with a linstock*" or forked stick used to hold a lighted match for firing the weapon, manages to kill two English officers, the Earl of Salisbury and Sir Thomas Gargrave. A stage direction informs us that they are standing "*on the turrets*," meaning evidently some place in the theater that is elevated above the main stage. Their talk just before this tragedy is of the advisability of devising military positions "at the north gate" and "the bulwark of the bridge" (1.4.22–67). We are thus to imagine these brave English officers cut down as they prepare to assault Orleans. The theater building is alive with the smoke and offstage noise of the fired chambers (which may well have been small ceremonial pieces used to fire salutes, or even powder chambers, rather than a full-size cannon, which would be difficult to manage). The assault is made three-dimensional by the action above and by forays of armed soldiers across the stage.

The tactical situation being pictorialized in the theater is that Charles and his soldiers, inspired by Joan, are attempting to drive off the besieging English army. In one *alarum* or foray after another, Talbot "*pursueth the Dauphin and driveth him*," only to be baffled by the diabolical Joan, "*driving Englishmen before her*" (1.5.0.1–4). Despite Talbot's heroic efforts, Joan manages to "*enter the town with soldiers*," that is, exit from the stage through a large door in the tiring-house wall signifying the "gates" of Orleans (1.5.14.1). Other short alarums and excursions are to no effect; Talbot is forced to concede that "Pucelle is entered into Orleans / In spite of us or all that we could do" (36–37). He and his forces exit as the trumpet sounds a "*Retreat*," signifying a withdrawal from battle.

As spectators, we are now aware that the tiring-house wall of the theater has taken on, for this sequence of action, the identity of the walls of Orleans. Scene 6 begins with *"Enter, on the walls, Pucelle* [i.e., Joan], *Dauphin, Reignier, Alençon, and soldiers."* Joan underscores the visual significance of their appearance above by proclaiming, "Advance our waving colors on the walls; / Rescued is Orleans from the English!" The walls remain a vital element of the action that night, when a French sergeant of the watch and two sentinels are seen there guarding the city. Talbot enters now on the main stage, assisted by Bedford, Burgundy, and their forces, *"with scaling ladders"* (2.1.7.1–2). Their plan is to enter the city by placing their ladders against the walls in the secrecy of night. They do so with a symmetry appropriate to the theatrical space provided for them. Bedford undertakes to ascend his ladder in "yond corner" while Burgundy takes up position at the opposite corner ("And I to this," he says), leaving to Talbot the middle position backstage: "And here will Talbot mount." They ascend in unison and appear to enter the city by vanishing into the tiring house at the level of the gallery, the very space where Joan and Charles have appeared earlier *"on the walls."*

The ensuing stage direction is helpfully specific: *"The French leap o'er the walls in their shirts. Enter, several ways, [the] Bastard [of Orleans], Alençon, [and] Reignier, half ready, and half unready"* (2.1.38.4–6). In other words, some of the routed French soldiers emerge from the tiring house (which we understand to represent for the time being the city of Orleans) at the gallery level and jump down on to the main stage, a vertical distance of as much as fourteen feet from the top of the gallery railing — a leap requiring agility and no doubt inspiring anti-French laughter among Elizabethan English spectators. Meanwhile their leaders emerge in total disarray at more than one doorway. (*Several* means "more than one.") Their conversation comically suggests that they have been caught so unprepared because they have been drinking, making love, or sleeping. The English have recaptured Orleans, and, when they emerge from the tiring house in the next scene, the main stage is now theirs as they occupy the interior of Orleans, so that Talbot can order that the body of the dead Salisbury be brought forth "here . . . in the marketplace, / The middle center of this cursèd town" (2.2.4–5).

The Elizabethan theater building has proved to be both flexible and visually specific during the entire sequence. The tiring-house facade with its doors and its gallery *"above"* is an imposing structure in which actors can represent themselves as manning the walls of a besieged city. The spatial relationship of that tiring-house wall to the main stage is a visually plausible representation of a besieged city and the dangerous

outside ground lying close to its parapets and towers. At the same time
this facade can immediately be put to other uses, without scenic change,
as the implied location of the action in *1 Henry VI* shifts back and forth
between the inside and the outside of Orleans, or indeed between England and France.

The battle for the tiring-house wall continues in *1 Henry VI*, as
though Shakespeare is flexing the muscles of his newly developed skill in
the representation of siege warfare. Joan's next exploit is to gain access
to Rouen, held by the English. The tiring-house wall takes on the identity of Rouen at the very start of this sequence, by one of Shakespeare's
simplest devices: his actors tell us where we are. "These are the city
gates, the gates of Rouen," declares Joan, as she and four French soldiers,
"disguised" as peasants *"with sacks upon their backs,"* stand before one of
the big doors in the tiring-house facade representing the gates of the
city (3.2.0.1–2). Their plan, a skulking one in contrast with the English
intrepidity in scaling the walls at Orleans, is to talk their way into the
city as "Poor market folks that come to sell their corn." Shortly after
they are admitted through this ruse, Joan appears *"on the top, thrusting out
a torch burning."* She is in some elevated location in the theater, using her
torch to signal to the Dauphin and his forces on the main stage, that is,
still outside the walls of Rouen, that she has found the best place for
them to make their assault: "No place to that, for weakness, which she
entered" (3.2.15–25). The plan succeeds for a time. The French recapture
Rouen, enabling Joan to enter *"on the walls"* once again in triumph. Yet
the triumph is short-lived. The English under Talbot are successful in the
ensuing alarums and excursions. Joan, the Dauphin, and Alençon flee in
disarray, while the aged Duke of Bedford, who has asked to be placed
in a chair "before the walls of Rouen" rather than miss the excitement of
the battle, dies in the happy realization that his side has won. As Talbot
exclaims, "Lost and recovered in a day again!" (3.2.91–116).

Later (much later historically) we see Talbot at Bordeaux in a familiar
stage configuration. "Go the gates of Bordeaux, trumpeter," he orders.
"Summon their general unto the wall." At this point a trumpet sounds
and the general of the garrison at Bordeaux enters *"aloft,"* in the gallery
to the rear of the stage. Once again, the tiring-house facade is made to
represent the walls of a besieged city. This time, however, Talbot is fatally outnumbered, owing to inadequate support from England. The
general of the garrison assures Talbot that the French are "strong enough
to issue out and fight," and that "the Dauphin, well appointed [i.e.,
equipped with an armed force], / Stands with the snares of war to tangle

thee" (4.2.1–22). This is a lucid demonstration of how a siege might be raised and how Shakespeare conveys this action in his theater. The besieging forces have adopted a strategy of surrounding a city and strangling its sources of supply for water, food, munitions, and the like. If, however, the besieged city is militarily strong enough to send forth soldiers to do battle, the defenders might be able to drive off the besieging army. They can do so more effectively still if they are reinforced by other military assistance brought in from other parts of France, and are especially in luck if the English do not have adequate reinforcements to bring up. Such is the case at Bordeaux. Talbot soon lies dead, along with his brave son John.

The tiring-house walls are defended from siege attack in later plays as well that deal both with civil war in England and with English military action in France. The Mayor and citizens of York, appearing *"on the walls"* in *3 Henry VI*, declare to the besieging forces of Edward IV that they have "shut the gates for safety of ourselves" (4.7.18). At Coventry, defenders appear *"upon the walls"* with the city of Coventry understood to be behind them in the tiring house (5.1.0.1–2). In *King John,* King Philip II of France, his son the Dauphin, the Duke of Austria, and others enter *"before Angiers,"* where they are joined by King John of England and his supporters. The open stage on which they stand represents the ground in front of the city's walls and gates, as is made clear when a trumpet sounds and a Citizen enters *"upon the walls"* to plead for a reconciliation between the opposing forces vying for control of Angiers. This Citizen remains on the walls as the opposing sides engage in indecisive battle and then send heralds *"to the gates,"* insisting on being admitted. The Citizen's reply underscores the spatial dimensions of the staging design: "from off our towers we might behold, / From first to last, the onset and retire / Of both your armies," he declares, adding however that he still cannot determine which army has prevailed. From his elevated vantage he proposes a marriage that will reconcile France and England, and the suggestion wins the kings' approval (2.1.1–561). Throughout this long scene, Shakespeare's theater is a theater of war.

Shakespeare creates the atmosphere of siege warfare not solely by his use of the tiring-house facade. He has other means as well, some of them verbal evocations of military maneuvers that we are to imagine rather than actually see. We do see the scaling ladders employed at the siege of Harfleur in *Henry V,* since they are specified in the opening stage direction of 3.1. His soldiers do presumably storm the walls as he urges them, "Once more unto the breach, dear friends" (3.1.1). At the same time, much is left for us to picture in our minds. What Henry alludes to is either the bringing up of a siege machine close to the walls in order to bombard a weak spot and open up a breach through which the besieging forces can then pour into the city, or a bombardment by means of "brass cannon" (line 11) to effect the same purpose. (These tactics, by the way, would have been quite impractical in Henry V's time, since soldiers trying to rush through such a breach would be subject to murderous cross-firing by the town's defenders; Holinshed's account of the siege of Harfleur contains no such business.) *"Alarum, and chambers go off,"* reads the stage direction at the scene's end, providing a cue for stagehands behind the scenes to fire off a round in a powder chamber in a loud burst of sound.

Moreover, the soldiers at Harfleur are busy digging mines and coping with countermines that we must imagine rather than actually behold in the theater. Captain Fluellen, bidden by Gower to "come presently to the mines" in *Henry V* in order to confer with the Duke of Gloucester, is unsparing in his disapproval of how the mines are being deployed. "Look you, the mines is not according to the disciplines of the war," he lectures Gower. "The concavities of it is not sufficient. For look you, th'athversary, you may discuss unto the Duke, look you, is digt himself four yard under the countermines" (3.2.53–61). Mines of this sort were tunnels dug under the enemy's fortifications in order to place explosives and thereby cause the foundations to collapse. As Captain Macmorris shrilly complains, "the work ish ill done; it ish give over. I would have blowed up the town, so Chrish save me" (89–91). Such operations do indeed hearken back to ancient times, as Fluellen, a devoted student of "the Roman wars" (96), is keenly aware. The diggers, called "pioners" or "pioneers" in this scene (86) and elsewhere (*Hamlet*, 1.5.172; and *Othello*, 3.3.362), were at the very bottom of the military hierarchy, like sappers of more recent date, for their job was both dirty and dangerous. Countermines were usually tunnels dug by the defenders to intercept the mines of the besiegers or to go beneath and undermine such tunnels, although in the present scene the French appear to have dug under the countermines of the besieging English. Perhaps that is what Fluellen means when he objects that all is not going "according to the disciplines of the war." In any event, a great part of the atmosphere of warfare in Shakespeare's history plays is conveyed through such dialogue and the evoking of things not actually seen.

The siege of Corioles in *Coriolanus* shows us that the stage conventions of such warfare apply in Shakespeare's plays not only to the English histories but to this tragedy, even to a tragedy set in ancient times; Shakespeare characterizes warfare according to the theatrical styles and conventions of his own day. The protagonist Marcius (not yet having been awarded the accolade of "Coriolanus") sets down before Corioles with Titus Lartius and other fighters. *"They sound a parley,"* that is, a trumpet summoning the enemy to a conference, whereupon two Senators enter, with others, *"on the walls of Corioles,"* in the gallery over the tiring-house wall. We recognize in this the customary configuration in Shakespeare's theater for the staging of a "parley" between the besiegers on the main stage and the besieged above, as in *King John.* The "gates" opening through a wide stage door into the tiring house representing the city thereupon become crucial in the ensuing action. Marcius *"Enter[s] the gates"* in pursuit of the fleeing Volscians *"and is shut in"* (1.4.1–46). The Elizabethan audience must now wait anxiously, for Marcius has dared to "Stand alone / To answer all the city" within the gates. When he emerges, at length, *"bloody"* (1.6.21), the audience knows that he has prevailed single-handedly. The sounds of drums, trumpets, and soldiers' shouts meanwhile provide the noise of battle. Alarums sound in the distance. Roman soldiers come onstage *"with spoils."* In the aftermath of victory, Coriolanus's soldiers *"all shout and wave their swords, take him up in their arms, and cast up their caps"* (1.6.75.1–2). Such is the theatrical sequence that introduces to the audience the eponymous hero of the play.

Just as Shakespeare and his acting company anachronized their stage renditions of siege warfare, post-Shakespearean productions have done so also, albeit with very different results. A Restoration revival of *Henry VI* in two parts by John Crowne at the Dorset Garden Theatre in 1680 and 1681 was much more interested in the portrayal of England's civil wars than in English exploits against the French, since the English nation had just gone through a terrible civil struggle in the mid-seventeenth century. Crowne's overriding interest in depicting the twin dangers of court factionalism and mob rule is evident in his choice of a title for his second part: *The Misery of Civil War.* Hence he played up the Jack Cade rebellion in *2 Henry VI,* along with the savage ritual killing of young Rutland and Edward IV's womanizing in *3 Henry VI* (suggestive perhaps of the notorious lechery of the Restoration monarch, Charles II). As a result, the battle engagements of the three-play sequence were heavily excised, especially those in *1 Henry VI.* Instead of staging military conflict through the use of Shakespearean alarums and sorties, Crowne preferred instructive tableaus: at one point, *"the scene is drawn, and there appears houses and towns burning, men and women hanged upon trees, and chil-*

dren on the tops of pikes." The device relied on scenic display rather than on live actors and their bodies.

The *Henry VI* plays were not often staged during the eighteenth and nineteenth centuries, and, even on the rare occasions when they were performed, the art of warfare played a distinctly minor part. The impetus for a revival of *1 Henry VI* at the Theatre Royal, Covent Garden, in 1738 was that "several ladies of quality" belonging to the Shakespeare Club wished to see all of Shakespeare's plays brought into production, including even this neglected masterpiece, which, as the playbill noted, had not been acted "these fifty years." An interest in the art of warfare was not among the considerations giving rise to this event. The tendency to group the *Henry VI* plays into a truncated one-evening entertainment, and to see them as fitfully interesting chiefly because of the glimpses they offer of the future Richard III, necessitated a heavy reduction of the fighting sequences. Edmund Kean's *Richard, Duke of York* at Drury Lane in 1817 was severely cut and supplemented with poetic passages from other dramatists such as George Chapman, John Marston, and John Webster in such a way that Kean could appropriate most of the good lines to himself. What generally happened instead of staging the *Henry VI* plays as absorbing chronicle plays in their own right was that passages from those earlier plays, especially *3 Henry VI,* were pillaged for additions to the text of *Richard III,* as in Colley Cibber's long-prospering production starting in 1700.

Only when directors and producers began seeing the *Henry VI* and *Richard III* plays as a series with lively potential for cyclical performance did serious stage warfare manage, as it were, to fight its way back into the repertory. Frank Benson mounted a cycle of six history plays in 1901, popularly known as "the Week of Kings," followed in 1906 by a production of the three *Henry VI* plays on successive nights. Even if the *Athenaeum* did complain that "Many have wished to see less scenery and more Shakespeare," the event opened up a sweep of history in which military conflict took on a strategic significance that was too easily lost sight of in the performance of individual plays geared to the egos of star actors and actresses in big roles (Joan of Arc, Queen Margaret, Henry VI, Suffolk) and emotionally intense scenes. At the Old Vic in 1923, Robert Atkins staged a swiftly paced two-part version of the *Henry VI* plays on an unadorned set. Barry Jackson at the Birmingham Repertory Theatre mounted individual productions of the three plays on successive years in 1951–1953. All three plays were restaged at the Old Vic in 1953, and then in 1957 in the final year of the Old Vic's ambitious undertaking of all the plays in the canon. Peter Hall collaborated with John Barton in a sequence named "The Wars of the Roses" at Stratford-upon-Avon in 1963, with the three *Henry VI* plays edited down to two by Barton, followed by a more complete *Richard III*. A television series in 1965, under the same title, boasted an impressive cast, nearly identical with that of the stage productions: Ian Holm as Richard of Gloucester, Peggy Ashcroft as Queen Margaret, Janet Suzman as the Lady Anne, Eric Porter as the Earl of Richmond, and Roy Dotrice as Edward IV. Jane Howell directed all four plays as a cycle for the BBC, ending with *Richard III* in 1983 with Ron Cook as Richard. Especially in these screen versions, military conflict, now eminently feasible, comes into its own.

To be sure, these filmed renditions, like the twentieth-century staged productions out of which they grew, make no attempt, even though they could certainly have done so, to reproduce the conditions of siege warfare that were so integral to Shakespeare's visualizations of armed conflict in his early history plays (which were themselves more a matter of theatrical convention than of historical reenactment). Charles Kean, in the heyday of nineteenth-century historical realism, attempted a lifelike siege of Harfleur in his *Henry V* at the Princess's Theatre in 1859, complete with war engines pointed menacingly at the town, stones flying in all directions, and then a Harfleur reduced to rubble, but such costly verisimilitude has long since disappeared. One sees in the various screen interpretations of *Henry VI* and *Richard III* no battlements, no scaling operations, no parleys with defending forces answering *"above"* from the besieged walls. The audience is not asked to use its imagination to suppose that an open theatrical space can be a besieged fortification at one moment and the inside of the town at the next. Instead, actors today adopt modern stage conventions of "Elizabethan" warfare, with armed men in one-on-one combat, parrying each other's swords and timing their choreographed blows so that the actors will not get hurt. This is not to criticize modern productions for making these choices; the point is rather that the language of stage gesture inevitably changes over time, and that actors necessarily employ the theatrical semiotics to which their audiences are attuned. Today's theater fighting is neither modern warfare nor Elizabethan siege warfare; it is an understood theatrical convention about the way Elizabethan warfare is "supposed" to look on the modern stage. The screen gives the director greater freedom to employ large numbers of extras armed in mail and steel helmets, along with archers, caparisoned horses, and all the rest, and yet here too "Elizabethan" warfare is a convention attuned to what audiences expect.

For all the attention to detail with which Shakespeare designs siege operations, he also shows us plenty of battles that are understood to take place in an open battlefield. Here a number of stratagems are at his disposal. Not infrequently, such battles are preceded by a series of proud vaunts hurled back and forth as the adversaries ready themselves for conflict. The purpose of such a meeting is nominally to see what might be negotiated (as in *King John*). Battle can sometimes be avoided, as in *King John* and in *2 Henry IV* at Gaultree Forest in Yorkshire (4.2). Sometimes, insults are traded in a highly antithetical ritual manner. In *King John,* at Angiers (where an open battle is in prospect, even though the city is under siege), the English and French kings exchange accusations about usurped royal authority while the women present, John's mother Eleanor and his widowed sister-in-law Constance, shrilly debate as to whether Constance's son Arthur is illegitimate. Philip the Bastard, meanwhile, heaps scorn on the Duke of Austria for presuming to celebrate his triumph over Richard Coeur de Lion (2.1.84–194). These exchanges of insults typically pair the antagonists in antithetically balanced staging. In *3 Henry VI,* prior to the battle historically fought between Towton and Sexton in Yorkshire, the Yorkists and Lancastrians taunt one another with charges of perjury, unnatural cruelty, and cowardice. The participants in this shouting match have every reason to be vengefully wrathful, since they have lost sons, fathers, and brothers to the opposite side in this bloody civil war of the Roses. Their defiant boasts make no pretense of seeking a peaceful resolution; the participants are working up their anger for the ensuing slaughter (2.2.61–177). Shakespeare may have learned something of the dramatic art of the flyting from Marlowe, whose *Tamburlaine* delights in such verbal gymnastics, as for example when Tamburlaine and his followers face off against the Turkish Emperor; in perfect symmetry, each leader has three chief subordinates while each wife is attended by a lady-in-waiting, enabling the dramatist to give the participants matching insults throughout the scene (*1 Tamburlaine,* 3.3).

Once the battle begins, Shakespeare's technique for dramatizing a battle is at once metonymic and Homeric. That is, Shakespeare calls upon the few extras available to him in the acting company to represent whole armies onstage in forays across the acting space, and intersperses this stage business with sequences of individual combats between the major contenders. The battle of Towton and Saxton in *3 Henry VI* begins in typical fashion with *"Alarum. Excursions"* (2.3.0.1). The next scene begins also with *"Excursions"* but is otherwise devoted to the clash of swords between Richard of Gloucester (the man who is to become Richard III) and the Lancastrian Lord Clifford. The one-on-one encounter between King Richard III and his successful challenger Richmond (soon to become Henry VII) is the fitting climax for *Richard III*, and as such is exploited in many a modern production: Ian McKellen's Richard, for example, in the film version of 1995 directed by Richard Loncraine, is pursued by Richmond through the steel girders of a building under construction as though these rivals are taking part in the final scene of an adventure thriller. Prince Henry and Hotspur fight for mortal odds at the end of *1 Henry IV;* the Prince's victory over his namesake (Henry Percy) signals his emergence into manhood and at least a temporary reconciliation with his father. Shakespeare reduces Hotspur's age by an entire generation in order to pair these opposites in dramatically meaningful symmetry; historically, Hotspur was about the age of Prince Henry's father. Shakespeare invents other one-on-one encounters, as when the Scottish Douglas kills Sir Walter Blunt outfitted to resemble King Henry IV, or when the King must defend himself against the mighty Douglas (5.4). *Henry V,* on the other hand, does not pit its hero king against any single opponent in the battle of Agincourt, perhaps because the Dauphin, Henry's antagonist earlier in the exchange of prebattle insults, is not a worthy contender. (In the quarto text, he is not even present at the battle.)

Shakespeare is certainly aware of the fact that he is dealing in theatrical shorthand. "Oh, for a Muse of fire, that would ascend / The brightest heaven of invention!" his opening Chorus to *Henry V* pleads. If only his acting company had "A kingdom for a stage" and "princes to act," they could show King Henry "like himself." On the eve of the great battle of Agincourt, the Chorus is especially apologetic that "oh, for pity!—we shall much disgrace / With four or five most vile and ragged foils, / Right ill-disposed in brawl ridiculous, / The name of Agincourt" (4 Chorus 49–52). The figure of "four or five" is not inaccurate; it is a plausible estimate of the number of hired men or extras that might be put to service in representing one of the greatest victories in all of British history. The Chorus is apologetic even for their weaponry and their skill as actors: their approximation of Agincourt will be "ridiculous," pitiful. "Can this cockpit hold / The vasty fields of France? Or may we cram / Within this wooden O the very casques / That did affright the air at Agincourt?" (Prologue, 11–14). The evidence suggests that in fact Shakespeare's acting company prepared such scenes with professional skill by taking lessons in fencing and other forms of stage combat. Yet nothing can reduplicate an actual field of battle. Theater necessarily deals through metonymy or synecdoche, whereby the name of one thing stands for another larger entity of which it is a part. The Chorus apologizes for such shortcomings, and yet at the same time sees in this necessary limitation of theater an invitation for the audience members to supply the rest by imagination, supplementing the actors' performance with their thoughts: "Into a thousand parts divide one man, / And make imaginary puissance" (24–25). Here then is the key to Shakespeare's dramatization of battle: it is an appeal to the audience's imagination, and as such it revels in what at first may have seemed a shortcoming.

Many are the ways in which Shakespeare asks us to "Piece out" the "imperfections" of his scene of battle. He relies on great speeches of exhortation. Henry V's famous rallying cry just before the Battle of Agincourt is addressed to "We few, we happy few, we band of brothers" (4.3.40–67)—an effective rhetorical appeal to Henry's soldiers to consider themselves lucky to be part of so small a band of English against so great a French army, while also a reminder to us that the actors are indeed few onstage, and that the "band of brothers" imaginatively includes us as audience as well, since we are now invited to take part vicariously in the risks and rewards of Agincourt. As spectators, we are exhorted to "see" horses when the actors talk of them, "Printing their proud hoofs i'th' receiving earth" (Prologue, 27). We are also invited to judge and compare, as when Richard III's mean-spirited appeals to hatred and paranoia on the eve of Bosworth Field are contrasted point by point with Richmond's inspirational reminder to his "loving countrymen" that "God and our good cause fight upon our side" (*Richard III*, 5.3.237–337).

Shakespeare often appeals to pity and horror in order to convey the full range of emotional response to conflict. Such scenes can become highly emblematic, as when, in *3 Henry VI*, a son who has unknowingly killed his father enters at one door, bearing the dead body, whereupon there enters "*at another door a father that hath killed his son, bearing of his son*" (2.5.54–113). No spectacle could more painfully drive home the harsh lessons of civil war, in which members of a single family are all too apt to find themselves on opposite sides of the conflict. This dilemma applies at the highest levels of state to the large royal family descended from Edward III, since Yorkists and Lancastrians alike go back to that great ancestry; it also applies at the local level to unnamed father and son,

son and father. The very anonymity of these sad figures underscores their metonymic function in representing untold numbers of similar interfamily tragedies. The emblematic and indeed markedly "unrealistic" character of this vignette is emphasized by the presence of King Henry VI, sitting alone on a molehill (line 14) and philosophizing on the vanity of human wishes while his mannish wife, Margaret, manages the battle for him.

Deaths are a great way of dramatizing the consequences of warfare and thereby relieving the potential tedium of too many alarums and excursions. Often the deaths are anticipated by famous last cries of valor or defiance. "A horse! A horse! My kingdom for a horse!" shouts Richard III at Bosworth Field. This is his last utterance. Whatever must be charged against Richard as tyrant and villain, he dies fighting. "Lay on, Macduff," the protagonist of *Macbeth* urges his nemesis, "And damned be he that first cries, 'Hold, enough!'" (5.8.33–34). These two great contenders exit fighting and then reappear in the midst of more combat, suggesting that the staging is to be elaborate and skillfully orchestrated. Lord Talbot dies in *1 Henry VI* in the company of his son and heir, whom he has urged to flee the battle and thus save the family line of descent only to be answered that such a flight would heap infamy upon them (4.6–7). *3 Henry VI* abounds in spectacular deaths: of young Rutland, of Richard Plantagenet, of Lord Clifford, of Warwick the great kingmaker, of the plucky young Lancastrian Prince of Wales, Edward, and of King Henry VI, murdered in the Tower of London by Richard of Gloucester (5.6).

As with siege warfare, open battlefield warfare in modern productions of Shakespeare's histories exploits a wide variety of ways to reinterpret the text in terms that are intelligible to modern audiences. Richard Loncraine's film version of *Richard III* (1995) begins with a scene (actually a sort of compilation of 5.5 and 5.6 in *3 Henry VI*) in which King Henry and his son, Edward the crown prince, both dressed in British military garb of the 1930s, are alone and apprehensively aware of military danger near at hand. Suddenly an armored tank breaks through the walls of their room. The two are gunned down by a menacing figure in a gas mask. Once the operation has been completed, the attacker unmasks, revealing the unmistakable features of Ian McKellen. It is Richard of Gloucester, carrying out the assassination of the Lancastrian royal line as he has promised to do. The Yorkist takeover is complete. Much later, as the new King Richard III now must fall before the onslaught of the Earl of Richmond (Dominic West), the warfare is again

4.1. Ian McKellen as Richard III, stalled in his jeep at the battle of Bosworth Field, bellowing his famous line, "A horse! A horse! My kingdom for a horse!" (5.4.13), in Richard Loncraine's film version of *Richard III* (1995), set in pre–World War II England at the time of an imagined fascist takeover.

aggressively twentieth-century. Richmond charges on screen in an armored vehicle, himself manning a machine gun on its upper deck. Explosions and fires are everywhere. When Richard's army jeep is mired in mud and unable to move, Richard angrily shouts, "A horse! A horse! My kingdom for a horse!" (5.4), thereby giving a comic spin to this notorious line by way of reminding the audience that it is watching a performance (see fig. 4.1). Indeed, the whole battle sequence, culminating in the death of Richard as he spirals down from the steel skeleton of a tall building, grinning demonically to the tune of "I'm sitting on top of the world," asks to be seen as a campy send-up of action or gangster film endings. (In fact, Loncraine is quoting James Cagney's death, as he shouts "Top of the world, Ma!" atop a burning oil tank at the end of the film *White Heat*.)

Laurence Olivier's *Henry V* (1944) glorifies warfare, no doubt in part at least because the film was commissioned by the British government as a means of bolstering morale in the war against Nazi Germany. Never mind that the enemy in Shakespeare's play is France; patriotism is an emotion easily aroused. The battle of Agincourt, filmed in Ireland, contains a long wordless sequence of French lords in full armor being hoisted atop their mounts by ungainly cranes (a completely unhistorical detail), of British soldiers positioning rows of sharpened stakes in the ground, of French cavalrymen urging their horses forward in a prolonged gallop, of British archers discharging simultaneously a barrage of arrows into the air, of brutal contact between the armies, of wounded horses flailing in the mud, and much more. Olivier's avowed intent is to visualize what the original production of the play in 1599 could convey only by the most approximate of theatrical shorthand: a fifteenth-century battle in all its splendor and gore. At the same time, Olivier is true to the spirit of Shakespeare's text by depicting this great battle as about leadership: about the disguised Henry's morale-boosting conversations with his soldiers on the night before the battle, his expertise in battle oratory, his setting a personal example by refusing to be ransomed, his magnanimity, his courage, and his devout insistence on attributing the victory to God (fig. 4.2).

Kenneth Branagh's film of 1989 could not fail to pay homage to Olivier. At the same time, in the wake of disillusionment about the Vietnam War and the Falklands conflict of 1982, the presentation of war takes a less glamorous turn. The Henry of this film (Branagh himself) is still very much a hero, but the cost of war is visibly greater and more personal. Here a long wordless tracking shot is devoted not to the battle itself, which has been sufficiently bloody, but to the aftermath, as Henry, surveying the slain on the battlefield, carries the body of a fallen boy from one length of the field to the other while the music sounds the "*Non nobis*" (see fig. 4.3). The practical purpose of this gesture is never explained; it is an emblem of Henry's deep concern with the cost of human lives. Then, too, Henry has had to confront the unpleasant reality of looting and stealing by his soldiers, including Bardolph, who is hanged, and Nym, who is also executed for what he has done.

Stage interpretations of Agincourt have run the gamut from patriotic fervor to iconoclastic denunciation of war. On the nineteenth-century stage, monumental and costly splendor was the order of the day, as in William Charles Macready's production at Covent Garden in 1839, featuring a series of pictorial panoramas by the painter Clarkson Stanfield (who was to provide similar background illustrations for *As You Like It* in 1842). One of these illustrations, for act 2, featured a diorama that moved while the Chorus spoke, portraying Henry's fleet as it left Southampton and crossed the English Channel to within sight of Harfleur, at which point the diorama merged ingeniously into the "actual" military encounter at that French city.

Far more common in recent years has been a marked bias against war. An RSC production at Stratford-upon-Avon in 1964, directed by Peter Hall, John Barton, and Clifford Williams in a time of mounting protests over the Vietnam War, underscored the nightmare terror of twentieth-

4.2. Laurence Olivier (in front, third from left) as Henry V about to set sail for France in Olivier's 1944 film version of *Henry V.* Two Cities Films/RGA. Courtesy Ronald Grant Archive.

century military conflict by its depiction of fatigued and poorly fed British troops coping doggedly with attrition and the relentless pounding of artillery. In the battle sequences of *Henry V* at Stratford, Ontario, in 1966, under the direction of Michael Langham, King Henry (Douglas Rain) displayed no regret or even recognition when the hanged Bardolph was dumped at his feet. Earlier, in 1956, this same director cast French-Canadian actors as the French warriors of this play, intentionally complicating the response to war of Canadian viewers. Michael Kahn, directing the play at Stratford, Connecticut, in 1969, interpreted the war as an imperialist adventure set in motion by calculating bishops and by King Henry's own egotistical yearning for glory. In the RSC production at Stratford-upon-Avon in 1984, directed by Adrian Noble, the arrested Bardolph was forced to kneel and was then strangled from behind, blood trickling from his head while King Henry received the embassy of the French herald Montjoy. In Michael Bogdanov's touring production for the English Shakespeare Company in 1986, Henry's supporters were rowdy football hooligan types carrying a banner in-

4.3. Kenneth Branagh (on the right) as Henry V at the battle of Agincourt, in Branagh's 1989 film version of *Henry V.* Although this Henry V is still very much the hero-king at Agincourt, Branagh's film examines in detail the human suffering and adventurism of war.

scribed "Fuck the Frogs"; during the battle, Pistol kicked and punched his French prisoner (4.4), while the bodies of the slaughtered boys who had guarded the luggage of the camp were unceremoniously piled on an ammunition truck (see T. W. Craik, ed., *Henry V,* 1995, pp. 87–91).

III

Thus far, this chapter has examined how the Elizabethan playhouse provided a space in which Shakespeare and his company could orchestrate sieges and open battles, and how those military engagements have been interpreted in subsequent performance history. Shakespeare also knew how to use his playhouse in other ways so as to give a powerful visual dimension to an ongoing story that was as much political as it was military. These elements of theater have also proved irresistible to modern producers as a key to widely varying interpretations.

Consider for example the sequence in *Richard III* leading up to Richard's acceptance of the English throne. Once he has ordered the execution of Lord Hastings for daring to support young Edward of York as king after the death of Edward IV, Richard needs to engineer his own "election" to the crown in place of young Edward by some sort of popular acclaim. Richard's henchmen, Lovell and Ratcliffe, present

"Hastings' head" (3.5.20.1) to the startled Lord Mayor as supposed evidence of Hastings's treason and then invite the Mayor, along with some fellow citizens, to meet with Richard at Baynard's Castle, an ancient fortified residence on the Thames in the city of London. Shortly thereafter, Richard and the Duke of Buckingham, entering *"at several doors,"* plot their strategy of deception in which Richard is to pretend reluctance in response to Buckingham's repeated offer of the crown on behalf of London's citizens. We understand that the main stage is now the courtyard of Baynard's Castle, from which the Mayor and citizens can look up in astonishment to behold Richard *"aloft, between two bishops"* (3.7.94.1). The two have already been named for us: they are Doctor Shaw and Friar Penker.

Richard's device, as Buckingham has advised, is to get himself quickly "up to the leads," that is, to the roof of Baynard's Castle, with "a prayer book" in his hand (47), so that he may appear to be at holy devotion. Some upper space in the theater, such as the gallery, presumably stands for the rooftop of the house. Catesby assists Buckingham in their beautifully orchestrated con game, conveying Buckingham's pleas to Richard and returning to the Mayor and citizens with Richard's excuses until Richard himself enters aloft in the role of a saintly man, reluctant to take on awesome responsibilities and loyal to the dynastic claims of his nephew Edward. This is a classic demonstration of the use of the upper acting area at its best, exploiting as it does the vertical separation of main stage and that upper acting area and requiring that only one speaker appear *"above."* (The clergymen say nothing.) Richard, in his commanding position above, speaks to two audiences, one onstage and one in the theater auditorium. At the scene's end the citizens troop off with Buckingham, having acquiesced to the clever deception, while Richard exits above with his clerical companions.

Laurence Olivier, in his 1955 film, fully exploits the resources of the camera by showing Richard in the gallery of a many-storied Jacobean mansion, high above his awed subjects, masking his own sinister appearance by two accompanying clergymen in full regalia. The result is a realistic portrayal of what one can imagine the scene to have looked like historically, with Olivier in period costume. Once the citizens have left, a gleefully triumphant Richard shinnies down into his courtyard on a rope, ringing a large bell in celebration of his success. Kevin Kline, as Richard in the New York Shakespeare Festival production of 1983, comically juggled a crucifix and a prayer book (the latter called for in the script). Richard Loncraine's 1995 film dispenses with the gallery; in-

stead, Richard is cloistered in some inner room, whispering conspirato-
rially with his confidence man, Buckingham (Jim Broadbent), as women
apply cosmetics to aid in the deception, whereupon he issues diffidently
forth to accept the citizens' offer of the crown. After they have left,
Richard and Buckingham burst out into the laughter they have barely
been able to suppress. Such appearances in Shakespeare's plays on the
"walls" invite a number of strategies for modern interpretation.

IV

Richard II is suffused with the stage language of political conflict. Its
first and third scenes are constructed on the principle of visual antithe-
sis. Two contenders, Thomas Mowbray Duke of Norfolk and Henry
Bolingbroke Duke of Hereford, lay their mutual accusations before
King Richard: on the one hand, that Mowbray plotted the death of the
King's youngest uncle, Thomas Duke of Gloucester, and on the other
that Bolingbroke is lying. Both litigants pledge their lives on the truth of
their accusations. The King, vowing impartiality, stands at the center of
this conflict in both a figurative and literal sense. The third scene then
stages a trial in the form of armed combat, with the two contenders
facing each other from opposite sides of the stage as the King and his
advisors presumably occupy the center backstage (fig. 4.4). "*When they
are set,*" reads the stage direction, "*enter the Duke of Norfolk in arms, defen-
dant*" (1.3.6.3–4). The Marshal asks him to name himself and his cause.
Thereupon "*The trumpets sound. Enter Duke of Hereford, appellant, in armor.*"
He too is asked to name himself and his cause. The legalistic and ritual
nature of the repeated exchange lends a solemn formality to the stage
pageantry of conflict. Richard is, both symbolically and in fact, the judge,
the arbiter, the presiding officer. Yet increasingly we learn that he may
be deeply implicated in the death of his youngest uncle. The hierarchical
order signaled by the stage arrangement is subverted by this secret.

John Barton, in his influential production of the play at Stratford-
upon-Avon in 1973, capitalized on the antithetical design of the first act
by interchanging the roles of the major contenders on alternate nights:
first Richard Pasco was Richard II to Ian Richardson's Bolingbroke,
and then the reverse. Two symbolic ladders reaching up behind the con-
testants during the trial proceedings underscored the symmetry of
confrontation (fig. 4.5). Scenery was essentially absent from a bare stage,
in marked contrast with ornate productions of the nineteenth century,
like that of Charles Kean at the Princess's Theatre in 1857, replete with

4.4. Mark Rylance as King Richard II (wearing the crown), Liam Brennan as Bolingbroke, and Terry McGinty as Mowbray in the scene of trial by combat in Rylance's *Richard II* (1.3), at the new Globe Theatre, London, summer 2003. By permission of the Shakespeare Globe Trust. Photo by John Tramper.

4.5. Richard Pascoe as Richard II (held aloft on a "throne"), Ian Richardson as Boling-broke (on a hobbyhorse, left), and Denis Holmes as Mowbray (right) in John Barton's pro-duction of *Richard II,* Stratford-upon-Avon, 1973. The ladders accentuate the antithetical staging of act 1, scene 3, with Bolingbroke and Mowbray on two opposite sides and King Richard presiding from an elevated position. Photo credit: Joe Cocks Studio Collection. Copyright Shakespeare Birthplace Trust.

Gothic architectural detail assiduously copied from Westminster Hall, St. Stephen's Chapel, and the like, along with a huge cast of extras. At His Majesty's Theatre in 1903, under the direction of Herbert Beerbohm Tree, Bolingbroke and Mowbray rode into the lists in scene 3 on horseback.

Once the unwise Richard has seized the dukedom of Lancaster belonging to Bolingbroke's father, John of Gaunt, and then rightfully to Bolingbroke himself on the death of his father, Richard finds himself cornered by his first cousin Bolingbroke, who has returned from exile to claim his violated rights. The scene of confrontation takes place at Flint Castle in Wales. This situation gives Shakespeare the opportunity to explore the expressive features of his playhouse. The tiring-house facade becomes the walls of Flint Castle, with the gallery as its parapet or battlements. Bolingbroke and his attacking army, represented by a few hired men in armor, are on the main stage. "What, will not this castle yield?" Bolingbroke asks, and is told (by Henry Percy, the "Hotspur" of *1 Henry IV*) that "The castle royally is manned." "King Richard lies / Within the limits of yon lime and stone" (3.3.20–26). The gestural language of "this castle" and "yon lime and stone" points deictically to the stage facade, picturesquely identified as Flint Castle throughout this crucial scene. Bolingbroke too describes the building he sees with visual particularity. "Go to the rude ribs of that ancient castle," he instructs the Earl of Northumberland, who thereupon advances to the tiring-house facade in order to deliver Bolingbroke's insistence that his banishment be repealed. Bolingbroke meanwhile marches with his forces about the main stage "without the noise of threat'ning drum, / That from this castle's tottered battlements / Our fair appointments may be well perused" (32, 51–53). His intent is that his military presence be felt by both spectators and the occupants of the stronghold. Bolingbroke knows how to use the mute language of physical threat.

The dramatic moment has arrived for Richard's appearance above. *"The trumpets sound. Richard appeareth on the walls"* (61.1–4). He shows himself, in Bolingbroke's own words, "As doth the blushing discontented sun / From out the fiery portal of the east / When he perceives the envious clouds are bent / To dim his glory and to stain the track / Of his bright passage to the occident." This familiar metaphor demands that Richard look authentically regal. "Yet looks he like a king," observes the Duke of York (63–68). Richard's role must have been assigned to the leading actor, Richard Burbage. Shakespeare gives him a commanding position above, looking down on those who are below as he delivers to them a compelling speech on the duty a subject owes the monarch. When Richard summons no less an authority than "my master, God omnipotent" to support his regal right, and predicts that heavenly vengeance will fall on those who rebel, his elevated position in the theater seems to support the very idea that this king is indeed God's deputy on earth.

Yet Richard is in fact powerless to resist the armed might of Bolingbroke, and he knows it. Accordingly, he dramatizes his own descent, his coming down to earth, his divesting himself of the illusion of godlike power. "Down, down, I come, like glistering Phaëthon, / Wanting the manage of unruly jades," he laments, as he exits from above to descend into the "base court"—the outer or lower court of the castle, but with connotations of the baseness and degradation he now must suffer (178–80). The sun image that was powerfully his at the moment of his entrance is now turned awry into the cautionary tale of a rash son who has mismanaged his father's sun-chariot and so must be thrown down. Richard must play his part in Bolingbroke's charade, which is that Bolingbroke and the rest will kneel to him and "show fair duty to His Majesty" (188) once he has yielded to Bolingbroke's inflexible condition of being restored to his dukedom of Lancaster. The King knows that now he is a king in name only. The elaborate ritual of his descent and their kneeling obeisance expresses in the language of stage action the crucial transfer of power that has thereby occurred.

The stage at Stratford, Ontario, designed by Tyrone Guthrie and Tanya Moiseiwitsch, showed in 1983 how successfully such a symbolic moment could be enacted on a presentational thrust stage created to incorporate the spatial features of the Elizabethan theater without attempting an exact historical reproduction. When Brian Bedford, as Richard, first showed himself on the upper platform, as though on the battlements of Flint Castle, he was indeed resplendent, in shining white garments sewn with silver and gold. His whole bearing was so splendidly regal that he seemed unquestionably entitled to the crown he wore upon his head. Bolingbroke and his followers on the main stage, in battle gear, seemed like usurpers, cowed by Richard's royal presence. The moment was highly metatheatrical: Richard established his claim to be the rightful king of England through the forceful charisma of Brian Bedford's performance. Yet Bolingbroke stubbornly held his ground, and the sham ritual of a negotiated surrender ran its disillusioning course. Richard's surrender in the theater was visibly one of physical descent, like that of the sun to which Richard compared himself (3.2.36–53).

The scene of Richard's deposition, excised from early printed texts of the play because it offered such a potentially inflammatory dramatization of the deposing of a king (as indeed proved the case when in 1601 the play was revived at the behest of followers of the Earl of Essex, on the eve of an abortive rebellion in his name), centers its stage action on the possession of crown, scepter, and throne. Who has the right to these tokens of royal authority? And when are the regalia actually brought onstage? The Duke of York enters as having come "From plume-plucked Richard," who, York says to Bolingbroke, "with willing soul / Adopts thee heir, and his high scepter yields / To the possession of thy royal hand" (4.1.109–11). Does York bring with him the tokens that Richard has promised to relinquish? A director gets to choose. At all events, a throne must be onstage from the start of the scene — a throne that for the nonce contains no occupant. Is this the moment for Bolingbroke's assuming that seat of high office? York bids Bolingbroke "Ascend his throne, descending now from him," i.e., from Richard, and Bolingbroke undertakes to do just that, but he is interrupted by the Bishop of Carlisle's passionate speech predicting the disastrous consequences of divine anger. The ceremony that Bolingbroke and York have devised to signal transfer of power is interrupted by a bishop who sees the event as nothing more than a usurpation.

Perhaps the moment for bringing onstage the royal regalia occurs when York exits briefly and returns with Richard (4.1.162.1). At once the crown becomes the focus of a struggle that is both symbolic and physical. What Bolingbroke and York hope for is a smooth transfer of power made possible by Richard's act of "giving" the crown to Bolingbroke. When asked by Richard why he has been summoned into this assembly, York gives a plain answer: "To do that office of thine own good will / Which tired majesty did make thee offer: / The resignation of thy state and crown / To Henry Bolingbroke." Thereupon Richard takes the crown, presumably from the cushion on which it is being held by some attendant, and extends it to Bolingbroke. "Here, cousin, seize the crown," he says. Not "take," but "seize." Richard continues, "Here, cousin, / On this side my hand, and on that side thine" (178–84). What has happened? Richard has put the crown partly into his rival's grasp, but has not let go himself. An unseemly tug-of-war is in prospect, one that is emblematic of what is at bottom a struggle for power rather than a legal transition of authority. "I thought you had been willing to resign," says Bolingbroke, indicating that the crown is not yet his. Yet Richard, having won this hand, knows that he must lose the game. He has dramatized the shoddiness of the proceedings, but proceed they must. He yields his crown and scepter to his hated opponent in a ceremony of divesting that is his own invention. No such ceremony has been known before, and so Richard makes it up. With his own tears he washes away the holy balm with which he was anointed king. This climactic action crystallizes a staging device that Shakespeare uses throughout *Richard II*, that of inverting and subverting the forms of hierarchical authority on which the monarchy rests.

Mark Rylance, in a production of the play at the new Globe Theatre in the summer of 2003, dramatized this conflict successfully by centering the event on Richard (played by Rylance) as a self-dramatizing young man more interested in winning applause for a stunning performance than in learning how to be a wise king. The metatheatricality of the interpretation admirably fitted the Globe stage, with its physical recreation of Shakespeare's original theater (see figs. 1.3 and 4.4 above). Rylance astutely saw that *Richard II* is about performance; as Richard himself puts it, "Thus play I in one person many people" (5.5.31). Rylance's King Richard was a superb actor, unfailingly able to center attention on himself and to insist that the royal appurtenances of throne, canopy, regalia, troops of attendants, and the magnificently ornate building in which they all were housed, were about him.

v

Two scenes in *1 Henry IV* are especially notable in their metatheatrical use of stage space. The first is the famous tavern scene (2.4) in which Prince Henry and Falstaff playact the roles of Prince Hal and his father, King Henry IV, with whom Hal must meet the very next day to account for his companionship with Falstaff and his neglect of princely duties. Falstaff is the embodiment of all that King Henry is not: he is irresponsible, fat, hedonistic, funny, given to excesses of the flesh, a thief, and a resourceful liar. The tavern scene is chiefly his, and is correspondingly fitted out with illiterate tapsters, frowsy women, tables, chairs, plenty of wine, and the like. The props of this scene become the props of the skit that he stages impromptu with Prince Hal about the latter's upcoming interview with his father. Urged by the Prince to take the role of King Henry, Falstaff immediately provides himself with the stage appurtenances he needs to be convincing as a player. "This chair shall be my state, this dagger my scepter, and this cushion my crown," he announces (2.4.374–75; fig. 4.6). These props are all real in the theater and help define the scene's tavern ambience. They are also, as the Prince hastens

4.6. Kevin Kline as Falstaff in Jack O'Brien's 2003 conflation of *Henry IV, Parts I* and *II,* at Lincoln Center, New York. In this famous tavern scene (2.4), Falstaff establishes himself on his "throne" with a cushion for his crown as he prepares to enact, parodically, the role of King Henry IV lecturing his wayward son for wasting his youth. Photo credit: Sara Krulwich/*New York Times.*

to observe, rather pathetic approximations of what they are supposed to represent. "Thy state is taken for a joint stool, thy golden scepter for a leaden dagger, and thy precious rich crown for a pitiful bald crown" (376–78). Theater must deal in metonymies, and this play-within-the-play is emblematic of theater. Falstaff as stand-in for King Henry proclaims by the very juxtaposition of actor and role how unlike are the Prince's two father figures. And yet Falstaff is superb as a mimic, or at least a stand-up improv artist. He plays Prince Hal with as much verve and comic genius as he demonstrates in enacting the Prince's father. Falstaff can look amusedly at both sides of a family quarrel, showing the kind of dialectical talent and multiplicity of points of view that Shake-speare himself employs as an essential technique of dramaturgy.

Modern productions have demonstrated an extraordinary range of interpretive possibilities in these playful encounters of Hal and Falstaff. Is Hal in charge of his own destiny as he moves toward manhood, or is he emotionally attached to a youthful hedonism he is reluctant to leave behind? At one extreme, Richard Burton played the Prince, in 1951 at Stratford-upon-Avon, as a young man who was gloomily aware of where he was going and what use he could make of Falstaff (Anthony Quayle) in the meantime; very little merriment emerged from this Hal, who knew from the start that the break with Falstaff was inevitable. Ian Holm, as Prince Hal in a 1964 production for the RSC, was detached and self-contained. Alan Howard, at Stratford-upon-Avon in 1975 under the direction of Terry Hands, was similarly mirthless in his role as king-to-be, taking delight neither in the antics of Falstaff (Brewster Mason) nor in the prospect of what it would actually be like to be king. Michael Pennington, as Hal in Michael Bogdanov's demystifying production of 1986 for the English Shakespeare Company, responded to a sterile and cold world of political maneuvering by being correspondingly manipu-lative and guileful. At the other end of the spectrum, Gerard Murphy, in an RSC production at the Barbican in 1982 as directed by Trevor Nunn, was emotionally dependent on Falstaff (Joss Ackland) to the extraordi-nary extent of sitting in his lap and cleaning up after Falstaff's messy breakfast. The fear and dislike felt by this young man for his humorless and unyielding father (Patrick Stewart) helped explain why this Hal had no desire to leave the cheerful confines of the Boar's Head Tavern.

Conversely, Falstaff as the Prince's companion has been interpreted in diverse ways, as an incorrigible but dear old toper, as an inventive liar, or as a calculating rascal who knows that his best trick is to please a youngster who is destined to become an immensely powerful monarch. Ralph Richardson, in John Burrell's Old Vic production of 1945 in Lon-don's New Theatre, was a sensitive, funny, witty companion whose en-dearing qualities contrasted vividly with the humorless abruptness and nervous energy of Hotspur (Laurence Olivier) and the gaunt sobriety of King Henry IV (Nicholas Hannen). Stacy Keach, at the New York Shakespeare Festival (Delacorte Theatre) in 1968, was a comically smug Falstaff, nearly innocent of having corrupted Hal and yet at once fasci-nating and repellent to a prince (Sam Waterston) who was awkwardly unsure of himself. Orson Welles, in his 1966 film called *The Chimes at Midnight* in the United Kingdom and *Falstaff* in the United States, made effective use of close-ups to show us a Falstaff (Welles himself) who is, beneath his jollity and badinage with the Prince, anxious about his future; he is at once charmingly witty and irresponsibly selfish, living for the moment while awaiting the blow that must eventually fall. Anthony Quayle captures a similar anxiety beneath the jesting in his performance as Falstaff in the BBC *1 Henry IV* filmed for television in 1979. Kevin Kline, in Jack O'Brien's conflation of parts I and II of *Henry IV* at Lincoln Center, New York, in 2003, was an intelligent, world-weary Falstaff always prudently measuring his resources (see fig. 4.6).

The play's second highly metatheatrical scene takes place at the battle of Shrewsbury, when Falstaff is called upon to play another role: that of the dying warrior. He does so with the kind of comic outrageousness that is his hallmark. Finding himself face to face with the mighty Douglas, who is known for his intrepidity and fierceness, Falstaff chooses the most practical expedient: he *"falls down as if he were dead"* (5.4.76.2–3). The action literalizes what Falstaff has just expatiated upon in his catechism on honor: honor is only a name, only air, belonging mostly to those who have died in battle. For that reason, concludes Falstaff, "I'll none of it. Honor is a mere scutcheon" (5.1.127–40). His falling down and playing possum instead of fighting it out is the pragmatic choice of one who understands that when one is dead one loses so many options.

At this same moment in the battle, and in this same spot, Prince Hal comes up against his great opponent, Hotspur, and wins. Hotspur lies dead at his feet, and so, amazingly, does Falstaff. Or so it appears. Hal graces each with an elegiac encomium, conceding in the case of Falstaff that "I could have better spared a better man" (5.4.104). The scene is emblematic: Hal seems now to have won honor from his rival, while at the same time bringing down the curtain on the rather dissolute drama he has acted out with Falstaff. Yet the Prince is deceived: Falstaff is not dead. Once the Prince has gone briefly offstage, *"Falstaff riseth up"* and proceeds to wound the dead Hotspur in the thigh as though having overcome him in the battle. His resurrection surprises the Prince when he returns a short time later, and perhaps surprises us too in the theater. Did we, as audience, realize that Falstaff was "dead"? An actor plays dead by lying still; he will get up after the show is over and live to act another day. Falstaff, and indeed Shakespeare as well, subverts the very conventions on which drama depends. We take it that Falstaff is "dead," and yet he is not. He rises irrepressibly, to live on into another history play (*2 Henry IV*) and to give Hal more grief of injured reputation until the very moment of the Prince's coronation as king. This is so like Falstaff.

He is bigger than life, but he is more than that: he seems bigger than art itself. He breaks the rules, determined not to go away.

Stage tradition offers two very different options concerning Falstaff at this moment. The nineteenth-century American actor James Henry Hackett, not untypical of the age in his long career as Falstaff from 1832 to 1870, played the moment for buffoonish slapstick comedy, winking and dodging his head as he lay prostrate, making no attempt to lead audiences to believe that he was "really" dead. Hackett's broad interpretation here was of a piece with his presentation throughout the play of an incorrigible old sinner who is discomfited at the Gad's Hill robbery, forced to crawl to safety at considerable cost to his dignity, caught out in a monstrous lie in the big tavern scene, impenitent about his mooching on Mistress Quickly, and guilty of every imaginable shenanigan (including flat cowardice) at the battle of Shrewsbury (see fig. 4.7). This was a Falstaff calculated to make the audience roar with laughter as he sat on a drum next to Henry IV only to tumble off when the King suddenly got up. Yet a very different and more subtle Falstaff emerges in the interpretations of Orson Welles, Anthony Quayle, Douglas Seale (at the Old Vic in 1955), and others: a Falstaff who knows perfectly well that he was set upon by Hal and Poins in the dark at Gad's Hill and that Falstaff's cue is to play the cowardly liar that they expect of him; to do so is to endear himself to the Prince by enacting the role of the Prince's jester. Such a Falstaff can have the presence of mind, when he falls prudently on the ground before the fearsome Douglas at Shrewsbury Field, to stay "dead" when Prince Hal comes upon the scene and to remain "dead" to the audience as well as to Hal until the Prince, having eulogized both Hotspur and the seemingly dead Falstaff, has left the stage. This is the time for Falstaff to rise and thereby defeat the Prince's hope that his companionship with Falstaff has come to an end.

It is because Falstaff—bigger than life and seemingly of larger dimensions even than the play itself—refuses to go away, that Prince Henry must make public his rejection of Falstaff at the end of *2 Henry IV.* Everyone is convinced that as king this young man will sanction the kind of lawlessness that Falstaff increasingly represents. Falstaff hobnobs with country justices of the peace who seem fully ready to jump on the gravy train that Falstaff's imminent rise to power appears to promise. They scurry off to London to join in the celebration. "The laws of England are at my commandment," crows Falstaff. "Blessed are they that have been my friends, and woe to my Lord Chief Justice!" (5.3.138–41). The danger of legal anarchy is real. The Lord Chief Justice himself has

4.7. James Henry Hackett (1800–1871) as Falstaff, presumably on his way to Shrewsbury. c. 1850. Hulton Archive. By permission of Getty Images, Inc.

no doubt that his days are numbered, now that the old king is dead. Prince Henry's brothers are glum.

The new Henry V is under a sharp necessity of repudiating Falstaff in such a public way that no one can mistake his signals. He promises to the Lord Chief Justice that "You shall be as a father to my youth" (5.2.118) and entrusts to him the custody of Falstaff as "The tutor and the feeder of my riots" (5.5.62). This is hardly fair to the endearing side of Falstaff that the Prince once enjoyed, and indeed productions of the play not infrequently side emotionally with Falstaff against the new monarch — as, for example, in the Old Vic's production in 1945 at London's New Theatre, with Ralph Richardson as a Falstaff who tried to banter with the new king in his coronation procession only to be cut off with a heartless "Reply not to me with a fool-born jest," or in Michael Bogdanov's English Shakespeare Company version at the Old Vic in 1987, in which the rejection of Falstaff was a cruel snub. Still, the rejection is politically prudent. What the new king has learned more than anything else is the grave importance of the public language of gesture in which he must now engage. It is a language that he has studied in his many playactings with Falstaff. Henry becomes a highly successful king because he enacts the role so well, without subverting the political meaning of his gestures as Richard II was so fatally inclined to do.

The new genre of the English history play, then, to which Shakespeare was such a major contributor throughout the 1590s, brought with it the necessity of a new stage vocabulary of warfare and of political conflict. Shakespeare's innovative solution was to embrace the seeming physical limitation of his theater as a challenge and indeed an opportunity to fashion a military world of the imagination in which his spectators were active participants. His artistry in creating such a visionary world matured remarkably from the *Henry VI* plays to *Henry V,* but in doing so never lost sight of the author's metatheatrical awareness that his history plays were created for the theatrical space in which Shakespeare worked.

ℒ5ℒ

Like a Strutting Player

STAGING MORAL AMBIGUITY IN
MEASURE FOR MEASURE AND
TROILUS AND CRESSIDA

More or less at the midpoint of his career as a dramatist, in the years around 1600 to 1604, Shakespeare seems to have reappraised his work and to have started off in new and experimental directions. His perfecting of the genre of romantic comedy reached its culmination in *As You Like It* (c. 1599) and *Twelfth Night* (1600–1602). *Henry V,* in 1599, brought to a victorious close a decade's nine-play-long exploration of English history down to the beginning of the Tudor reign in 1485. The plays to which he next turned have generally been grouped together by modern scholars (since the late nineteenth century) as the "problem plays." The list of such plays varies to an extent, sometimes including *Hamlet,* especially since it was written about the same time. The plays most commonly regarded as problem plays are *Measure for Measure, Troilus and Cressida,* and *All's Well That Ends Well.* The purpose of this present chapter is to ask in what ways these plays, in which themes, genres, and language are so strikingly innovative, are also experimental in their uses of the Elizabethan stage and in modern production. The focus will be mainly on *Measure for Measure* and *Troilus and Cressida.*

I

The Duke is a figure of theatrical control in *Measure for Measure.* He has come under a good deal of heavy critical weather of late, in essays and in the contemporary theater; he is often seen as manipulative, intruding into people's lives, playing with them insensitively for his own purposes.

He is all of these things, but to offer this only as a negative judgment of tyrannical behavior is to miss an essential point. The Duke is the embodiment of theatrical contriving. He does what the dramatist does: from behind the scenes he moves his characters about, putting them at risk, testing them, while at the same time taking care in a comedy that they are spared from irreparable harm. He deceives them to see how they will behave under the supposed circumstances in which they find themselves, just as the playwright fills his stage with characters who are crucially unaware of matters about which we as audience are informed. The Duke is, in many ways, like the playwright, controlling, coping with new circumstances, and engineering a final scene of discovery. The Duke, like the playwright, ultimately forgives and recovers his characters.

One of the Duke's deceptions is to adopt a religious disguise to which he has no right. As a theatrical device, this must have seemed particularly striking to Shakespeare's original audience, with its keen interest in religious controversy and in allegations of duplicity on the part of Catholic Jesuit priests in England. The Duke offers spiritual counsel to those who think they are about to die. In the real world this would seem presumptuous to the point of blasphemy. The theater is not, however, the real world, and to confuse the two is to misread an essential theatrical metaphor in *Measure for Measure*. The Duke makes use of a power that is like "power divine" (5.1.377), enabling him to observe, judge, and correct the human failings of his subjects. He operates like that divine power through mercy and justice. Yet he is himself not a divinity. He is two things: he is an absolute ruler in a culture that often idealized kingship as embodying divine authority on earth, and he is a surrogate for the playwright, whose authority over the world that he creates in the theater is limited only to the important extent that the theater is not the real world.

Being in some ways like both a divinity and a playwright, the Duke is mysterious and unique. His reasons for leaving his public office in Vienna to spy into corruption are ultimately unknowable, but depend to an extent on his realization that as a person who is himself above the vicissitudes of fleshly temptation he has failed to comprehend the depth of his subjects' human failings. His visitation among them is like an incarnation. With each character what he must do is uncover the human weakness, put it to the test, show how inadequate the individual is to achieve self-control without help, and then provide the necessary assistance.

The Duke has good reason to believe that Lord Angelo is not all that he appears to be. The Duke has known that the "well-seeming Angelo" once declined to go through with a marriage to Mariana when her dowry was lost at sea (3.1.215–25). The Duke also has reason to suspect that Angelo can be tempted by power. "Hence shall we see, / If power change purpose, what our seemers be," he says to Friar Thomas by way of explaining his request for a religious garb and identity (1.3.53–54). In the real world, no ruler in his right mind would turn over complete authority to one whom he suspects in this way. As a figure of theatrical control, on the other hand, the Duke's manipulations are productive. Angelo discovers, to his utter dismay, that being given seemingly absolute power does indeed tempt him to the most heinous of crimes, that of assaulting the virginity of a young religious novice about to become a nun, and then of ordering the secret execution of her brother by way of covering up that first crime. Angelo is horrified at the discovery. He realizes that some terrible thing in him compels him to a series of actions that are deeply repugnant to the law-abiding image he has had of himself. Angelo's soliloquies are as tortured and unhappy as those of a tragic protagonist. He is a lost soul.

What is the Duke's strategy in all this? Realistically considered, the plan is sadistic. As a device of theater, on the other hand, it operates according to a structural plan with beneficent intent. Arguably, Angelo is a more complete human when he knows the depravity of which he is sadly capable. He becomes a part of humanity by acknowledging his uncontrollable weakness. To be weak is to realize that one needs help. Angelo's greatest problem is that he thinks no one is watching over him, that there is no one to restrain him when his thoughts turn vicious. We know of course that the Duke is watching, but Angelo does not. He has no choice other than to live out the nightmare of his own iniquity, with no apparent end in sight other than the despair of knowing that, like Macbeth, he is a murderer who cannot stop himself from murdering. This is a devastating realization, but it is also emotionally health-giving at last. Angelo continues to resist this help, trying to brazen it out with Isabella in a scene of public confrontation by citing his presumed reputation for integrity and by using the simple weight of his authority. He is egged on in this by the Duke, who is putting Angelo to his last test. Angelo fails once more, taking the expedient of trying to save his own skin at the expense of justice. The Duke has known that Angelo would prove to be morally weak at this critical juncture. Yet when, in a climactic theatrical gesture, the friar's hood is pulled from the Duke's head by Lucio, revealing the Duke in his full royal identity and showing to Angelo that he has been observed all the while by an unseen higher authority, we hear unmistakably the relief in Angelo's voice. "O my dread lord," he says to the Duke, "I should be guiltier than my guiltiness / To think I can be undiscernible, / When I perceive Your Grace, like power divine, / Hath looked upon my passes" (5.1.374–78). Angelo sees that it is far better to be apprehended and executed for his crimes than to be allowed to continue as a tyrant and murderer. Such a dealing out of "measure for measure" would not only reestablish justice in the state; it would also save Angelo from the agonies of a tortured conscience.

Having made this crucial point, the Duke is then in a position to forgive Angelo. In point of fact, Angelo has done neither of the things for which he is so sorry: he has not ravished Isabella, and he has not succeeded in having Claudio executed. He intended to do both, and he believes he has done so, with the result that the Duke has been able to observe once more how Angelo will continue to lie until he is openly discovered. Yet Angelo has not actually committed the crimes he intended to commit because the Duke has arranged it this way. The Duke has planned the bed substitution allowing Mariana to be Angelo's lover in the dark of night instead of Isabella, and the Duke has planned the substitutions in the prison that spare the life of the condemned Claudio. The Duke is thus the playwright who has dramatized Angelo's story of a potential crime and punishment that finally need not be either. The Duke is the embodiment of a dark comic providence in this play.

The Duke's dramaturgical strategies with Claudio work along similar lines. Although Claudio is not as heinously guilty as Angelo, Claudio has much to learn. He has broken the draconian law of Vienna against fornication. His offense in this seems mild, and is shared by the woman he is to marry, Juliet, who confesses to the Duke as seeming friar that their "offenseful act" was "mutually committed" (2.3.27–28). That is, they have made love in anticipation of a marriage that has been delayed for reasons of dowry settlement. "She is fast my wife," Claudio tells Lucio, "Save that we do the denunciation lack / Of outward order" (1.2.144–45). Still, Claudio has broken the law, and it is a law that the Duke endorses. The Duke supports the "strict statutes and most biting laws" that are the "needful bits and curbs to headstrong steeds" (1.3.19–21), because Vienna is awash in fleshly carnality. The Duke's first task, as seeming friar, is to counsel Claudio on the necessity of self-control. This is a lesson that Claudio is prepared to heed, if only because he has been arrested. He acknowledges to Lucio that his unwelcome confinement in prison comes "From too much liberty." "As surfeit is the father to much fast, / So every scope, by the immoderate use, / Turns to restraint" (1.2.125–28). *Measure for Measure* is a "problem play" in good part because human carnality is such a problem.

Like Angelo, Claudio will presumably be a better person ultimately if he can come to terms with his share of human frailty. In order to steer him in that direction, the Duke employs a very stern test indeed: disguised as the friar, he lectures Claudio on the vanity of human wishes. "Be absolute for death," he admonishes the young man, and goes on to detail a host of reasons why any thoughtful person should be out of love with life. Human existence is an hourly affliction of diseases, unfulfilled hopes, and inexorable decline toward senility. Why should one fear death, "That makes these odds all even"? (3.1.5–41). Claudio, condemned to be executed, sees the spiritual benefit of preparing for a cessation of all his unhappiness. The homily is a commonplace of church doctrine delivered in this instance by a bogus friar, but it makes a deep impression on Claudio.

Can Claudio withstand the temptation to hope still for life? This temptation comes to him in the form of his pious sister, who, faced with the choice presented to her by Angelo of saving her brother's life by surrendering her virginity to Angelo's lust, hopes instead that her brother's sense of honor will make him wish to die under Angelo's sentence rather than be the pander to vice. "Then, Isabel, live chaste, and brother, die; / More than our brother is our chastity" (2.4.185–86). This is much more than squeamishness on Isabella's part; it is a test for Claudio, one that the Duke will watch with great interest. Claudio thinks of himself as brave and unflinching in the face of death when death is inevitable. When, however, he learns from Isabella that there is a way to save his life, however shameful, he collapses into begging her help. "Sweet sister, let me live. / What sin you do to save a brother's life, / Nature dispenses with the deed so far / That it becomes a virtue" (3.1.135–37; see fig. 5.1). This is just what Isabella has feared, that Claudio would be prepared to practice a kind of incest out of his sister's shame. She hysterically rebukes him and leaves him alone to ponder his own cowardice and failure of nerve.

Claudio is given no more lines and very little presence onstage throughout the remainder of the play in which to convey his emotions. He is left to himself in prison expecting to be executed at any moment, then is strangely rescued by the friar (i.e., the Duke), and at last is brought onstage with his identity concealed in order that the revelation of his being still alive may serve as the play's last important surprise to Isabella and the rest. His unveiling, like that of the Duke earlier in this final

5.1. W. Holman Hunt, *Claudio and Isabella* (1850–1853). In *Measure for Measure* (3.1), Isabella brings to her brother the news that he must die under Lord Angelo's sentence unless Isabella yields to Angelo's lust. By permission of the Tate Gallery, London.

scene, is a big moment theatrically, and yet Claudio says nothing. Much has been made in recent criticism and stage practice (see below) of Isabella's silence when the Duke offers to marry her; the silence of Claudio is no less wondrous. What is Claudio thinking? Modern productions have shown a range of possibilities: he can be grateful and overjoyed, or conversely suspicious and antagonistic. If the former, he and Isabella have perhaps learned to forgive each other and themselves for the mutual failures of their searing encounter in the prison. Through the Duke's incessant manipulations, they may have discovered how their own frailties can teach them to forgive.

Isabella's odyssey as a pupil of the all-seeing manipulative Duke is no less strange and wonderful. She is of course a more innocent character than Angelo and Claudio. Yet she too, under the pressure of the Duke's temptation, collapses into failure. That is when she turns on her brother in something very close to hatred. "Take my defiance, / Die, perish!" she shouts at him. "Might but my bending down / Reprieve thee from thy fate, it should proceed. / I'll pray a thousand prayers for thy death, / No word to save thee" (3.1.145–49). Claudio has of course failed her utterly, and he now knows it. Even so, this novice to the monastic life she has hoped to embrace experiences a failure of charity. " 'Tis best thou diest quickly," she declares, as she turns on Claudio and prepares to leave.

Like Claudio, Isabella is given no words to express her remorse. Instead, her opportunity to show the charity that has eluded her comes in the form of the Duke's last temptation for her. Just as the Duke gives Angelo enough rope to hang himself in the final scene by holding out to him the illusory prospect of escaping detection, the Duke misleads Isabella with the temptation to seek vengeance for the seeming execution of Claudio. No one other than the Provost knows that Claudio is alive. What should be done to Angelo? Is not this a situation demanding "An Angelo for Claudio, death for death"? How else are we to interpret the proverbial wisdom insisting that "Like doth quit like, and measure still for measure" (5.1.417–19)? The Duke intensifies the pressure on Isabella by arguing that her brother's ghost will rise from his grave to haunt her if she does not ask for rigorous justice. The Duke insists that his sentence is definitive, whether she intervenes or not: "He dies for Claudio's death" (451). Yet Isabella kneels, in another of the play's climactic theatrical gestures around which the resolution of the plot revolves. She does so partly because Mariana has begged her to spare the erring male that Mariana still craves for her husband, and to that extent Isabella's kneeling is a gesture in defense of marriage, however imperfect an institution that may be. Isabella herself, in a traditional reading of the play at least, turns away from her quest for the life of a nun to opt instead (surprisingly, perhaps) for marriage. At the same time, Isabella's kneeling expresses charitable understanding of human failure. "Look, if it please you, on this man condemned / As if my brother lived," she bids the Duke. "I partly think / A due sincerity governed his deeds, / Till he did look on me" (452–55). Her use of the conditional "as if" is prophetic, because Claudio does live and so measure need not be quit with measure. That Isabella has passed the Duke's test with such vibrant success is perhaps one reason that he proposes marriage to her.

With the engaging but incorrigible Lucio, the Duke needs to proceed with a course of correction more attuned to the genre of dramatic satire than romantic comedy. Lucio is unrepentant as a rake and as an undoer of reputations. He needs to be taught a lesson about whoremongering and about slander. The Duke learns much from him, to be sure, about how fragile a reputation for integrity can be if the owner is innocently unaware of appearances. Lucio is irresistibly funny, but he is also irresponsible, like Falstaff, and he needs to be brought to account. Hence the Duke's course of correction, having taught Lucio nothing through exhortation, must resort to arbitrary restraint. Lucio must marry Kate Keepdown, with whom he has fathered a child without any intention of caring for her or the baby. Because men's sexual thrustings have consequences, Lucio must be forcibly obliged to bear responsibility. The lesson is essentially that imposed on Angelo, and on Bertram in *All's Well That Ends Well* (see below). In biblical language, as ye sow, so shall ye reap.

All these plots through which the Duke plays with the lives of his subjects culminate in a final scene of discovery and closure. As in *As You Like It, Twelfth Night,* and *The Tempest,* the denouement takes the theatrical form of removal of disguise: three, in fact. The first, the unveiling of Mariana, is preceded by a riddling catechism. Are you married? asks the Duke of the veiled figure standing before him. "No, my lord." Are you a maid? "No, my lord." A widow, then? "Neither, my lord" (5.3.177–82). The puzzle invites Lucio to suggest that the woman may be a "punk," or whore, but the more serious intent is to introduce a riddle the answer to which is a key to the exposing of Angelo. This exposure is also an unveiling, one that is metaphorically attuned to the several physical unmaskings with which the play ends.

The Duke's unveiling by Lucio, after the Duke has left the stage and then returned as the friar, is a stunning moment of revelation for the characters onstage except for the Provost and Friar Peter, who are privy to the Duke's contrivances. Angelo realizes that he has been watched and apprehended in his criminality; Escalus, his well-meaning associate in administering the law, is disburdened of the mistakes he has made in adjudging the rival claims of Angelo and Isabella; Isabella herself sees that she has been providentially rescued from a plight like that of Susanna among the Elders; and Lucio sees that his days of gentlemanly hedonism are drawing rapidly to a close.

This disclosure also sets in motion the final unveiling, that of Claudio. Here at last dramatic resolution can take place, for Angelo has not committed murder after all. Isabella, after having shown the charitable stuff of which she is made once she has reflected on her own weaknesses, is rewarded with the recovery of a brother she thought lost. Claudio, having readied himself to die, is restored to life and to a sister's love. The strange marriages with which the play concludes — Isabella's (perhaps) to the Duke, Mariana's to an Angelo whose penitence may or may not last, and Kate Keepdown's to a rakish husband whose view of such a marriage is that it is "pressing to death, whipping, and hanging" (533) — signal a closure that is conventionally the way for comedies to end, however unorthodox and experimental in this present instance. The ending strongly confirms the sense in which all the dramatic excitement in the play is of the Duke's contriving. The play is his theater, his place of imagination, in which to work his stage magic and impose his own quixotic sense of order. In Shakespeare's own theater, these metatheatrical devices would have seemed wonderfully pertinent to the theatrical space in which they occurred, with the "heavens" above bearing silent but visible witness to a *theatrum mundi* or theater of the world where justice on earth can only hope to approximate that of the divine cosmos and indeed may seem at times to be mocked by its own huge imperfection.

Performance history underscores this sense of the Duke's centrality as a controlling and manipulative figure; it also reveals how divergent are the possible interpretations of this enigmatic figure and of the play as a whole. The play seemed so morally offensive to audiences during the three centuries lying between its first-known performance on December 26, 1604, and the twentieth century that it was generally ignored or turned into something almost unrecognizably different. Samuel Pepys, seeing a production in February 1662 in Lincoln's Inn Fields of something called *The Law against Lovers,* greatly admired the "dancing and singing" of a "little girl" who turned out to be Beatrice's younger sister, Viola, imported into the plot of *Measure for Measure* along with Beatrice and Benedick from *Much Ado about Nothing* to give audiences something they were sure to like. Benedick was given a new identity as Claudio's brother, while Beatrice was transformed into a ward of Lord Angelo. In this new guise, Benedick and Beatrice undertook to rescue Claudio and Beatrice's cousin Juliet from incarceration. Angelo, it turned out, was no villain after all but was merely testing Isabella, whom he loved so sincerely that he was ultimately permitted to marry her. The low comedy of Pompey and Mistress Overdone was removed to make room for more song and dance in a happy finale. Charles Gildon's *Measure for Measure, or Beauty the Best Advocate,* at Lincoln's Inn Fields in 1699–1700 with Thomas Betterton and Anne Bracegirdle as Angelo and Isabella, did away with the *Much Ado* accretions but continued to eliminate the below-stairs characters; Lucio appeared in scene 1 only. Angelo was again a redeemable character, having married Mariana in secret, so that the bed "trick" was no extramarital trick after all. Claudio and Juliet were similarly a married couple, so that their fornication was no fornication. Respectability reared its indomitable head throughout, while operatic flourishes turned much of the play into an elaborate masque. In such bowdlerized and musically enhanced guises, a semblance of *Measure for Measure* stayed in the repertory throughout most of the eighteenth century, but even in this adapted form the play generally proved too much for nineteenth-century tastes; it appeared in the theater only fitfully. Richard Wagner's operatic version of 1842 named *Das Liebesverbot* (The prohibition against love) cast Angelo as a romantic hero.

When twentieth-century productions, such as Tyrone Guthrie's at the Old Vic in 1933 starring Charles Laughton, ventured at last to give the play more or less as written, they were at first greeted with outraged protests. More recently, *Measure for Measure* has itself become a vehicle for protest against sexism and patriarchal abuses of authority. Peter Brook, in an austere production at Stratford-upon-Avon in 1950 with John Gielgud as Angelo, juxtaposed the sordid and the sacred in a way that was deliberately jarring and uncomfortable (fig. 5.2). Estelle Kohler, in John Barton's production for the RSC at Stratford-upon-Avon in 1970, was so shocked and bewildered by the Duke's sudden proposal of marriage at the end of the play that she gave him no answer, leaving him to wander offstage a disappointed and unhappy wooer. Since Shakespeare's script does indeed provide no lines for her to reply, directors and actresses since then have seized the moment as one of feminist self-assertion in which the woman actually gets to choose. Martha Henry, at Stratford, Ontario, in 1975, under the direction of Robin Phillips, was

5.2. Rosalind Atkinson as Mistress Overdone and Leon Quartermain as Lucio, with two gentlemen, as they discuss the news of Claudio's arrest for fornication in 1.2 of Peter Brook's 1950 production of *Measure for Measure* for the Royal Shakespeare Company in Stratford-upon-Avon. Photo credit: Angus Bean. Copyright Shakespeare Birthplace Trust.

the living embodiment of resentment and pent-up fury at a man's world in which not only she but other women, including Mariana and Juliet, were victimized. In a Court Theatre production in Chicago in 1979, directed by Nick Rudall, the actress playing Isabella (Kate Goring) was instructed to touch the hand of the Duke hesitantly as they left the stage, implying assent, but failed to do so on one night during the run when a substitute actor took the part of the Duke; as she explained privately afterward, this particular actor just didn't turn her on.

Angelo, in performance, has run the gamut from anguished sinner, as in Tim Pigott-Smith's sensitive rendition in the BBC television version of 1978–1979, to sadomasochistic and puritanical monster: in Marius Goring's performance at Stratford-upon-Avon in 1962, Angelo was at once publicly arrogant and privately addicted to self-flagellation. He is usually seen as glad or at least willing to marry Mariana at the play's end in return for his life's having been spared, or even more as an acknowledgment that he can scarcely deserve to be forgiven and accepted by her, but Barbara Gaines's production for the Shakespeare Repertory Company of Chicago in 1995 would have none of this; as Greg Vinkler, playing Angelo, turned to leave the stage with pardon in hand, he curtly rebuffed the arm offered to him by Mariana as his new (and evidently unwelcome) partner in marriage.

The Duke is perhaps the most controversial character of all in this perplexing drama. The present chapter has attempted to make a case for him as a kind of benign if quixotic playwright figure, controlling the lives of others as dramatists do their characters with a view to testing and deepening them as persons under stress. Performance history makes plain that other choices are available. The Duke's management of the lives of his subjects, undoubtedly officious, can quickly become capricious and even sadistic. In Keith Hack's production at Stratford-upon-Avon in 1974, Barrie Ingham's Duke was himself seriously responsible for the universal corruption in his city of Vienna. His manipulative interference in people's lives was deeply resented and seen as hypocritical. Lucio's satiric jabs at the Duke for being a secret lecher hit home; this Duke was no better than the Angelo whom he entrapped and brought before the bar of a ludicrously compromised justice. Correspondingly, in some recent productions Lucio has become an ingratiating rake, a raisonneur for the play, as in Lenny Baker's enactment of the role for the New York Shakespeare Festival production in Delacorte Theatre, as directed by John Pasquin, with Meryl Streep as Isabella and Sam Waterston as the Duke. The street-life comic characters too have come into their own, nowhere more so than at Stratford, Ontario, in 1985, where Michael Bogdanov's cast led off each performance with a cabaret prelude involving quantities of black leather, strobe lighting, a police raid, and the inviting of audience members to come onstage and join with transvestite dancers in a little fun before the play itself began. Yet whether or not the play is seen in traditional or revisionist terms, the important truth remains that the Duke is an intensely theatrical figure, supervising the action in such a way as to cast him in a role strikingly similar to that of theater director.

II

In *Troilus and Cressida,* perhaps the most experimental of Shakespeare's plays, the playwright pursues an opposite strategy: that of a dramatic narrative over which no character has control. Instead of a presiding figure fulfilling the scheme of a comic providence, this play features choric commentators whose role is to watch and observe as the chaotic and unpredictable destiny of war overwhelms its participants and victims, including the lovers of the play's title. Not coincidentally, *Troilus and Cressida* is a play that does not fit comfortably into any identifiable dramatic genre. It is a history play in that it chronicles the most famous war in ancient history; it is the tragedy of Hector, the greatest of the Greeks, who, along with Patroclus and some unnamed soldiers, is dead at the play's end; and it is a kind of satirical black comedy about a love affair and a war related in such a way as to stress the absurd. With fitting ambiguity, it was placed by the editors of the great Shakespeare folio edition of 1623 between the history plays and the tragedies.

The play's very title emphasizes multiplicity of points of view. Troilus and Cressida are unlike each other; theirs is a mutual attraction of opposites. Troilus is a prince of the Trojan royal family; Cressida is the daughter of a priest who defects to the Greek side and then bargains for his daughter to join him. Troilus is sick with an enervating desire for Cressida, unable to think of anything else until he possesses her; she is wary, attracted to him but fully conscious that men are wooers only until the moment of sexual surrender. Troilus thinks that Cressida is the most important thing in the world to him, but when the necessity of war requires that she be sent away to the Greeks in exchange for a Trojan prisoner of war whom the Trojans need, Troilus acquiesces in her departure; Cressida, for her part, cannot believe that he is willing to let her go, since she has finally cast her lot with him. Gendered differences undermine their relationship as surely as does the war itself. Who is right or wrong in this dismal story of a failed love affair? The only sure thing is that the names of the lovers will live forever as emblems of the Forsaken Man and the Inconstant Woman. Their go-between, her uncle Pandarus, will go down in history as the Pander.

The war is no less indeterminate. After so many fruitless years on the

Phrygian plain, the disheartened Greeks quarrel among themselves and long for home. The Trojan leaders cannot agree on the justice of their side of the conflict: are they right to keep Helen, whom Paris abducted in part because the Greeks had taken away Priam's sister Hesione (2.2.77)? Helen and Paris have become vapid sybarites, hardly inspiring as emblems of a worthy cause. As Diomedes bitterly says of Helen, "For every false drop in her bawdy veins / A Grecian's life hath sunk; for every scruple / Of her contaminated carrion weight / A Trojan hath been slain" (4.1.71–74). The wisest of the Greeks, Ulysses, is also the most ready to give Machiavellian advice, as he plays the oafish Ajax off against the sulking Achilles. The predictable result is pointless carnage and the tarnishing of once-bright reputations. In his anxiety about fame, Achilles butchers the great Hector and earns for himself throughout eternity the name of bully.

In the absence of any controlling figure, Shakespeare gives us a number of wry commentators who point out the absurdity of this war. The point of view is multiple and satirical. Thersites, despised by his fellow Greeks and considered by Hector to be too insignificant and pitiable a soldier even to be worth killing, takes morbid delight in images of disease. "I would thou didst itch from head to foot. An I had the scratching of thee," he taunts Ajax, "I would make thee the loathsomest scab in Greece" (2.1.26–28). His extensive list of ailments includes the dry serpigo, ruptures, catarrhs, dirt-rotten livers, sciaticas, the bone-ache of syphilis, and much more (5.1.17–24). Adept satirist as he is, Thersites can do a superb mimicry of Agamemnon's hubristic self-seriousness, or old Nestor's palsied fumbling on his gorget, or Ajax's fatuous self-absorption in his forthcoming contest with Hector (1.3.151–75, 3.3.274–99). This incessant theatricality puts us in mind that we as audience are in the theater, watching a play; as Ulysses puts it, Thersites is "like a strutting player, whose conceit / Lies in his hamstring," thinking it rich "To hear the wooden dialogue and sound / Twixt his stretched footing and the scaffoldage." Ulysses, like Hamlet, is not amused by "Such to-be-pitied and o'erwrested seeming" (1.3.153–57). Small wonder that Ulysses is miffed, since Thersites' scabrous metaphors deprive the military leaders on both sides of any vestige of heroism or human decency: Nestor is a "stale old mouse-eaten dry cheese," Ulysses a "dog-fox," Achilles and Ajax both "curs," Diomedes a "dissembling abominable varlet," and Troilus a "scurvy doting foolish young knave." Cressida is no better than a "whore" (5.4.2–15). Thersites' satiric point of view underscores the connection between men's competition over women and their competition on the field of battle. "All the argument is a whore and a cuckold," observes Thersites in choric fashion (2.3.71–72). The Trojan war began over women, and in turn it dooms the love affair of Troilus and Cressida.

Pandarus is another wry choric observer of lust and war, acting as go-between but powerless to do anything to stop the onrush of a blind destiny that will engulf the participants. His love song, performed for Paris and Helen, is a languid testimonial to love's power to wound and enervate. As Paris observes of Pandarus to Helen, "He eats nothing but doves, love, and that breeds hot blood, and hot blood begets hot thoughts, and hot thoughts beget hot deeds, and hot deeds is love" (3.1.114–30). Pandarus teases his niece about her sexual surrender. He seems to be driven by a prurient curiosity, along with a deep emotional attachment to Troilus. He is far more concerned about Troilus's unhappiness when Cressida is returned to the Greeks than he is about her welfare. Rejected at last by Troilus, Pandarus provides the play with a sardonic epilogue in which the members of the audience are leeringly invited to think of themselves as "Brethren and sisters of the hold-door trade," his partners in pandering (5.10.51). His choric function serves, like that of Thersites, to reduce war and love to their lowest common denominator.

Other commentators, standing to the side and unable to control what they observe, add to the multiplicity of this universal disablement. Ulysses lectures sagely on the ways in which the heavens themselves "Observe degree, priority, and place, / Insisture, course, proportion, season, form, / Office, and custom, in all line of order" (1.3.85–88), and yet is unable to convert that great principle of harmonious hierarchy into high-minded advice for his fellow Greeks. In the council meeting of the Trojans, Hector argues in defense of "moral laws / Of nature and of nations" that speak aloud to have Helen returned to the Greeks (2.2.184–85), but then chooses to pursue the war as a matter of family honor. Cressida sees perceptively into the weakness of women, vulnerable in time of war and too apt to let the error of their eye direct their mind (5.2.113), but this knowledge does not save her from giving in to circumstances. Hector's wife Andromache speaks with the visionary insight of one who has dreamed prophetically about the danger Hector faces as he goes into battle, but her foreknowledge does little more than to offer a sad ironic comment on Hector's fate. He goes to war because "The gods have heard me swear" (5.3.15). We know that Hector will not heed his sister Cassandra's prophetic warnings, because, according to legend, Apollo has rendered useless the very power of prophecy that he gave her when she refused him as a lover; such knowledge does nothing to change her unhappy plight. Character is fate in such a way that the participants in the story have no choice but to act out what destiny has decreed. Because the story has been often told, its outcome is predetermined by history.

No scene in the play is more experimental in its multiplicity of points of view, or more expressive of historical determinism, than the long scene in the Greek camp as Troilus, escorted by Ulysses, visits by night the tent where Cressida now resides with her father Calchas and where she is aggressively courted by the Greek officer Diomedes. Thersites is there as well, tagging along after Troilus and Ulysses in voyeuristic hopes of witnessing a sordid scene. "They say he [Diomedes] keeps a Trojan drab and uses the traitor Calchas his tent," Thersites comments as the scene is about to begin. "I'll after. Nothing but lechery! All incontinent varlets!" (5.1.97–99). Thersites' role is to conceal himself out of sight of the rest, from which vantage point he can hurl his acerbic comments at the audience. "Roguery!" he exclaims. He interprets salaciously and pruriently: "How the devil Luxury, with his fat rump and potato finger, tickles these together! Fry, lechery, fry!" When Cressida asks Diomedes, "What would you have me do?" Thersites offers his view of what Diomedes must have in mind: "A juggling trick—to be secretly open." Thersites paces the scene as a sort of lewd theatrical stage manager, specifying the props that are needed, as when he calls for Cressida to produce the sleeve that Troilus has given her as a love token: "Now the pledge, now, now, now!" Thersites even provides a couplet by way of epilogue as the wooing of Cressida by Diomedes comes to a close with Cressida's confession of turpitude: "A proof of strength she could not publish more, / Unless she said, 'My mind is now turned whore'" (5.2.19–117). Thersites is the interpreter of this little dramatic interlude, unobserved by the others, closest to us as audience in that he knows and sees all, even though he can control nothing. We are unavoidably drawn in by his gleeful and demeaning view of what we see through his eyes.

Troilus and Ulysses, meanwhile, occupy the middle position of those who observe Diomedes and Cressida while they are simultaneously being observed by Thersites. They too are understood to be concealed from the objects of their gaze, though Shakespeare's original staging clearly must have required that the audience see all. We also understand that it is night because we are told as much and because Diomedes carries a torch as he proceeds to Calchas's tent, enabling Troilus and Ulysses to follow him in the dark. "Follow his torch," says Ulysses privately to his companion (5.1.86), and then, as they arrive at their station, "Stand where the torch may not discover us" (5.2.5). Torches signal nighttime activity to an Elizabethan audience watching the play in the full light of day. Cressida "comes forth" to Diomedes, and the coy ritual of wooing begins. Troilus's role is that of the disappointed lover and angry rival, impatient to the point of distraction, having to be restrained by Ulysses in urgent asides. The new lovers, meantime, are oblivious to what is going on around them as they engage in a tug-of-war over Troilus's sleeve. Diomedes plays hard to get, suavely confident of his own masculinity and knowing that Cressida has few options other than to take up with him.

The scene is then framed, after the wooers' departure, by Troilus's lament for a Cressida who is no longer the Cressida he has loved. "The bonds of heaven are slipped, dissolved, and loosed," he laments, leaving only "The fragments, scraps, the bits and greasy relics / Of her o'ereaten faith" (160–64). When Troilus and Ulysses then exit, having been summoned by Aeneas, Thersites is left alone to provide still another epilogue, this time for the play-within-the-play that includes Ulysses and Troilus. "Lechery, lechery, still wars and lechery; nothing else holds fashion. A burning devil take them!" (198–200). This exquisitely crafted nighttime scene thus displays its rhetorical and theatrical shape as a series of concentric circles one inside the other. Its dramaturgy is well fitted to the unadorned Elizabethan stage, with its columns providing a means of miming concealment. The scene's intricate design of layers within layers is also well suited to the play's persistent use of multiple points of view. No one is in charge. Destiny holds sway.

Production history emphasizes the experimental and theatrically self-aware dimensions of this remarkable play. Evidently it was not a success in Shakespeare's own day. A revised title page and newly added epistle to the reader for a second version of the 1609 quarto goes so far as to claim that the play was "never staled with the stage, never clapper-clawed with the palms of the vulgar." Even though the original title page does offer the play to the reader "as it was acted by the King's Majesty's Servants at the Globe," these contradictions suggest controversy and failure to win popular support. The play was too advanced for its day, and indeed proved so down to the twentieth century; in the long interim, it was either shunned as too dismaying or rewritten so as to be palatable. John Dryden's *Troilus and Cressida, or Truth Found Too Late,* 1679, changed matters around so that Cressida was the victim of a sad misunderstanding, driven to suicide by her unhappy fate, whereas Troilus, learning the truth about her too late, killed the treacherous Diomedes and was then slain in battle. This adaptation was occasionally revived, from 1709 to 1734, whereas Shakespeare's original had no life in the theater at all until it was rediscovered in Germany in 1898 and then in London, by Charles Fry in 1907 and William Poel in 1912. Poel produced the play on an experimental bare stage, using Elizabethan acting conventions of rapid entry and exit without scenic change. Poel took the part of Pandarus, with Edith Evans as Cressida and Hermione Gingold as Cassandra.

Other directors soon discovered that *Troilus and Cressida*, with its self-aware theatricality and mixed-genre experimentalism, was admirably attuned to a world increasingly disillusioned about war and rapidly changing social mores. An all-male production by the Marlowe Society at Cambridge in 1922 caught a mood of war-weariness in the aftermath of World War I. Michael Macowan, at London's Westminster Theatre in 1938, chose modern dress in order to remind audiences of the play's relevance to the pessimism so widely felt about Neville Chamberlain's appeasement of Hitler in that year and the growing dread that war was again imminent (fig. 5.3). Glen Byam Shaw, directing the play for the RSC at Stratford-upon-Avon in 1948 with Anthony Quayle as a pathological and blithering old Pandarus and Keith Mitchell as a brutal Achilles, took away from the love affair of Troilus and Cressida (Laurence Harvey and Muriel Pavlow) any romantic illusions and from the war any coherent sense of purpose. Tyrone Guthrie, at the Old Vic in 1956, set the play in the *fin de siècle* Edwardian attire of the German and Austrian empires, in a time of rapidly approaching social change and military conflict, with Helen (Wendy Hiller) lounging languidly on a grand piano while Pandarus (Paul Rogers) played waltzes (fig. 5.4). Thersites (Clifford Williams) was a cynical war correspondent. John Barton revisited the play several times between 1960 (with Peter Hall as codirector) and 1976, in a time of growing social unease about the redefining of sexual mores, racial conflict, and increasingly radical protests on campuses and in cities against the Vietnam War. In 1968, Alan Howard as Achilles flaunted homosexuality in a male world where all combat was voluptuous, whether in the bare-loincloth wrestling of Hector and Ajax or on the battlefield. The male anatomy was no less persistently on display in 1976. At the Aldwych in 1981, under Terry Hands's direction, Achilles (David Suchet) and Patroclus (Chris Hunter) were passionately desirous of each other in a way that the play's other love relationships seemed to lack, though the orgy of groping that accompanied Helen's sole appearance in 3.1 was certainly intense enough.

5.3. Oriel Ross as Helen and Max Adrian as Pandarus, in act 3 of Michael Macowan's 1938 production of *Troilus and Cressida* for the London Mask Theatre Company. Courtesy of the Manders & Mitcheson Theatre Collection.

5.4. Helen (Wendy Hiller) lounges on a piano and flirts with Paris, while Pandarus (Paul Rogers) plays waltzes, in act 3 of Tyrone Guthrie's modern-dress production of *Troilus and Cressida* for the Old Vic, 1956. V&A Images/Victoria and Albert Museum.

The RSC's production at Stratford-upon-Avon in 1996, directed by
Ian Judge, was similarly a marathon of both homoerotic and heterosex-
ual display in which sex was easy but long-term emotional commitment
nowhere to be found. Helen (Sally Dexter) in Sam Mendes's 1990 production at the Swan Theatre in Stratford-upon-Avon was brought on
as a gold-wrapped package to be untied and opened, like a birthday
present for Paris; Achilles (Ciaran Hinds) was a menacing gang boss in
black leather and greasy hair to match; Pandarus (Norman Rodway, who
also played the Chorus) was a wheezing, giggling chap in a natty blazer
as though he were the barker for a circus act; Thersites (Simon Russell
Beale) was a skid-row bum in a skullcap and flasher's overcoat decorated
with a gay-lib button (fig. 5.5). Mark Wing-Davey's production at the
Delacorte Theatre in New York in 1995 found sordidness in every aspect
of the play: bored Greek officers watched television as Ulysses (Stephen
Skybell) spouted oratory about order and degree; a giant prop dildo
responded with upward gestures as Pandarus (Stephen Spinella) sang
about the "dying" and the "groans" of love. Thersites (Tim Blake Nelson)
added new obscenities to the sardonic gloatings provided in Shakespeare's text.

Because the play so eloquently deconstructs its own medium of theater, incessantly calling attention to playacting and self-representation,
Troilus and Cressida has proved itself ready-made for Brechtian interpretation. The Berliner Ensemble made this point, in 1986, in Manfred
Wekwerth's expert deployment of that ensemble's collaborative playing
and use of techniques calculated to disengage the audience from stage illusion, all aimed at a performance that was a social and political act. The
arrival of Cressida (Corinna Harfouch) in the Greek camp, for example,
was comically deflated by the unexpected appearance of Ajax, jogging
back and forth across the back of the set and not even stopping to beg
for a kiss as he warmed up for his encounter with Hector (see Gary Taylor, *Reinventing Shakespeare,* 1989, pp. 298–304). Howard Davies, pro-
ducing the play for the RSC in 1985, chose as his *mise en scène* the era of
the Crimean war, with flash photographers, machine guns, field tele-
phones, a firing squad for the massacre of Hector, and Thersites (Alun
Armstrong) as a "Geordie waiter" creating havoc in the Greek officers'
mess.

Disillusionment about male sexual rapaciousness has become a central focus of many recent productions, as in 1985, when Juliet Stevenson
played Cressida as caught up in a nightmare of male violence and man-
handling of women, finding herself left no other choice finally than to

5.5. Simon Russell Beale as Thersites as a skid-row bum, in Sam Mendes's 1990 production of *Troilus and Cressida* for the Royal Shakespeare Company, Swan Theatre, Stratford-upon-Avon. Photo by Donald Cooper.

accede to her dehumanizing role as the love object of sex-starved military men. Suzanne Burden, cast as Cressida in Jonathan Miller's 1981 BBC television version, found herself out of synch with Miller and with the actor playing Troilus, Anton Lesser; the two men saw Cressida as sexually aroused and aware of her power as the object of men's desires, whereas the actress interpreted her role as one in which she was unprotected and abandoned by her father to become a plaything of the Greek generals. In all these mordant interpretations, Cressida's surrender to Diomedes in act 5 took on a timeliness aptly suited to the metatheatricality that is strongly implicit in Shakespeare's text. No play is more capable than *Troilus and Cressida* of making Shakespeare seem thoroughly modern.

III

A word or two about *All's Well That Ends Well.* The play centers its action around riddles, rings, disguises, and substitutions — especially the substitution of the so-called "bed trick" in which one woman secretly replaces another as the man's sexual companion. These theatrical motifs are intertwined. The solving of the play's central riddle depends on the exchange and identification of rings, while the fulfillment of the riddle depends upon disguise and the bed substitution.

The word "ring" appears far more often in this play and in *The Merchant of Venice* than elsewhere in Shakespeare. In *All's Well*, two rings are essential to the plot: Bertram's ring that he reluctantly gives to Diana as the asking price for her virginity, and another ring that Helena places on Bertram's finger during the night encounter that he supposes to take place with Diana. The surprise, as we learn only in play's denouement when Bertram gives this ring to old Lafew as a promise to marry Lafew's daughter (since Bertram's wife, Helena, is now presumed dead), is that this second ring was originally the French King's; he gave it to Helena as an assurance that he would come to her aid if ever necessary (5.3.84–87). It is reputedly a magical ring (102–5), and is thus associated with Helena's mysterious gift of curing the King's seemingly incurable disease. She is of course in back of the ring business, as also of the switching of bed partners in the play's famous bed trick so much like that of *Measure for Measure.* In that play, the bed trick was the Duke's idea; here it is Helena's. Accordingly, we can see her as another figure of manipulative theatrical control, and with ambiguous qualities that are like those of the Duke. Her tactics raise questions of moral propriety. Like the Duke, she disguises herself in religious garb in order to deceive and trick her wayward husband into accepting the marriage and his responsibility as father of her child. At the same time, many persons in the play, including the King, Lafew, and Bertram's mother, are convinced that (in the King's words) "some blessèd spirit doth speak / His powerful sound" in all that Helena does (2.1.162–78).

Not surprisingly, then, in performance history Helena has proved to be an enigmatic and contradictory figure. In Tyrone Guthrie's landmark production in 1953 at Stratford, Ontario, and then at Stratford-upon-Avon in 1959, the ethical dubiety of Helena's manipulations seemed thoroughly in keeping with the universal desolation of Guthrie's pre–World War I French African *mise en scène.* Helena was no less unremittingly aggressive in her pursuit of Bertram in Noel Williams's production at Stratford-upon-Avon in 1955. On the other hand, she has increasingly come to be seen as the victim of sexist abandonment by a callow and unsympathetic young man, as in John Barton's production in 1967 and Trevor Nunn's in 1981, both at Stratford-upon-Avon. Helena has thus become, like the Duke in *Measure for Measure* and Thersites in *Troilus and Cressida,* a key to the play's success in performance as the embodiment of an ambiguous controlling or choric figure through whom the dramatist, making adroit use of stage props and techniques such as rings, disguises, and substitutions, shapes his dramatic narrative of paradox and riddle.

ℒ 6 ℒ

The Motive and the Cue for Passion

ROMEO AND JULIET, HAMLET, AND OTHELLO IN PERFORMANCE

Just as Shakespeare innovated with staging in his experimental problem plays in the early 1600s, he explored new ways of staging tragedy as well. Tragedy was, for him, an essentially new genre at this point in his career as dramatist. He had written one early tragedy, *Titus Andronicus* (c. 1589–1592), borrowing its staging methods as well as its revenge themes from successful hits of the late 1580s like Christopher Marlowe's two-part *Tamburlaine* and Thomas Kyd's *The Spanish Tragedy,* but Shakespeare otherwise had not pursued tragedy as a genre with the intense interest that was to emerge in 1599–1600 and afterward. His early history plays, to be sure, dramatize tragic events and are sometimes called tragedies in their titles, as in the case of an early version of *3 Henry VI* called *The True Tragedy of Richard Duke of York, and the Death of Good King Henry the Sixth* (1595). Nevertheless, because these plays are concerned with the historical events of England's civil wars of the fifteenth century, their generic form is more sequential and narrative than tragic in structure, and as a group they move forward to the triumph of Henry Tudor, Queen Elizabeth's grandfather, over Richard III at Bosworth Field in 1485. Even though Shakespeare's early four-play historical sequence culminates in what is called *The Tragedy of King Richard the Third* on its 1597 quarto title page, the form of the sequence as a whole is not unlike that of the great English religious cycles of the late Middle Ages in which the often unhappy events of human history are seen as a prelude to the victory of goodness over evil in a great cosmic struggle determining the fate of humankind. *The Tragedy of Richard II* (1597), the first play in Shakespeare's second four-play historical sequence, ends with the death of that king but simultaneously with the rise of King Henry IV and hence of the dynasty that will produce Henry V.

Romeo and Juliet, written in the mid-1590s, is a tragedy, but in an unusual sense: its first two acts are for the most part so delightfully comic that the play seems aptly partnered with Shakespeare's romantic comedies of the same period, such as *A Midsummer Night's Dream.* It is as though Shakespeare held off from engaging intensely with tragedy until he had perfected the genres of romantic comedy and history play, and perhaps until he felt himself ready for such a daunting enterprise. His experiments with the problem plays (and *Hamlet* is sometimes listed in the roster of problem plays) signal a new direction in the early 1600s. The purpose of this chapter is to examine the ways in which Shakespeare approached the staging of tragedy, first in a play (*Romeo and Juliet*) with significant affinities to romantic comedy, and then in two plays (*Hamlet* and *Othello*) through which Shakespeare helped redefine the greatness of a genre that is preeminently associated with his name. *Julius Caesar* (1599) will be discussed briefly in chapter 7.

I

"My dismal scene I needs must act alone," says Juliet, as she prepares to drink the sleep-inducing drug that the Friar has given her lest she be obliged to marry Count Paris (4.3.19). Her scenic image calls attention to a theatrical self-awareness in *Romeo and Juliet* (1594–1596) that manifests itself in several key scenes. Repeatedly, the physical stage, with its tiring-house facade and gallery above, is visually identified with the house of the Capulets and with Juliet's chambers in particular, and then finally with the Capulets' burial vault. This visual linkage is unusually versatile, making use of vertical ascent and descent and displaying a protean ability to turn inside to outside. Modern productions have found in these stage images an invitation to explore in diverse ways the visual implications of Shakespeare's great tragedy of young love.

The theatrical image-building begins with the play's fourth scene, after an opening sequence of violence between the two feuding families of Capulets and Montagues and two scenes in which the Capulets encourage the suit of Count Paris for their daughter Juliet's hand. Romeo, having been urged by Benvolio to attend the "ancient feast" to be held that night at the Capulets' house, joins Benvolio, Mercutio, and *"five or six other masquers"* in scene 4 as they get ready for the evening's festivities.

Torchbearers are at hand, functioning as in act 5 of *Troilus and Cressida* and indeed as always in Shakespeare's theater as a signal to the audience that it is nighttime. "Give me a torch. I am not for this ambling," says Romeo. "Being but heavy, I will bear the light" (1.4.11–12). He thus makes metaphorical and punning use of a useful stage prop. The revelers listen to Mercutio's dazzling jeu d'esprit on the subject of Queen Mab and dreams, and prepare to enter the Capulet house as party crashers. (Mercutio is invited, but certainly not Romeo and Benvolio.) How is their entrance to be staged in the Elizabethan theater?

The stage directions provide the clue. As scene 4 ends and 5 begins, the direction reads, "*They march about the stage, and Servingmen come forth with napkins.*" This informative note bridges the two scenes with a continuous action; no scene break is to be found in the early printed texts of this play. As the revelers promenade about onstage, miming the action of approaching and then entering the feasting hall, servants come on with napkins over their arms to signal that they are prepared to bring on food and drink. The revelers do not exit; they simply stand to one side until it is time for Capulet and his friends to come onstage at line 16: "*Enter all the guests and gentlewomen to the masquers.*" The stage has, by a theatrical sleight of hand, become the interior hall of a space earlier identified as the outside of the Capulet house. "*Music plays, and they dance*" (26.1). Romeo and Juliet meet and kiss. All too soon, it is time to leave. Shakespeare makes clever use of the exits at the scene's end by having Juliet inquire of her Nurse the names of the guests leaving one by one, so that she can find out who it is she has danced with.

The magic of stage transformation proceeds apace. "*Enter Romeo alone,*" begins act 2. Romeo is unwilling, even unable, to leave, after the transforming experience of meeting Juliet at the dance. "Can I go forward when my heart is here?" he exclaims. "Turn back, dull earth, and find thy center out." He retires to one side, or conceals himself behind a stage pillar, as his friends, Mercutio and Benvolio, come onstage looking for him. "He ran this way and leapt this orchard wall," ventures Benvolio. We understand that Romeo is concealed from them, on the other side of an imagined barrier, like Troilus and Ulysses in act 5 of *Troilus and Cressida.* Mercutio, pretty drunk it seems, invokes Romeo in some remarkably bawdy language, and then exits with Benvolio as the two of them give up on their search. "Go then, for 'tis in vain / To seek him here that means not to be found," says Benvolio as the scene ends. Yet it is not a scene break after all, for Romeo, still onstage, echoes Benvolio's verse line with the pairing line of a couplet: "He jests at scars that never felt a wound" (2.2.1). "Found" and "wound" rhyme in Elizabethan English. The unauthorized quarto text of 1597, the corrected and authorized quarto text of 1599, and the folio text of 1623 all choose not to provide any numerical indications of scene interval at this point. Indeed, the scene markings throughout are the work of subsequent editors. The concerns of some nineteenth-century actor-managers and editors that "act 2, scene 1" and "act 2, scene 2" needed to be outfitted with differentiating scenery (the first for an alleyway separated from the Capulet garden by the "orchard wall" and the second for the garden itself), with a curtained interval allowing for a quick change of scenery, is entirely spurious as a theatrical response to the demands of Shakespeare's text.

The stage is now transformed imaginatively, by the language of Romeo and his friends, into the garden or orchard of Juliet's family's house. We are now on the inside of that garden wall with Romeo. He looks up and sees a light. "But soft, what light through yonder window breaks?" It appears in Juliet's window—not a balcony, as erroneously imposed by later staging tradition. She is evidently in the upper acting area, as if at her window. The staging arrangement is admirably suited for this famous love scene: he speaks up to her from below as she timorously but lovingly answers and then darts back twice into the tiring house to answer the Nurse's call. They part thus, she above and he from the main stage. That stage throughout has been the garden lying below her window, and the tiring-house facade itself a passable likeness of the Capulet house.

The lovers are closely associated with this stage setting. When the sad time is come for the now-banished Romeo to bid his young wife farewell, the stage direction specifies *Enter Romeo and Juliet aloft*," together now at her window (3.5.1). Shakespeare's theater cannot show them in bed together as in the film version by Franco Zeffirelli (1967) or in the comparable love scene in *Shakespeare in Love* (1996), nor would it choose to do so; Juliet is played by a boy actor. Indeed, the Elizabethan staging is physically chaste; the lovers are separated for the most part, together only for moments. This present moment is indeed brief, for Romeo must descend from Juliet's window, evidently doing so by climbing down in full view of the audience from the gallery. The rope cords that Romeo has provided via the Nurse (2.4.185–87, 3.2.34–35) for just such a purpose are now pressed into service. Once he is on the main stage, we imagine him once again in the garden from which he wooed her earlier, separated by a vertical distance. When the Nurse sounds a note of alarm, Romeo leaves.

We might suppose that the remainder of this long scene is to be acted aloft, since that space is so closely associated with Juliet's chambers, but it is not. According to the first and unauthorized quarto text of the play (1597), Juliet *"goeth down from the window"* (3.5.67.1). That is, she disappears above and quickly descends behind the scenes so that she can reemerge on the main stage to confront first her mother and then the Nurse and her father about the impending marriage with Count Paris. Although the 1597 quarto is generally unreliable as a text, this particular stage direction (not in the second quarto or the folio) may well reflect direct experience of the play in performance. This is a busy, crowded scene, unsuited to acting in the gallery above. Seemingly for that reason, Shakespeare has Juliet descend to the main stage, and he asks us to understand that it is now her chambers. Such transformations are not uncommon, as we have seen earlier in the bridging of scenes 4 and 5 in act 1.

It is here too, on the main stage, that Juliet drinks the drug given her by the Friar and then falls into her bed—presumably a curtained bed thrust onstage from one of the doors or the discovery space (4.3.58). Here she remains hidden from view, comatose, while Capulet and his wife bustle about with preparations for the wedding and chaff with their servants. Our knowledge that Juliet lies silently behind the curtains all this while (4.4) creates a dramatic irony leading up to the Nurse's going to those curtains and opening them, only to discover Juliet seemingly dead. A passage of mourning (4.5) ensues without a scene break, depending for its dramatic tension on our knowledge as audience that the grief is misdirected. Yet we also sense that the mistaken mourning anticipates a genuine tragedy still to come.

The play's final scene at the Capulets' burial monument requires a good deal of stage business. Paris arrives with his page, bearing flowers, perfumed water, and a torch. The torch, as always, signals nighttime. Paris strews Juliet's "bridal bed" with his gifts of sorrow (5.3.12), and, hearing a noise, retires to one side. Romeo arrives next, with his boy bearing a torch, a mattock, and a crowbar. Romeo takes these instruments, bids the boy begone, and evidently mimes the action of gaining entrance to the tomb: "Thus I enforce thy rotten jaws to open," he says to the "womb of death" in which Juliet lies (45–47). Whether a stage structure was employed in the original production is questionable, though it is often provided in subsequent stage history; Juliet needs to be visible to the audience once Romeo has discovered her, and the sequence of their two suicides must be acted where the audience can see. The spoken references to "This vault" (86) and to "The stony entrance to this sepulcher" (141) help create the imagined setting and need not be literalized in the theater.

What is needed is a sense of recapitulation. "Methinks I see thee, now thou art so low, / As one dead in the bottom of a tomb," Juliet said earlier as Romeo climbed down from her window in his farewell (3.5.55–56). The sad deaths of the lovers take place in the theater in the very spot where Juliet imagined her tragedy to begin. Shakespeare's theater is an unusually vital, and often neglected, element in the thematic construction of *Romeo and Juliet*.

Until recently, directors and theater managers have tended toward verisimilar representations of Shakespeare's love tragedy, thereby gaining in visual splendor while giving up the original presentational staging that made for such flexible shifts from exterior to interior or from one part of the theater space to another while maintaining a continuity of understood location. The persistence of the word "balcony" in critical discussions of this play is symptomatic. The word will not go away, even though it never appears in Shakespeare's script; Juliet appears at her "window" in 2.2 (line 2), and she bids farewell to her new husband for the last time in 3.5 by saying, "Then window, let day in, and let life out" (line 41), as Romeo climbs down from her window to begin his journey of banishment. Indeed, Shakespeare never uses the word "balcony" in any of his writings. It is a technical term of Restoration and eighteenth-century staging, carried forward to this day. Any production is of course free to locate the encounters of Romeo and Juliet where it chooses; Zeffirelli visualizes the "balcony" scene in his 1968 film in a sensuously attractive way, with Olivia Hussey as Juliet, in a low-cut gown, on a balcony not far above ground level while Leonard Whiting as Romeo breathlessly clamors to reach her through the surrounding shrubbery. "Oh, wilt thou leave me so unsatisfied?" he cries (2.2.125), in a reading of the line charged with erotic premise by his nearness to the object of his desire. Later, we catch a brief glimpse of them as newly married, naked in bed, as the hour of Romeo's sad departure nears. Film can take us to these locations without losing dramatic momentum. The Elizabethan theater, with its upper acting area over the stage, could present Juliet at her "window" in a space that might indeed look like a balcony in our terms; Gwyneth Paltrow, as Juliet in *Shakespeare in Love* as played in an Elizabethan playhouse, gives us just such an effect. Stage history reminds us, on the other hand, that in the Restoration and eighteenth century a location like this would have been effected by painted scenery mounted on movable screens. An engraving of 1753 shows Maria Isabella Nossiter as Juliet on a very substantial balcony in the Theatre Royal at Covent Garden, receiving the attentions of Spranger Barry as Romeo (fig. 6.1). It is this kind of scenic literalism, compounded in the nineteenth century by the building of more massive sets, that necessitated the scene breaks and changes of scenery that Shakespeare's script eschews.

The same Restoration idea of decorum that demanded painted scenery also insisted on a play that fulfilled the age's sense of poetic justice, and so a tragicomic version, in which the young lovers did not die after all, became popular as a substitute for Shakespeare's tragedy. Even in a tragic unfolding of the story, the ending was revamped for melodramatic effect: Romeo stayed alive long enough after having drunk poison to be able to share with Juliet the agony and the ecstasy of their last moments on earth. This ending, taken from Thomas Otway's classical adaptation of 1679 called *Caius Marius,* was repeated by Theophilus Cibber's revival of *Romeo and Juliet* in 1744, by David Garrick in 1748, by Hector Berlioz in his symphonic interpretation of 1839, and by Charles Gounod in his operatic version, *Roméo et Juliette,* of 1867. Stage sets became more impressive and costly, especially in Garrick's enclosed vault for Juliet in act 5, with trees on all sides and the moon visible in the sky. So striking was this stage image that it inspired contemporary illustrators and engravers like R. S. Ravenet in 1753 to publish engravings for wide distribution (fig. 6.2). The increasing trend in the nineteenth century toward grand sets resulted, for example, in Henry Irving's revival at the Lyceum Theatre in 1882, with vaulted arches, ironwork grill gates, and stone staircases leading down into the Capulets' tomb, while the moon looked down on the melancholy scene. Not to be outdone, Mary Anderson, at the Lyceum in 1884, built onstage a passable replica of the Piazza Dante in Verona, complete with handsome gardens and authentic architectural detail. As Romeo and Juliet lovingly conversed in the Capulets' garden in 2.2, the audience feasted its eyes on a cascade of descending terraces receding into a distant moonlit haze. The Renaissance costumes were festooned with satin and brocade. Elaborate machinery made possible the transformation of houses into gardens and cloisters into tombs; as one contemporary observer wonderingly remarked, both Friar Laurence's cell and Juliet's chamber were "turned inside out in full view of the house." No cost was spared in the quest for verisimilar effects.

Splendid as this kind of theater no doubt was, and innovative in its own way as interpretation of Shakespeare for the age in which it was produced, it led to a reaction in favor of simplified sets and continuous action. William Poel, in 1905, revived the spirit of original staging in his

The Garden Scene in the celebrated PLAY of Romeo and Juliet.

ACT 2ᵈ SCENE 2ᵈ.

Alack there lies more Peril in thine Eye, than twenty of their Swords.

London Printed for John Ryall at Hogarths Head Fleetstreet.

6.1. Spranger Barry as Romeo and Maria Isabella Nossiter as Juliet in the so-called balcony scene of *Romeo and Juliet* (2.2), at Covent Garden in 1753. The balcony tradition derives from stagings such as these in the eighteenth century. Shakespeare never uses the word "balcony" at all. His Juliet is at her "window." From an engraving by William Elliott (c. 1753), after a painting by R. Pyle. By permission of The Harvard Theatre Collection, The Houghton Library.

6.2. George Ann Bellamy as Juliet and David Garrick as Romeo in Juliet's vault, in act 5 of Garrick's 1748 production of *Romeo and Juliet* at Drury Lane, London. In a departure from Shakespeare's text, Juliet awakens before Romeo dies. The moon shines through broken clouds on an elaborate set of trees and the burial vault in all its Gothic splendor. Paris lies dead in the lower right corner. From an engraving by R. S. Ravenet (1753), after a painting by Benjamin Wilson. By permission of The Harvard Theatre Collection, The Houghton Library.

production for the Elizabethan Stage Society. John Gielgud followed suit at the New Theatre in 1935 with a single permanent set for the entire performance. Laurence Olivier and Gielgud traded off the roles of Romeo and Mercutio; Peggy Ashcroft was Juliet, with Edith Evans as the Nurse. Insisting that *Romeo and Juliet* is "a play of wide spaces in which all scenery and decoration can easily become an irrelevance," Peter Brook, at Stratford-upon-Avon in 1947, created a set to match his words. Glen Byam Shaw's single set for the same theater in 1954 was geometrically abstract, with concentric circles and curved pathways suggesting the public square of an Italian city such as Verona. Joseph Papp's production for the New York Shakespeare Festival in Delacorte Theatre in Central Park, 1968, took place on scaffolding and a runway extending into the seating area where the scene at Juliet's window was located.

Such experimentalism has naturally gone hand in hand with other transformations. Ron Daniels, responding to rapid changes in social mores in the 1960s and 1970s, set the play in a kind of urban jungle of graffiti-marked walls in his 1980 production at Stratford-upon-Avon. The Young Vic, in its production at Birmingham in 1982, took on the issue of racial conflict by casting the Montagues as blacks and the Capulets as whites. Michael Bogdanov, at Stratford-upon-Avon in 1986, envisioned the play in post–World War II mafioso Italy. Jerome Robbins, Robert Wise, Stephen Sondheim, and Leonard Bernstein collaborated in the immensely successful adaptation *West Side Story* (1957, filmed in 1961), set in New York's Spanish Harlem. The Goodman Theatre's production of *Romeo and Juliet* in the 1980s, directed by Michael Maggio, chose an Italian urban world of gang warfare as its *mise en scène*. Terry Hands, directing at Stratford-upon-Avon in 1973, saw Mercutio as a troubled figure, angry, alcoholic, and erotically attracted to Romeo.

Directors for the screen have enjoyed the freedom to move the camera where they wish, and have generally done so, with visually opulent results and a corresponding tendency to replace language with images and theatrical imagination with verisimilar effects. Zeffirelli (1968) certainly does all this, choosing to show us what physical desire between two handsome people is like and how violence can disrupt the quiet of Verona's streets. The sun-baked piazzas and winding alleyways of an ancient Italian city are filled with the brightly colored costumes of a travel poster. Handsome young males in tights and codpieces seem ready to step out of an Italian Renaissance painting by Ghirlandaio or Mantegna. Baz Luhrmann's *William Shakespeare's Romeo + Juliet* (1996) is metacinematically aware of its upbeat MTV style, as it cuts frenetically from image to image and indulges in funny anachronistic jokes (as when the use of the word "sword" in Shakespeare's script is wryly justified by the inscribing of that word on the barrel of an automatic weapon, or when the failure of Friar Laurence's warning letter to reach Romeo in time is attributed to the attempted-delivery notice of a "Post Post Haste" express-mail system hung on the doorknob of Romeo's exile home in Mantua), and yet this film too opts for a lot of scenic realism. The *arriviste* Capulet mansion is a monument to the vulgar display of wealth, with a grand staircase descending into a hall built on the scale of Grand Central Station. Romeo (Leonardo DiCaprio) and his buddies, dressed in Hawaiian shirts, hang out in the seedy Sycamore Grove Amusement

Park or shoot pool in the Globe pool hall. Tybalt (John Leguizamo) and his Capulet gang display their contempt for the Montagues in gangland style. A gas station goes up in flames. Helicopters circle over the city (a composite of Miami and Los Angeles, shot actually in Mexico City) as Prince Escalus struggles vainly to maintain law and order. A television anchorwoman (the real TV newsreader, Edwina Moore) pronounces the prologue as though introducing the evening news. Juliet's mother (hilariously portrayed by Diane Venora) is a pill-popping, chain-smoking socialite preparing for a huge bash of a party so that her laid-back daughter (Claire Danes) will take an interest in the social catch of the season, Dave (i.e., Count) Paris (Paul Rudd), whose face has just appeared on the cover of a weekly newsmagazine. Friar Laurence (Pete Postlethwaite) is a New Age priest, counseling his young protégés in a swank chapel such as one would find only in L.A. or Miami. Juliet's Nurse (Miriam Margolyes) is an endearing caricature of a modern-day Hispanic housekeeper.

II

"What would he do, / Had he the motive and the cue for passion / That I have?" asks Hamlet in soliloquy (2.2.560–62). He is referring in consciously theatrical language to the First Player's just-ended recitation on the death of Priam. Hamlet is intensely interested in the players who have chosen this opportune moment to visit Elsinore. He engages them to play a tragedy about a regicide that evening in the presence of Hamlet's uncle and mother, the king and queen of Denmark. He himself will write a speech of "some dozen or sixteen lines" to be inserted into their script. He knows the players well from their previous visits and welcomes them with genuine warmth, noting that the boy player's voice appears to have changed since their last encounter (421–29). It is Hamlet's idea to have the First Player recite his Virgilian piece about vengeful Pyrrhus and the destruction of Troy, for Hamlet knows the speech well enough to have memorized it; he intones some thirteen lines of its blank verse with what Polonius calls "good accent and good discretion" before handing the rest of it over to the First Player (466–67).

Hamlet is a keen student of the theater. His tastes are refined, distinctly nonplebeian. The speech about Priam he so much admires is one that "pleased not the million; 'twas caviare to the general. But it was — as I received it, and others, whose judgments in such matters cried in the top of mine — an excellent play, well digested in the scenes, set down with as much modesty and cunning." There were no "sallets" or spicy improprieties in the lines "to make the matter savory," no "matter in the phrase that might indict the author of affectation." It was written in "an honest method, as wholesome as sweet, and by very much more handsome than fine"—that is, more well-proportioned than showy (2.2.436–45). Later, Hamlet inveighs against the "groundlings," that is, those who stand around the stage in the yard of the public theater, who "for the most part are capable of nothing but inexplicable dumb shows and noise" (3.2.10–12). He deplores overdone acting, which, "though it makes the unskillful laugh, cannot but make the judicious grieve, the censure of the which one must in your allowance o'erweigh a whole theater of others" (25–28). This is a remarkable statement for an actor (Richard Burbage) to make in a public theater, virtually surrounded on three sides as he is by "groundlings" who have paid to see him act. Presumably those spectators are being asked to take a joke. Still, the passage underscores the seriousness of Hamlet's attachment to drama of the very greatest sophistication.

Hamlet's fascination with theater takes what is for Shakespeare an unusually topical turn when Hamlet learns from Rosencrantz and Guildenstern (in a passage added to the folio text, not found in the earlier quartos) that the visiting players who have come to Elsinore are on tour in the provinces. Why, he asks at once, would the "tragedians of the city" choose to go on tour, when their privileged situation in the metropolis would presumably give them the commercial advantage that Shakespeare's own company enjoyed in London? "How chances it they travel? Their residence, both in reputation and profit, was better both ways." They would do better both professionally and commercially if they stayed in the city. The fact that "the city" remains unnamed invites us to read the passage in English and contemporary terms. And indeed the circumstances are strikingly relevant to Shakespeare's London in the years 1599 to 1601, when *Hamlet* was written and produced. An "aerie" of "little eyases," that is to say a nest of young hawks, "are now the fashion" on the theater scene, and "so berattle the common stages"— the adult playhouses — "that many wearing rapiers are afraid of goose quills and dare scarce come thither." That is to say, many persons of fashion are afraid to patronize the adult companies for fear of being held up to ridicule by the boy actors and their satirical plays. The boys "cry out on the top of question and are most tyrannically clapped for't." There has been "much to-do on both sides" in the battle between the boy and adult companies, especially since they are egged on by a fascinated public. "There was for a while no money bid for argument unless the poet and the player went to cuffs in the question." The boys "carry it away . . . Hercules and his load too" (2.2.326–62).

This last phrase sounds like a transparent reference to the Globe Theatre as visualized in the emblem of Hercules bearing the world on his shoulders, and indeed the passage as a whole seems to refer to a so-called War of the Theaters or Poetomachia between the adult and juvenile theaters that was in full swing at the time Shakespeare wrote *Hamlet*. To an extent it was a clash of personalities among Ben Jonson, John Marston, and Thomas Dekker, but it also had commercial and artistic implications for the institution of the theater, and it is for that reason that the subject is taken up so seriously and at such length. Will satire at the second Blackfriars theater sweep all before it and damage the kind of theater for which Shakespeare wrote, to such an extent that the adult companies will be driven out of business? Shakespeare airs the controversy in *Hamlet* with obvious interest but with his customary tact and fair-mindedness, just as he seems not to have been a major contender in the War of the Theaters itself.

Hamlet often thinks in theatrical metaphors and calls the audience's attention to the theatrical space in which they are beholding the play. When, for instance, Hamlet describes to Rosencrantz and Guildenstern how he has lost all his appreciation for life, he gestures to the theater building in which he is standing. "This goodly frame, the earth," he muses, "seems to me a sterile promontory; this most excellent canopy, the air, look you, this brave o'erhanging firmament, this majestical roof fretted with golden fire, why, it appeareth nothing to me but a foul and pestilent congregation of vapors" (2.2.299–304). The stage roof above Hamlet, the so-called "heavens" of the theater, is, evidently, spangled with images of the celestial cosmos of sun, moon, and stars. It is a "canopy," an "o'erhanging firmament." Hamlet need only gesture in its direction or lift his eyes upward to give an immediate spatial dimension to his words. He himself is on the main stage, representing the earth on which we live, with the heavens above and the terrifying underworld beneath — a space that in *Hamlet* is associated with Ghost of Hamlet's father who "*cries under the stage*" like some "fellow in the cellarage" (1.5.158–60). Hamlet's theater thus visualizes the cosmos in which he must struggle with his task of avenging a dead father. That cosmos is embodied in a handsomely decorated theater building; its parts and its spatial relationships are symbolic of an understood order in the universe. Yet order in this play is subverted by a ruling monarch who has murdered his brother in order to take away the throne and his brother's wife.

In the conflict between a visual symbolic order and the reality of criminal behavior lies the problem that presents itself to Hamlet the actor.

The play *Hamlet*, among its other amazing accomplishments, is an astute critical defense of theater at its highest potential. Much of Hamlet's discourse on theater has to do with proper and improper acting styles. Instructing the visiting players as they are about to go onstage, he bids them to speak the speech as he has pronounced it to them, "trippingly on the tongue." Hamlet has been coaching them. They are not to saw the air too much with their hands, but to deliver the whirlwind of their passion with temperance and smoothness. Nothing offends Hamlet so much as "to hear a robustious periwig-pated fellow tear a passion to tatters, to very rags." Such overacting "out-Herods Herod," exceeding the noisy fury of that familiar stage tyrant from the religious cycle plays. Hamlet will have no strutting and bellowing, of the sort that Ulysses deplores in *Troilus and Cressida.* Instead, Hamlet insists on a drama that will "hold as 'twere the mirror up to nature, to show virtue her feature, scorn her own image, and the very age and body of the time his form and pressure" (3.2.1–35). Presumably, Shakespeare's audience would be able to recall plays that they had seen in an overacted style; "Pyramus and Thisbe" in *A Midsummer Night's Dream* parodies the sort of thing that Hamlet has in mind. *Hamlet* as a play is serious about reform of the English stage.

The play-within-the-play staged by the visiting players, to which Hamlet has contributed and over which he presides as patron and a kind of chorus ("You are as good as a chorus, my lord," says Ophelia), is intent on holding a mirror up to its onstage audience. It dramatizes a regicide for spectators among whom is sitting the murderer of Hamlet's own royal father. It shows a king who is much like Hamlet's own father as Hamlet remembers him: kindly, solicitous of his wife, and philosophical about death. It also stages a queen who protests her undying loyalty to her royal husband but who will prove inconstant; as Hamlet assures his audience, "You shall see anon how the murderer gets the love of Gonzago's wife" (3.2.261–2). That Gertrude is made miserably uncomfortable by having to watch this business is made evident by her complaint that "The lady doth protest too much, methinks" (228). Hamlet turns the knife in the wound until the spectator with whom he is most concerned — Claudius — can bear no more. The play Hamlet sponsors is designed to "show virtue her feature" in the person of the wise old king and "scorn her own image" in the reprehensible conduct of the murderer and the queen. This play's overtly didactic purpose is nothing less than to show "the very age and body of the time his form and pressure"—that is, to anatomize, by uncovering and denouncing crime, the "unweeded garden" that Denmark has become (3.2.22–24, 1.2.135).

Hamlet is sharply critical of acting styles in the play-within-the-play. "Begin, murderer; leave thy damnable faces and begin," he bids the player of Lucianus, who is about to pour poison into the ear of the sleeping king (3.2.250–51). Hamlet wants no mugging in his play. By implication, he suggests that the real murderer sitting in the audience, Claudius, is a bad actor. Yet the critique is multifaceted, since Lucianus is "nephew to the King" that he is about to murder (242). Hamlet is the nephew of Claudius, and Hamlet has been exhorted by his dead father to seek revenge on the murderer Claudius. Is Hamlet criticizing himself for making damnable faces instead of proceeding to do what he has to do? Hamlet has already berated himself for just this kind of overacting coupled with inaction. "This is most brave," he bitterly castigates himself, "That I, the son of a dear father murdered, / Prompted to my revenge by heaven and hell, / Must like a whore unpack my heart with words, / And fall a-cursing, like a very drab, / A scullion!" (2.2.583–88). In his unsparing honesty with himself, is Hamlet half-persuaded that he is himself a bad actor?

Claudius serves as one antithetical model to Hamlet in the matter of good and bad acting styles; Polonius is another. Whenever Hamlet and Polonius meet, the conversation is apt to turn to acting. As they wait for the play-within-the-play to begin, Hamlet remembers that Polonius "played once i'th'university." Polonius recalls those days with evident self-satisfaction: "That did I, my lord, and was accounted a good actor." "What did you enact?" asks Hamlet. "I did enact Julius Caesar," is the reply; "I was killed i'th' Capitol; Brutus killed me." Hamlet cannot resist an insulting if clever multiple pun: "It was a brute part of him to kill so capital a calf there" (3.2.96–104). What an unfeeling jab! It is prompted no doubt by Polonius's long-winded fatuousness in praising the visiting troupe as "The best actors in the world, either for tragedy, comedy, history, pastoral, pastoral-comical, historical-pastoral, tragical-historical, tragical-comical-historical-pastoral, scene individable, or poem unlimited" (2.2.396–400). Only a Polonius could come up with such pedantry. Polonius is proud of his critical talents, enabling him to declare solemnly that with good actors "Seneca cannot be too heavy, nor Plautus too light" (400–401). His judgment of the First Player's disquisition on the death of Priam is that "This is too long." "It shall to the barber's with your beard," Hamlet tauntingly replies (498–99). Polonius has ventured to criticize the very speech that Hamlet has just praised to the skies as pleasing to the judicious while proving to be "caviare to the general," that is, too good for the uninformed tastes of the general populace. Polonius is a barbarian of their ilk. "He's for a jig or a tale of bawdry," Hamlet dismissively says of him to the players (500). More than anything else, perhaps, Hamlet wishes to be as unlike Polonius as possible. The theatrical links between them irritate him.

How then is Hamlet to act in his own real-life play? How is he to fulfill his role as avenger? How should he respond as an actor to "the motive and the cue" that prompt him to proceed with his own performance? His intense dislike of Claudius and Polonius offers negative clues. Hamlet has no wish to adopt the "damnable faces" of a stage villain or to saw the air with his arms like a ranting maniac. There are ways in which he would not wish to kill his uncle Claudius. One of them presents itself when Hamlet finds Claudius at prayer.

"Now might I do it pat, now 'a is a-praying," Hamlet says as he sees the man defenselessly before him, on his knees, unaware of Hamlet's presence (3.3.73). The moment seems at first irresistibly opportune: Hamlet knows now that his uncle did commit the murder, based on Claudius's guilty reaction to the play-within-the-play about regicide, and so do we know of that guilt even more directly, since Claudius has admitted the deed in soliloquy as he attempts to pray. It is one of the rare instances in which we see and hear Claudius with his guard down. (An earlier brief instance occurs at 3.1.50–55.) Why does Hamlet not end the business forthwith? Two answers present themselves. One is Hamlet's own, that killing a man at prayer would be to send his soul to heaven and thus save him from divine punishment. This sounds like a rationalization, though, for Hamlet must realize that Claudius's attempt at penance for having committed murder is not likely to succeed in cleansing his soul. Instead, a theatrical reading of motive suggests itself. Hamlet would not think well of himself if he killed this man in cold blood, however heinous and premeditated Claudius's own crime may have been, and we too would turn away from Hamlet in some revulsion as the play's protagonist. *Hamlet* would end too soon, and with the wrong ending.

Instead, Hamlet kills Polonius. He does so in an attempt to fulfill his father's wish and his own hope to kill Claudius "When he is drunk asleep, or in his rage, / Or in th'incestuous pleasure of his bed, / At game, a-swearing, or about some act / That has no relish of salvation in't" (3.3.89–92). Here is a plan that Hamlet can endorse with real enthusiasm. Accordingly, he marches off to his mother's private chambers, finds her alone, hears a man's voice behind the curtains, and lunges with his rapier. The logic of acting thus forthrightly seems unassailable. What other man than Claudius would be hiding in the Queen's chambers? Yet it is Polonius who falls through the curtains and lies in a pool of his own blood. Hamlet's conclusion from this is that he has mistaken once again. What seemed like right-minded action has proved to be wrong. His assuming the role of bloody avenger thus will lead to further consequences, ones in which Hamlet must pay a price for his mistake.

Persuaded at last that some providential scheme will make use of him as an actor in its own play, Hamlet submits to that destiny. Dispatched to England as a danger to the state, Hamlet manages to spring a trap on his escorts (Rosencrantz and Guildenstern) and return to Denmark. He has shown himself capable of decisive action in the interim, boarding a pirate ship in a fierce encounter and dooming Rosencrantz and Guildenstern to their certain deaths. He remains committed to the unfinished business of revenge. Yet, having learned how his own best-laid plans have gone so awry, he places himself at the disposal of the providence in which he believes. His belief is well placed, too, or so it seems, for the ending is a fulfillment in action that is perfectly suited to the part he now wishes to play. Unpremeditatedly he does indeed kill his uncle — unpremeditatedly in the sense that the occasion is sudden and Hamlet's quick response a kind of justifiable self-defense. Claudius has practiced on Hamlet's life with the poisoned sword and poisoned cup, so that Hamlet's visceral reaction seems fully justified in the theater. No moral complexity affixes itself to Hamlet's dispatching of the King. The act is, emotionally at least for us, not a cold-blooded regicide, not a repetition of what Claudius did to the older Hamlet, not an eye for an eye that will raise the specter of unending reciprocity.

Moreover, the ending brings about the death of Hamlet, a thing that he has longed for since the very beginning of the play. The final action allows Hamlet to die not as a guilty suicide but as hero and victim of a plot. Laertes freely forgives Hamlet for having slain him, and begs pardon for having entered into the kind of dishonorable conspiracy to commit a secret murder of the sort that Hamlet never even contemplates. Hamlet is that rare thing in dramatic literature, a multiple killer (Polonius, Claudius, Laertes, Rosencrantz, Guildenstern) whom we forgive and admire because he acted nobly. He is reconciled with his mother, who is also a victim. Shakespeare has devised for Hamlet and for *Hamlet* an ending that elegantly fulfills the protagonist's desire to be a great actor on the stage of Danish history. The ending is ironized, to be sure, by Horatio's profound questioning of Hamlet's providential interpretation; to Horatio the story is one "Of carnal, bloody, and unnatural acts, / Of accidental judgments, casual slaughters, / Of deaths put on by cunning and forced cause" (5.2.383–85). Fortinbras's presence, and his upcoming role as king of Denmark and Norway, further complicate our response to a play that is at once a tragedy of human greatness and a tragedy of waste. Nonetheless, Hamlet has found in his last moments an acting style that is true to his own critical perception of what theater at its best is all about.

Hamlet's intense preoccupation with the theater would seem to call for a performance style that is also theatrically self-aware, and in a sense this has always been true, since the role has been coveted by the leading actors of all eras as a vehicle for their finest acting capabilities. To most of the great actor-managers of the eighteenth and nineteenth centuries, this also meant enhancing their performances with pictorial splendor. William Charles Macready won praise in 1838 for "a series of glorious pictures" in his production at the Theatre Royal, Covent Garden. The palace of Elsinore, in Charles Kean's production in the same year at Drury Lane, featured separate and elaborate sets for a guard platform in two sections, for the royal court and the theater in which "The Murder of Gonzago" was played before Claudius and Gertrude, for the Queen's private chamber, and for Ophelia's burial ground. Scene changes from one location to another were elaborate and time-consuming. The decision to build the guard platform in two separate parts is symptomatic of the visual literalism of such a production: Kean was providing theatrical particularity to Shakespeare's text in which, at 1.4.61, Hamlet vows to follow his father's Ghost when it beckons him to "a more removèd ground," and then exits at the end of 1.4 with just that purpose in mind, reentering with the Ghost in what editors since Edward Capell have labeled as 1.5. Yet these scene divisions do not appear in the early printed texts. Edward Capell's decision (in his 1768 edition) to provide a scene division here was presumably prompted by the fact that Hamlet and the Ghost do exit and then reenter according to the original stage directions, and by Capell's experience of contemporary staging of Shakespeare's plays in discrete scenes with a curtain to mark the intervals.

Charles Fechter, at the Princess's Theatre in 1861, set the play in a Viking landscape, with the actors dressed as Scandinavian warriors in cross-gartered leggings. In Henry Irving's production at the Lyceum in 1885, set in the fifth or sixth century, Hamlet encountered his father's Ghost amid an impressive structure of battlements and massive rocks over which hung the moon, slowly fading as dawn appeared over an expanse of water and as the lights of the palace glimmered in the background. Ophelia was buried in a graveyard picturesquely set on a hillside.

More recent productions have paid close attention to the play's remarkable potential for swift-moving and self-aware theatricality. *Hamlet* in modern dress began with H. K. Ayliff at the Birmingham Repertory Theatre in 1925, followed by Tyrone Guthrie at the Old Vic in 1938, who saw the play as thematically relevant to a mood of anxiety and gloom at the imminent approach of World War II. A Freudian interpretation of Hamlet's indecisiveness, taken in good part from Ernest Jones's *Hamlet and Oedipus* and indeed from Freud himself, informed Laurence Olivier's influential film of 1948, with its fascinated interest in Gertrude's chambers where the Queen is interrogated by her son (fig. 6.3), and then in Hamlet's obsession with death and the burial of Ophelia in the final act (fig. 6.4). Joseph Papp's *Hamlet* for the Public Theater in New York, 1968, took psychological interpretation a good deal further by showing audiences a manacled Hamlet (Martin Sheen) in a coffinlike cradle at the foot of his uncle and mother's bed. Grigori Kozintsev's Russian film *Hamlet* of 1964 took on the political resonance of artistic resistance to totalitarianism; Kozintsev himself had been imprisoned by Stalin's Soviet regime. Hence, the walls, drawbridge, and huge spiked portcullis of Elsinore Castle were images of a state prison. For Peter Hall, directing *Hamlet* at Stratford-upon-Avon in 1965, "politics are a game and a lie."

At Wisdom Bridge Theatre in Chicago in 1985, directed by Robert Falls, Claudius was a Great Communicator in the style of movie-actor turned governor of California and then president of the United States, Ronald Reagan: Claudius himself never appeared onstage in 1.2 for his first big scene of explaining the necessity of his marriage to Gertrude, but was instead seen on television monitors to left and right, while the stage itself was given over to his advance men and PR experts setting up for a press party where the "spin" of the new administration was being manufactured. Fading and torn posters of the previous king hung from the walls as a bleak reminder of an administration now nearly lost to memory. Polonius (Del Close) was a businessman in a three-piece suit taking down conversations on his tape recorder; Hamlet (Aidan Quinn) was a young rebel with a cause, spray-painting "To be or not to be" on a bulkhead and then stepping back admiringly to observe, "Now, *that* is the question."

Michael Almereyda's low-budget film *Hamlet* of 2000 (fig. 6.5) is no less witty and reflexively aware of its medium: Hamlet (Ethan Hawke)

6.3. Laurence Olivier as Hamlet, with Eileen Herlie as Gertrude, in her chambers (*Hamlet*, 3.4), just before Hamlet stabs the unseen man whose voice he hears behind the arras. From Olivier's 1944 film.

6.4. Laurence Olivier as Hamlet interrupts the burial of Ophelia in act 5 of Olivier's 1944 film.

6.5. Ethan Hawke as Hamlet in a ski cap with Diane Venora as his mother and Kyle McLaughlin as Claudius on a Manhattan street, in Michael Almereyda's *Hamlet* (2000).

is an alienated and geeky young man obsessed with digital cameras and filmmaking, savvy enough to detect the recording mechanism that Polonius (Bill Murray) has planted on Ophelia in anticipation of Hamlet's interview with her. On an overnight flight to England under the armed escort of Rosencrantz and Guildenstern, Hamlet has the presence of mind to check their luggage as they are asleep. Discovering in their laptop the incriminating request from Claudius that the king of England order Hamlet's execution, Hamlet simply backspaces and inserts in the place of his name that of Rosencrantz and Guildenstern. Anachronisms of this sort are not simply gimmicks to underscore the "relevance" of Shakespeare to today's audiences; at their best, they are comments on the nature of acting and theatrical illusion that seem in keeping with the text's abiding interest in theatrical reflexivity.

Film can of course encourage visually realistic splendors. Franco Zeffirelli's *Hamlet* (1990) is so mesmerized by spectacular scenic effects — as for example in the very beautiful hillside graveyard where Ophelia is put to rest — and so caught up in its exploitation of matinee-idol stardom (Mel Gibson as Hamlet, Glenn Close as Gertrude, Alan Bates as Claudius, Helena Bonham Carter as Ophelia, Ian Holm as Polonius, Paul Scofield as the Ghost) that the film seems to settle for such crowd-pleasing enjoyments as sufficient in themselves. Kenneth Branagh's uncut four-hour film of 1996–1997 contains some brilliant acting, notably that of Derek Jacobi as Claudius, Julie Christie as Gertrude, Kate Winslet as a distraught Ophelia, and Richard Briers as a politically sagacious Polonius; at the same time, it too flirts with Hollywood name recognition in its drafting of Jack Lemmon (Marcellus), Gérard Depardieu (Reynaldo), Charlton Heston (the Player King), Robin Williams (Osric), and Billy Crystal (the Grave-digger) in cameo appearances. Exterior shots of Blenheim Palace gates, vast mirror-hung interiors, earthquake tremblings at the sound of the Ghost's voice, and an action-film ending in which Fortinbras's soldiers quite unnecessarily jump over railings and smash a lot of windows, all point toward the kind of spectacle that filming can invite. A more thoughtful and theatrically conscious Hamlet is to be seen in Kevin Kline's superb televised performance in 1990 for PBS, with Dana Ivey as Gertrude, Diane Venora as Ophelia, Brian Murray as Claudius, and Michael Cumpsty as Laertes — a screening that had the bad luck to appear more or less simultaneously with Zeffirelli's blockbuster and so has been undeservedly forgotten.

III

"Divinity of hell!" exclaims Iago as he lays before the audience, in soliloquy, his plan of cunning deception aimed at Othello and Desdemona. "When devils will the blackest sins put on, / They do suggest at first with heavenly shows, / As I do now." His plan is to counsel Cassio to seek the aid of Desdemona in recovering favor lost with Othello when Cassio allowed himself to get drunk on watch. The plan is entirely plausible, as Iago wryly explains to us. Desdemona is easily persuaded by appeals for help; she is fond of Cassio; and her new husband, Othello, is so infatuated with her that he can deny her nothing. "How am I then a villain," Iago asks us, "To counsel Cassio to this parallel course / Directly to his good?" (*Othello*, 2.3.342–46). Iago is amused by the ingeniousness of the puzzle he sets before us. We perceive a number of salient points about him. He is a consummate actor, who takes pride in his acting skill; he delights in using that skill to hurt others; and he associates his power of deceptive acting with that of devils, who conceal their "blackest sins" with "heavenly shows" in order to mislead their victims. Acting is thus fraught with the potential for dangerous evil.

Certainly Iago is the great actor in *Othello* (c. 1603–1604), like the titular figure of *Richard III*. Othello's role is as imposing, but does not demand the versatility of deceptive playacting we find in Iago. Performance history records numerous instances of leading players for whom the roles of Othello and Iago have proved to be equally attractive; Laurence Olivier played Iago at the Old Vic in 1938 and then Othello at the National Theatre in 1964 and on film in 1965. Some major actors have teamed up in pairs, alternating the roles of Iago and Othello on successive nights, including Edwin Booth and Henry Irving at London's Lyceum Theatre in 1881, and Richard Burton and John Neville at the Old Vic in 1956.

Like a consummate actor, Iago is superb at deception while also eager to reveal his true nature to us so that we can appreciate his skill. The layers of deception are complex. He is perfectly candid in the opening scene with Roderigo about his hatred for Othello and his reasons for arousing Brabantio from sleep so that the old senator will arrest and bring charges against Othello for eloping with his daughter, but Iago never lets Roderigo know how he, Roderigo, is being no less deceived and used. Indeed, Iago is at his best as a comic deceiver with Roderigo, since we lose no sympathy for this "snipe" and are ready to be amused by Iago's maneuverings. He manages to persuade Roderigo that Desdemona is in love with Cassio merely on the plausible grounds that she is bound to seek a partner of her own race, age, and complexion, and that therefore, somehow, she will be receptive to Roderigo's gifts as inducements to love. Those gifts that Roderigo has to fork over are not small; the jewels that Iago has had from this pathetic young man are enough, in Roderigo's words, that they "would half have corrupted a votarist" (4.2.195–96). Iago has promised to deliver them to Desdemona, but of course he has pocketed them himself. Roderigo is a dismal version of Sir Andrew in *Twelfth Night,* whom Sir Toby persuades to send for more money in an illusory pursuit of the Countess Olivia.

More is to come, each incident of outwitting made more astonishing than the last by Roderigo's increasing resistance to the deception. Iago talks Roderigo into picking a fight with Cassio, a fight that does indeed lead to Cassio's dismissal but with what benefit for Roderigo is hard to make out; as he complains to Iago afterward, "My money is almost spent; I have tonight been exceedingly well cudgeled; and I think the issue will be I shall have so much experience for my pains, and so, with no money at all and a little more wit, return again to Venice" (2.3.358–62). One might think that even an insignificant creature like Roderigo would have learned his lesson, but no, Iago succeeds in drafting his young charge into the much more dangerous assignment of assaulting Cassio in the dark with intent to kill (4.2.212–22). We know that Iago's private worry is that Roderigo will finally call him to "a restitution large / Of gold and jewels that I bobbed from him / As gifts to Desdemona." Iago will be the gainer whether Roderigo kills Cassio or Cassio Roderigo (5.1.11–19). And so Roderigo goes to his ignominious end, having been wounded in the encounter with Cassio and then stabbed to death by Iago in one of his many roles, that of the avenger of criminal outrage. "Kill men i'th' dark?" Iago piously exclaims as he coolly dispatches the one who has assisted in his villainies and who now knows too much. Iago is indeed an "inhuman dog," as the dying Roderigo proclaims him; he is also remarkably clever at deception.

It is as the tempter and deceiver of Othello, of course, that Iago is at his most inventive and diabolical (fig. 6.6). He is an intensely theatrical figure. His soliloquies are strategically placed in such a way that we are led by him through the play; he is the prologue, the master of ceremonies, the engineer of the plot, and its most engaging commentator all in one. In his first soliloquy, after having persuaded Roderigo that Desdemona is bound to seek out a lover more of her own age and complexion than Othello, Iago confesses privately his hatred for the Moor as he devises his scheme:

> Cassio's a proper man. Let me see now:
> To get his place and to plume up my will
> In double knavery. — How, how? — Let's see:
> After some time, to abuse Othello's ear
> That he is too familiar with his wife.
>
> (1.3.393–97)

To whom is Iago talking? Partly to himself, perhaps also to us, as he disarmingly takes us into his confidence and boastfully puts on display his formidable powers of contriving a plot. His plot, as it turns out, is the plot of the play *Othello*.

Richard III similarly plays the role of theatrical master of his own revels, as, in soliloquy, he coolly informs us as audience that he will proceed first against the life of his brother Clarence, then lay amorous siege to the Lady Anne, and then take advantage of the imminent likelihood that God "will take King Edward to his mercy / And leave the world for me to bustle in" (*Richard III*, 1.1.32–41, 144–62). The link between Richard and Iago is instructive, for both are seen as diabolical. As theatrical figures, they operate like the Vice, the inventive, chortling tempter of the morality play tradition who boasts to the audience of his plans and appears to be motivated by a delight in evil for its own sake. Shakespeare's vice figures (Edmund in *King Lear* is another) are more

6.6. Kenneth Branagh as Iago goads Othello (Laurence Fishburne) into jealous thoughts about his wife in Oliver Parker's 1995 film of *Othello.*

humanized: they are motivated by perversely human desires even though their love of evil is also somehow innate. On the one hand, Iago is consumed by jealousy and hatred of others, and needs emotionally to ruin their happiness because he himself is so eaten by envy. Misery loves company. At the same time, Iago is propelled forward in his plotting by sheer love of mischief-making. He would not waste his valuable time on Roderigo, he tells us, "But for my sport and profit" (*Othello,* 1.3.385–87). Both sport and profit are essential to him; he enjoys the game for its own sake while also furthering his dangerous ambitions.

Iago's second soliloquy serves as choric close to the scene in which he has talked Roderigo into picking a fight with Cassio on watch after Cassio has had too much to drink. The soliloquy achieves a number of theatrical tasks. It reveals once again Iago's jealous fear that he has been cuckolded by Othello—a scenario so wholly implausible as to convince us that his jealousy is pathological. He more or less admits the groundlessness of his fear earlier, when he concedes, "I know not if't be true; / But I, for mere suspicion in that kind, / Will do as if for surety" (1.3.389–91). Now, at the end of act 2, scene 1, he lets us know that he worries about still another sexual rival: "I fear Cassio with my nightcap too" (2.1.308). He gives us no reason for this anxiety. Iago is a "jealous soul," in the words of his long-suffering wife, Emilia. Such men, as Emilia knows only too well, "are not ever jealous for the cause, / But jealous for they're jealous. It is a monster / Begot upon itself, born on itself" (3.4.160–63). Yet for all his acutely irrational suffering, Iago functions as the theatrical manager of his own play. He lays out his plan now to disturb Othello's mind with jealous fear of his new wife. He sees his course, though the details are still to be worked out as opportunities present themselves. Iago is a brilliant innovator. "'Tis here, but yet confused," he says of his plan; "Knavery's plain face is never seen till used" (2.1.312–13). The uncertainty about details arouses our curiosity; Iago will not spoil his story by telling it ahead of time, though he creates expectation by announcing his overall intent. His choric observations punctuate the stage action with moments of ominous stillness and structure the play's ascent through exposition and plot complication with architectonic precision.

Iago's methods, as he opportunistically makes use of what comes to hand, exploit stage properties and theatrical devices of concealment and overhearing. The handkerchief presents itself to him when Emilia finds it and dangles it before her husband as an inducement for him to be nice to her. Iago has asked her many times before to obtain Desdemona's handkerchief, even when he didn't quite know how he could employ it; now it fits perfectly into his well-shaped plot. It becomes a device of illusion, that preeminently theatrical art by means of which stage objects are invested with meaning through the power of suggestion. Othello is Iago's audience, led by the nose as asses are to believe that the handkerchief betokens Desdemona's sexual guiltiness. Iago is a master of timing, knowing just when to produce the handkerchief as seemingly tangible evidence. His persuading Othello to be jealous makes use of other sorts of theatrical illusion as well. He urges Othello to watch and see whether Desdemona will plead for the reinstatement of Cassio as Othello's lieutenant. Iago has already set the business in motion by suggesting to Cassio that he ask Desdemona to help him by interceding with Othello. Iago knows that she will agree, and that her doing so will seem to confirm Othello's fears. Desdemona thus becomes an unwitting actor in Iago's scenario, playing the role he has designed for her. Cassio too plays such a role, having been put in a needy situation by Iago's contriving: it was Iago who got Cassio drunk on watch and set on Roderigo to start a fight, so that Iago is the author of Cassio's dismissal from Othello's service. One step leads logically to another: Iago is superb at devising a script in which the plot follows the rules and logical sequences of superior dramatic construction.

The climax of Iago's plotting takes the form of theatrical overhearing, and it occurs in act 4 where the climax of a good play ought to occur. Iago prepares his onstage audience, Othello, by leading him to expect what Iago wants him to see and "hear." When Cassio's mistress, Bianca, enters with the handkerchief that Cassio has left with her to have the work copied, Iago stage-manages a little play-within-the-play consisting of Cassio and Iago himself in conversation and with Othello as concealed audience. The talk is about Bianca, a subject that sends Cassio into gales of laughter, but to Othello's predetermined senses it must be about Cassio's sexual achieving of Desdemona. Othello is out of earshot but has no doubt as to what is being said. Iago has brilliant theatrical instincts; that is part of the reason he is so appealing in the theater. Yet what he accomplishes as theater artist is also dismaying. It calls into question the "truth" of theatrical image-making, and suggests forcefully that a diabolical plotter can devise more effective theater than those who are more ingenuous and naive.

The diabolical intent of Iago's scripting is especially insistent in the last act, as his revenge play draws toward its catastrophe. Iago is the deviser of the plot against Desdemona, having prompted Othello to "Strangle her in her bed, even the bed she hath contaminated" (4.1.208–9). Othello does just as Iago has directed. Fittingly, then, both men are repeatedly associated with images of damnation. "Oh, the more angel she, / And you the blacker devil!" exclaims Emilia when Othello tells her has just killed Desdemona. "Thou dost belie her, and thou art a devil," Emilia continues. Othello is at this moment persuaded that it is Desdemona herself who is "like a liar gone to burning hell," but he concedes that salvation and damnation hang on the question. "Oh, I were damned beneath all depth in hell / But that I did proceed upon just grounds / To this extremity," he insists to Emilia (5.2.133–44). When he learns too late that Emilia is right, Othello concludes that he must certainly be damned. "When we shall meet at compt," he says to the corpse of Desdemona, "This look of thine will hurl my soul from heaven, / And fiends will snatch at it." He positively implores the devils of hell to "Blow me about in winds! Roast me in sulfur! / Wash me in steep-down gulfs of liquid fire!" (282–89). Iago, meantime, is likened to the devil himself, the Father of Lies, though, as Othello grimly notes, the comparison does not deny that Iago is in fact a man. "I look down towards his feet; but that's a fable." That is, Iago has human feet, not cloven as the devil's are fabled to be. "If that thou be'st a devil, I cannot kill thee," Othello says as he lunges at Iago but manages only to wound him before Othello is disarmed. "I bleed, sir, but not killed," Iago replies, as though to confirm Othello's fear that Iago really is a devil and hence somehow immortal.

Iago is dramatist and stage manager for most of the play but not of the final action. He is exposed finally as liar, villain, and murderer by his wife, who has bravely ventured to challenge the custom requiring that wives be silently obedient to their husbands. "'Tis proper I obey him, but not now," she declares to the assembly gathered around Desdemona's deathbed (5.2.203). Othello learns too late of the innocence of the wife he has killed, but at least he does learn that he has acted wrongfully, and is so remorseful and unforgiving of himself that he takes his own life as a gesture of reprisal and compensation. Iago's lies, so theatrically effective that they seem to call in question the veracity of the truth itself, are shown for what they really are. The play's powerful moment of reversal and discovery is one finally in which the stage language of illusion no longer subverts but illuminates.

Because *Othello* is such a domestic tragedy, productions on stage and screen have not gone in heavily for scenic effects. Even though Venice would seem to beckon with its splendid architecture and Cyprus with its exotic eastern Mediterranean locale, directors have generally focused instead on the personal tragedy engulfing the main characters. Orson Welles's film of 1951–1952, remastered in 1992, is something of an exception with its windswept landscapes and eighteenth-century battlements of Mogador citadel in Morocco where Welles shot on location. Then, too, Verdi's opera *Otello* (televised live from the Metropolitan Opera in New York in 1948 and 1978, and filmed at Milan's La Scala opera house and on location in 1986–1987 as directed by Franco Zeffirelli with Placido Domingo as Otello and Justino Diaz as Iago) begins with a splendid storm scene reminiscent of those at the start of *Twelfth Night* and *The Tempest* that theater directors have found so visually inviting. Yet even in these versions the drama of marital and racial conflict is the center of attention. Many interpretations in film and television are focused in this way, often indeed because they originated as stage productions. Stuart Burge's 1965 filming, with Laurence Olivier in Caribbean blackface, was essentially a capturing by the camera of a highly successful stage production at the Old Vic in 1964, more closely seen on film than in the theater but still patently a drama conceived for a limited space. The BBC's *Othello,* first shown on television in 1981, with Anthony Hopkins as Othello, Bob Hoskins as Iago, and Penelope Wilton as Desdemona, does invoke the scenic splendor of Venice at times, but mainly focuses on a marital tragedy.

Janet Suzman's generally excellent video version is essentially a televising of a culturally significant stage production in Johannesburg, in 1988, with a black South African actor (John Kani) as Othello and a white South African actress (Joanna Weinberg) as Desdemona. Suzman, herself a South African, thus confronted head-on the issue of race in the last days of apartheid, shortly before that system of racial discrimination ended. Since much of the film was shot in the theater itself, scenic effects (apart from an opening sequence of elopement in a Venetian gondola) play a small part in its tense drama of racial conflict. Ted Lange's Rockbottom Productions *Othello* in 1989 similarly employed mixed-race casting in a film taken directly from a Los Angeles stage version, with black actors Ted Lange as Othello and Hawthorne James as Iago, and with white actress Mary Otis as Desdemona, offering the play as a comment on race relations in late twentieth-century Los Angeles. Trevor Nunn's superb televised *Othello* (1990) is yet another production taken from a stage original, in this case the RSC's version at the Other Place in Stratford-upon-Avon, with Willard White as Othello, Ian McKellen as Iago, and Imogen Stubbs as Desdemona. Its small-theater intensity, translated here to the small screen of television, is claustrophobic and private. The best moments of Oliver Parker's 1995 film of *Othello,* with Kenneth Branagh as Iago and Laurence Fishburne as a physically impressive Othello, are those in which Iago's poison does its fatal work on Othello in the intimacy of their man-to-man conversations (see fig. 6.6 above).

Productions onstage and on screen positively invite an intense interest in artistry of performance. Few plays can equal *Othello* as showcases for bravura, reputation-enhancing acting. Edmund Kean, Edwin Forrest, Edwin Booth, Ira Aldridge, Tommaso Salvini, Paul Robeson, Orson Welles, Earle Hyman, James Earl Jones, and Christopher Plummer, to name only some, were famous as the Othellos of their day, ranging in style from venerable majesty to explosive violence. The pairing and exchanging of the roles of Othello and Iago by two well-known actors, as with William Charles Macready and Charles Mayne Young in 1816, Macready and Samuel Phelps in 1839, Henry Irving and Edwin Booth in 1881, and Richard Burton and John Neville in 1956, bespeaks a competitive rivalry in showmanship. Laurence Olivier, who played *Othello* in the National Theatre production of 1964 mentioned above, and then in the 1965 film, had played Iago at the Old Vic in 1938, opposite Ralph Richardson as Othello. Raul Julia, at the New York Shakespeare Festival in 1979, and Ben Kingsley, at Stratford-upon-Avon in 1985, have vividly demonstrated the tortured unhappiness and capacity for violence lurking beneath the dignity and calm of Othello as he first appears in the play. Personal tribulations in the lives of actors have added to the notoriety, as in Edmund Kean's notorious dissipations, Edwin Forrest's divorcing of his wife for adultery and then being found guilty of a similar offense himself in the 1830s and '40s, Ira Aldridge's claim of descent "from men of royal siege" (1.2.22) in Senegal and his highly publicized marriage to a white woman in the mid-nineteenth century, and Paul Robeson's relationship with his Desdemona, Uta Hagen, in a rivalry with her husband, José Ferrer (playing Iago), in the 1940s.

Correspondingly, the role of Iago has never ceased to be an actor's plum. Frank Finlay, opposite Olivier's Othello in the National Theatre's 1964 production and subsequent film, is Cockney-accented and ill-bred but menacingly resourceful, more than a match for his several victims. Bob Hoskins, in the BBC *Othello* of 1981, is a loutish, giggling psychopath of lower-class origins, incessantly putting himself on show to the audience and daring us to applaud his craft. In Janet Suzman's 1988 South African version, Richard Haddon Haines is appropriately a police state fascist, utterly persuasive in his paranoid fear that blacks will take away white folks' women. The casting of a black actor, Hawthorne James, as Iago, opposite a black Othello (Ted Lange) and a white Desdemona (Mary Otis) in Rockbottom Productions' version of 1989, fascinatingly complicated the equations of racial conflict in a way that put unusual demands on the actor playing Iago. Ian McKellen, in Trevor Nunn's 1990 televised version, is superb as the outwardly sociable and "honest" soldier who writhes within from jealous rage. Kenneth Branagh, as Iago in Oliver Parker's film of 1995, is an adept manipulator, well equipped to shatter the seeming calm and dignity of Laurence Fishburne's Othello. Like *Romeo and Juliet* and *Hamlet,* the play of *Othello* never makes better sense than when it is seen as about the art of performance.

ℒ7ℒ

A Poor Player That Struts
and Frets His Hour upon the Stage

ROLE-PLAYING IN *KING LEAR, MACBETH,*
AND *ANTONY AND CLEOPATRA*

Shakespeare's tragedies of the mid- and late 1600s take up themes that seem appropriate to middle age and advancing years: the decline of virility, concern about aging, fear of being forgotten or mistreated by ungrateful children, the longing for adventure as one senses the diminution of one's capabilities, the irrational craving for success and power as affirmations of one's importance in the face of impending dissolution. Shakespeare was in his forties in 1604 and afterward, still relatively young in our terms today but verging on the late years for a man who died on, or very close to, his fifty-third birthday.

What staging concepts and methods seemed appropriate to him as he moved toward the culmination and completion of his career as a writer of great tragedy? Shakespeare was at the height of success, in an acting company that enjoyed royal patronage as England's premier troupe. His command of his theatrical medium was unparalleled. At the same time, one senses in the late tragedies an increasing skepticism about matters of religious faith and an increasing anxiety about humanity's penchant for evil and self-destructiveness. Shakespeare seems especially uneasy about the capacity for malicious harm in those who, playwright-like, practice deception, even if dramatic illusion can also be a force for good. One manifestation of this dialectical instability of artistic expression takes the form of self-reflexiveness. The language of theater in these plays becomes a supple vehicle through which Shakespeare explores the powerful and at times frightening implications of what it means to be a dramatist. We have encountered these artistic preoccupations already, especially in *Hamlet* and *Othello*.

I

"Pat he comes, like the catastrophe of the old comedy," says Edmund in *King Lear* (c. 1605–1606) as he sees his brother Edgar approaching. "My cue is villainous melancholy, with a sigh like Tom o' Bedlam" (1.2.137–39). Edmund's overtly theatrical language is appropriate to one whose villainous function strikingly resembles that of Iago in *Othello*. Like Iago, Edmund is envious of others' advancement over him. Like Iago and also like Richard III, he takes us into his confidence in chortling soliloquies, keeping us informed of his plans as he moves upward by means of one successful scheme after another. He is superbly adept at fooling others by his ability to don roles as a skilled actor does. Consequently, Edmund is to an extent the master plotter of *King Lear,* fulfilling the role of dramatist as he assigns the characters to various parts in a narrative aimed solely at his triumph. His success is so nearly complete that by the end of the play he has expanded his ambitions beyond the subplot to which he is at first assigned — the story of the Earl of Gloucester and his two sons — to the point that he is now the Duke of Cornwall and the lover of King Lear's two elder daughters. He is in a position to challenge the Duke of Albany for the throne. King Lear and Cordelia are in his custody, enabling him to give a secret order for the death of the play's heroine, much as Iago plots the death of Desdemona. A major difference, however, is that Edmund's brother Edgar is also versatile in adopting various roles and disguises. Edgar's skill as actor serves as a crucial counterbalance to that of Edmund. The theatrical language of role-playing can be a force for evil or for good, or sometimes an uncertain mix of both.

Edmund's opening soliloquy establishes him as a fascinating villain, one whose justifications for what he plans to do are intellectually challenging. Why should an illegitimate son or younger son (Edmund is both) be deprived of hopes of inheritance by "the plague of custom" (1.2.3)? Does not the goddess Nature herself encourage a profoundly skeptical rejection of worn-out ideologies through which human society has imposed arbitrary limits on personal ambition? Is not the intelligent person who can discard these outmoded social mores in a position to gain tactical advantage over others who submit to the conventions of morality and law? Edmund's father, the Earl of Gloucester, is a credulous believer in portents and "spherical predominance" as if human behavior were the consequence of "planetary influence" and "a divine thrusting on" (106–36). Edmund finds it all too easy to persuade this old man that his elder son, Edgar, is plotting against his life. Edmund then counsels his brother to be on guard against their father's wrath, to arm himself, and to flee. Edmund draws his sword on his brother, pretending that he does so "In cunning" because this is what their father will expect him to do; once Edgar has fled, Edmund wounds himself to lend credibility to his story of having attempted to apprehend Edgar, and persuades the enraged Earl that Edgar was "Mumbling of wicked charms" as he escaped (2.1.29–38). In rapid succession, we have watched as Edmund has played the boastfully soliloquizing villain, the loyal son concerned for his father's safety, and the loyal brother concerned only for Edgar's welfare. Both his father and brother are taken in by Edmund's act, for it is smoothly and plausibly performed. "Loyal and natural boy," Gloucester says in gratitude for Edmund's presumably having saved the old man from Edgar, "I'll work the means / To make thee capable"—that is, legally able to inherit as the "true" son (2.1.84–85). The word "natural" captures the irony of the situation: Edmund was born out of wedlock, but he is also, as Gloucester now sees him, one who is capable of the "natural" feelings of loyalty and affection that Edgar seems to have abandoned. We as audience, knowing all, are obliged to admire Edmund's intrepidity and expertise in engineering this reversal even while we are given ample reason to be distressed by the result.

The disinheriting of Edgar means that Edmund has stepped into the role of heir to the earldom of Gloucester, a title that is bestowed upon him once his father has been apprehended as a traitor for assisting the mad Lear and thereby aiding and abetting a French invasion of England. Cordelia has asked her new husband, the King of France, for an army in order that she might rescue her father from the barbaric way in which he has been rejected by Goneril and Regan, and, since this requires a French army on English soil, any who come to the assistance of her and her father are by that definition engaged in treasonous activity. Edmund uses this legal definition of treason as his justification for informing on his father to the Duke of Cornwall, who has taken the administration of justice and national defense into his own hands. Edmund plays the role to Cornwall of a loving son who is torn between his family loyalties and his duty to the state in a time of military crisis. "How, my lord, I may be censured, that nature thus gives way to loyalty, something fears me to think of," he laments to the Duke (3.5.3–5). We know that this pretense of deep reluctance is only a cover to earn the admiration and support of Cornwall. "I will persevere in my course of loyalty," Edmund concludes, "though the conflict be sore between that and my blood." The word "blood" again plays on the irony of Edmund's deception: it can variously mean family loyalty, blood descent, filial instincts, and self-assertive lust. Cornwall is quite taken in. "I will lay trust upon thee, and thou shalt find a dearer father in my love," he assures Edmund (22–27). Edmund has thus found another father.

Once Cornwall is dead, in a scuffle with a servant over the blinding of Gloucester (3.7.75–101), Edmund's means of supplanting this father is to lay amorous siege to Cornwall's widowed duchess, Regan. Edmund does well in his role as lover. To both Regan and Goneril, he is intensely masculine. "Oh, the difference of man and man!" exclaims Goneril as Edmund departs from her on an important embassy concerning the war. "To thee a woman's services are due; / My fool usurps my body" (4.2.26–28). Goneril has only contempt for her husband, the Duke of Albany; Edmund is to her an exciting lover, one for whose favor she competes in deadly contest with her sister. Regan, by now a widow, has a tactical advantage over Goneril in that no husband stands in her way. Her intent is to promote Edmund to the dukedom of Cornwall as her consort. "Witness the world that I create thee here / My lord and master," she defiantly proclaims in the presence of Goneril and the Duke of Albany, who have good reason to fear the ambition of Regan and of Edmund (5.3.79–80). Edmund has come remarkably close to the throne of England itself. His one powerful rival for power, the Duke of Albany, mistrusts him as a "Half-blooded fellow" (82) and adulterer who is wholly unfit by lineage and temperament to share authority in the conduct of the war, much less to rule as monarch, but Edmund has the potent backing of Regan and the dukedom that she now bestows upon him.

Edmund's daring bid for absolute power helps explain why he accepts the challenge of a stranger knight to armed single combat. The proposed duel is on its face one that he need not even bother to consider: the challenger is anonymous, a figure out of medieval romance. Goneril, for one, is astonished and dismayed at Edmund's going through with the fight. "This is practice, Gloucester," she admonishes him when he has fallen before the challenger. "By th' law of arms thou wast not bound to answer / An unknown opposite. Thou art not vanquished, / But cozened and beguiled" (154–57). Her interpretation of the law of arms is correct; Edmund has taken what appears to be a needless chance and has lost. Yet he does seem to have had a good reason. The Duke of Albany is alerted by now to the fact that Edmund and Goneril are sexual partners and have plotted against the life of Albany himself. The incriminating letter containing this information has been given to him by the anonymous challenger. It is the letter that Edgar retrieved from the pockets of Goneril's steward and messenger, Oswald, whom Edgar killed in defense of his father, old Gloucester (4.6.259–74). Edgar is the anonymous challenger. Edmund does not know this, but he does understand the terms of the challenge, which are those of medieval trial by combat: whoever wins will appear to have been favored by the gods, since trial by combat is postulated on the idea that the armed contestant who swears truly will be fated by the gods to prevail over a false opponent. Edmund, not believing in the gods or in the binding nature of oaths, figures that if he defeats the anonymous challenger he will have proved his innocence to those who do believe in divine justice, no matter what charges Albany might bring against him. The idea is ingenious, and might indeed have worked if Edmund had won. But he does not. His last assumed role, that of the champion of truth, evades him.

Edgar's repertory of roles is no less protean. Finding himself a hunted fugitive with a price on his head, Edgar chooses the disguise of Tom o' Bedlam, a lunatic patient of London's Bethlehem Hospital turned out to beg for his daily bread. "My face I'll grime with filth, / Blanket my loins, elf all my hair in knots, / And with presented nakedness outface / The winds and persecutions of the sky," he resolves (2.3.9–12). In this pitiable outfit he is an apt partner for the mad King Lear and the Fool during the storm scenes of act 3. His talk as poor Tom is chiefly of the devils that torment him, with names like Flibbertigibbet, Smulkin, Modo, Mahu, Frateretto, and Hoppendance or Hoberdidance — names that Shakespeare found in Samuel Harsnett's *Declaration of Egregious Popish Impostures* (1603). He complains of the Prince of Darkness and of the foul fiend that haunts him in the voice of a nightingale or the shape of a gray cat (3.4, 6).

When he sadly encounters his eyeless father who has been blinded by Cornwall as a presumed traitor, Edgar adapts his disguise as poor Tom to the charitable purpose of leading his father to the cliffs of Dover, where Gloucester hopes to end his wretched life by suicide. Once at Dover, Edgar's peasantlike role modulates into that of a person who speaks more cultivated English than poor Tom: as the blind Gloucester says to him, "Methinks thy voice is altered, and thou speak'st / In better phrase and matter than thou didst" (4.6.7–8). When the two of them are then encountered by Oswald, who sees an opportunity to earn a reward by executing an "old unhappy traitor," Edgar adopts the protective coloration of a heavy Somerset dialect. " 'Chill not let go, zir, without vurther 'cagion," he replies to Oswald's demand that he let go of Gloucester's arm (238). This disguise makes use of a standard rustic speech on the London stage.

Subsequently, in the fifth act, Edgar is the anonymous challenger of Edmund who defeats his brother in mortal combat and then finally reveals who he is. "My name is Edgar, and thy father's son," he tells the dying Edmund (5.3.172–77). As Edmund says, "The wheel is come full circle." Edmund has met his just end in the person of his doppelganger, his virtuous other self; the very similarity of their names suggests the extent to which they are paired as opposites. Edgar is Edmund's nemesis. His perseverance in goodness is the final refutation of Edmund's skeptical assault on moral value and charitable forbearance.

The scene of Gloucester's attempted suicide at Dover shows Edgar as actor and also as dramatist in a particularly theatrical light. In his disguise as the lowly peasant charged with escorting Gloucester to his intended rendezvous with death on Dover cliffs, Edgar has to consider what to do about his father's suicidal despair. He decides against revealing who he is to his father, despite his understanding that Gloucester is now despairing most of all for the way he has attempted to destroy his eldest son. Perhaps the young man fears that the shock would be too great. Instead, Edgar chooses a well-intending deception in the form of a little drama to be acted out by his father and himself. He leads the old man to a spot that he declares to be the edge of an immense seaside cliff. Here he describes to the blind Gloucester in detail all that one might see if one were in such a place: gatherers of samphire (an edible herb) halfway down the cliff face, fishermen on the beach the apparent size of mice because of the great distance, a ship looking no larger than its ship's boat, and the like (4.6.11–24). Gloucester bids that he be left alone and falls forward, intent on ending his life. He lands, anticlimactically, on the floor of the theater stage. Perhaps both we as audience and Gloucester are meant to be disoriented by this development: up to this point the scene has been orchestrated as a "real" scene would be in a theater without scenery, relying on verbal description to convey a sense of great height and danger. Are we not to "understand" by such devices that Gloucester "really is" at a cliff's edge? Is Edgar as stage magician practicing tricks on us? We discover with surprise that we are in the theater and that Gloucester is unhurt.

Why is Edgar doing this? Evidently his purpose is to allow his father to work through his suicidal intent without suffering harm. "Why I do trifle thus with his despair / Is done to cure it," he confides to us (4.6.33–34). Edgar's plan involves an abandonment and even demonizing of his former role as peasant. Adopting now a new persona as a well-spoken Englishman finding the old man at the presumed foot of the cliff, he persuades Gloucester that he has fallen from a great height without harm, that his survival is "a miracle," and that at the top of the cliff can now be seen a strange horned monster with eyes like moons and a thousand noses. "It was some fiend," he pronounces. Edgar invents a mythology in which a devil has tempted Gloucester to suicide from which he has been providentially saved. "Therefore, thou happy father," he counsels the old man, "Think that the clearest gods, who make them honors / Of men's impossibilities, have preserved thee" (55, 69–74). "Father" means "old man," but we as audience also savor the wordplay: Edgar addresses Gloucester as his own father. Gloucester is persuaded that the gods indeed desire him to live until called by them to his final rest, and understands that they are rebuking him for attempting to end his suffering before his time. The outcome is heartening: Gloucester is cured of his despair, and father and son are reunited, even if the father does not yet realize that his companion is literally his son. At the same time, the scene Edgar has devised is one of deception. Presumably he chooses this course because he knows that his father needs to believe in gods. We are aware, in the theater, that the story and its staging are theatrical artifice. The gods themselves are nowhere to be seen in *King Lear;* instead, Edgar invents gods as a transparent theatrical fiction.

Edgar's constantly shifting roles enable him to become the play's most intelligently skeptical and choric commentator. He soliloquizes on what it is like to be in danger of his life for purported crimes that he did not commit, obliging him to bury his identity: "Edgar I nothing am" (2.3.21). Throughout the storm scenes, he intermittently steps outside his role as poor Tom with pitying asides for Lear's tribulations: "My tears begin to take his part so much / They mar my counterfeiting" (3.6.59–60). Comparing his own sufferings with those of the King enables him to bear his own injustices more easily: "He childed as I fathered!" (110). He learns from his own mistakes: when he starts to comfort himself by reflecting that things cannot get worse for him, he encounters his blinded old father in despair and immediately chides himself for having defined suffering only in his own terms. Things can get worse, and have done so. "I am worse than e'er I was," he realizes, meaning that he is worse in that his father is so unhappy. "And worse I may be yet," he continues. "The worst is not / So long as we can say, 'This is the worst'" (4.1.1–28). As long as we mortals are able to draw breath, the one thing we can count on is that things may get worse. This is a bleak philosophical view, but it has the immense strength of counseling us to expect nothing. To be thus armed against the vicissitudes of fortune is to be ready for anything. Edgar's stoic wisdom enables him to persevere, to pity, to help those who deserve help, and to rise above misfortune through the consolations of philosophy.

Thus prepared, Edgar enters into his final playacting role of anonymous knight-challenger. By revealing his identity as Edgar through unmasking, he brings his story to its painful but clear resolution. As the unmasker who has played the stage manager and theater magician, Edgar recalls for us similar devices used in the resolution of earlier plays like *As You Like It, Twelfth Night, All's Well That Ends Well,* and *Measure for Measure.* With astonishing versatility, Shakespeare uses a device of closure he had perfected in his comedies as his way of ending the Edgar-Edmund plot in his most devastating of tragedies.

Edgar occupies an odd role in the performance history of *King Lear,* one that Shakespeare surely did not anticipate: for about a century and a half, he was transformed into a kind of romantic hero who married Cordelia as part of a newly written happy ending. Such was the revised version put together by Nahum Tate in 1681. Tate was responding to audiences who found the death of Cordelia an intolerable refutation of the principle of poetic justice, according to which virtue should eventually be rewarded and vice punished. Shakespeare's play was far too pessimistic for the Restoration and eighteenth century in its frightening implication that the gods take no care of human suffering or perhaps even do not exist; Doctor Johnson later confessed that, as editor of his great edition of Shakespeare published in 1765, he was able to get through Shakespeare's original text of *King Lear* only because editorial duties required him to do so. Accordingly, in Tate's happily ending *History of King Lear,* first performed at the theater in Dorset Garden in 1681, the play restored Cordelia to her father and married her to Edgar. In defense of Tate it should be noted that he was following in part the lead of Shakespeare's sources, including the chronicle accounts of Lear's supposed reign, *The First Part of the Mirror for Magistrates* (1574 edition), and an anonymous play called *The True Chronicle History of King Leir* (c. 1588–1594), in which Lear and his daughter were happily reunited, although the marriage to Edgar was Tate's idea.

Since the love interest of Edgar and Cordelia ran throughout Tate's

Lear, this version had no need for the King of France. More significantly, the entire Edmund-Edgar plot had to be recast and shrunk in size, with a resulting elimination of the existential debate between these brothers as to how to cope in a godless universe; indeed, those very ideas were repugnant to the neoclassical age. Edgar still went in disguise for a time, but not as "a poor shift to save his life"; instead, his "generous design" was to aid Cordelia. Gone too was the French invasion, so that the happy ending could be seen in a political light as the triumphant return of established monarchy — an object lesson not lost on audiences in 1681 who had recently celebrated the Restoration of English monarchy (in 1660) and were now facing new constitutional crises that were to result in 1688 in the end of the Stuart dynasty.

King Lear thus became, through the minimizing of the Edgar-Edmund plot and the elimination of the Fool, a melodrama about the King and his daughter. It was very much a play about a king, not simply an aging father as in many modern productions; in the performances of Thomas Betterton, Barton Booth, James Quin, and especially David Garrick, Lear wore royal costume, even in the storm scenes. Garrick appears thus in a 1761 engraving of a theater-based painting by Benjamin Wilson (fig. 7.1). Even though the blinding of Gloucester was shown onstage in Garrick's production (as in Tate's), other painful happenings were ameliorated. Lear arrived in time to forestall the suicidal leap of Gloucester at Dover cliff. Much of this expurgation of violence and injustice continued on into the nineteenth century, even when the tragic ending was haltingly reintroduced, first by William Charles Macready at Covent Garden in 1834. Macready deleted the blinding of Gloucester and the suicidal attempt at Dover. Samuel Phelps at Sadler's Wells in 1845 and Henry Irving at the Lyceum in 1892 generally followed suit.

In more recent productions, the saga of Edgar and his family has been restored to its rightful place in the text, and accordingly has taken on an appalling bleakness that seems dismayingly appropriate to a world torn by military, political, and social conflict. Strongly influenced by Jan Kott's view, in *Shakespeare Our Contemporary* (published in English in 1964 but known earlier through its Polish original), of *King Lear* as existential nightmare, Peter Brook mounted a production at Stratford-upon-Avon in 1962, followed by a film in 1970, in which the painful scenes of physical torture are truly numbing. The Duke of Cornwall (Patrick Magee) scoops out the right eye of Gloucester (Alan Webb) with a spoon, at which point the screen goes dark and is then filled with the disfigured face of Gloucester. When a nameless servant wounds Corn-

7.1. David Garrick as King Lear in the storm scenes of act 3, in Garrick's 1756 stage production at Drury Lane. From a mezzotint by J. McArdell, based on a painting by Benjamin Wilson, 1761, based in turn on Garrick's stage production. By permission of The Harvard Theatre Collection, The Houghton Library.

wall in the ensuing scuffle, Regan (Susan Engel) bludgeons that man to death. King Lear (Paul Scofield) and Gloucester on Dover beach in act 4 are two ruined old men, clinging to each other amid a world in total collapse; they have no hope of learning from their suffering other than to know what suffering can be like. The gruesome deaths of Goneril (Irene Worth), Regan, and Cordelia (Anne-Lise Gabold), reported in Shakespeare's script as taking place offstage, are all vividly filmed by Brook. Edmund, for his part, becomes a brutish and unrepentant villain in his open adultery with the lustful Goneril (we see them abed together) and his making no attempt at the end to save the life of Cordelia. Surrounded by such carnage, Edgar too is driven to violence: he impales Oswald on his pike like a squealing animal, and, in his climactic encounter as the anonymous challenger with his brother Edmund (Ian Hogg), Edgar sinks his ax into Edmund's neck with a massive blow that ends the encounter before it has hardly begun. Brook's presentation of Edgar is symptomatic of much recent criticism, in which Edgar's behavior toward his ruined father has been seen as puzzlingly self-serving and perhaps vindictive. Even when, in some other productions, Edgar is seen in a less negative light, he is apt to appear slow-witted and complacently naive, unprepared for the disillusionments he successively encounters and lacking the piercing intellect and suave charisma of his brother.

Brook's weighty challenge to the more humanistic interpretation of tradition has had followers. Increasingly, in a world unfamiliar with the powerful royal absolutism of early modern Europe, Lear and Gloucester are seen in performance as old, frail men who capture our attention more as fathers than as monarchs. In Nicholas Hytner's 1990 modern-dress production for the RSC, John Wood was a rather ordinary-looking senior citizen in rumpled jeans and a worn jacket, while Gloucester and Edgar were dressed in faded cast-off garments. In the BBC's 1983 televised production with Laurence Oliver as the king (fig. 7.2), Goneril (Dorothy Tutin) and Regan (Diana Rigg) are calculated and heartless in their treatment of their father, while Edmund (Robert Lindsay) betrays to us his restless ambition as he plots ruthlessly against his naively trusting brother Edgar (David Threlfal). Akira Kurosawa's *Ran* (1985) is no less apocalyptic than Brook's *Lear,* especially its frightening portrayal of the Lady Kaede (Mieko Harada), the remorselessly ambitious and homicidal daughter-in-law of the old Lear-resembling warlord Hidetora Ichimonji (Tatsuya Nakadai). In the pattern of gender reversals deployed by Kurosawa (the king has three sons, not daughters), the Lady Kaede takes on some of the menacing aspect of Edmund in Shakespeare's play. Yet even this film softens the horror of its grim tale by the humanity of Hidetora's rejected son Saburo (Daisuke Ryu), of Hidetora's other daughter-in-law Sue (Yoshiko Miyazaki), and of her brother Tsurumaru (Takeshi Nomura). These three figures, the approximate equivalents of Shakespeare's Edgar and Gloucester, suffer patiently and gain in stoical wisdom even as they eventually pay the inexorable price of choosing to be charitable in a world of greedy competition for power. In the final moments, the blind Tsurumaru alone survives, having been left with no companionship or assistance in the ruined world suggested by the film's title, *Ran,* or "chaos." Similarly, the bleakness of Grigori Kozintsev's 1970 Russian film version is alleviated to some extent in its concluding sequence by a stirringly chivalric duel between Edmund (Regimantas Adomaitis) and Edgar (Leonhard Merzin).

In recent interpretations, then, the role-playing of Edgar and Ed-

7.2. Laurence Olivier as King Lear, in Granada Television's 1983 production, directed by Michael Elliott.

mund is generally to be understood against a background of existential meaninglessness in which human action, whether intended for good or ill, is deprived of efficacy and meaning. No one is finally in charge in most modern performances of *King Lear*, not the gods, nor the villains, nor the few survivors. The textual indeterminacy of this play, in which the early quarto and folio versions even fail to agree as to who delivers the final speech (Albany in the quarto, Edgar in the folio), finds its modern-day equivalent in a dramatization of anarchy.

II

"Life's but a walking shadow, a poor player / That struts and frets his hour upon the stage / And then is heard no more," Macbeth ponders, in growing awareness that his end is rapidly approaching. "It is a tale / Told by an idiot, full of sound and fury, / Signifying nothing" (*Macbeth*, 5.5.24–28). Such is Macbeth's recasting of Jaques's Seven Ages of Man in *As You Like It*. The metatheatricality of his observation recalls Ulysses' wry observations on the "strutting player" in *Troilus and Cressida* and Hamlet's scorn for the "robustious periwig-pated fellow" who "out-Herods Herod" in his striving "to tear a passion to tatters, to very rags." Macbeth's despairing interpretation of the shape of human life is not a Shakespearean "lesson" to be examined as if it delivers the choric "meaning" of the play; indeed, it is answered to a significant extent in *Macbeth* (c. 1606–1607) by the loyal and courageous decency of Macduff, Malcolm, old Siward and his son, and others who risk their personal safety and that of their families for the good of the commonweal, much as Edgar's role-playing is an essential countervailing force to Edmund's artful villainy in *King Lear.* Macbeth's famous quotation does nonetheless underscore the dramatist's awareness that his characters act out their destinies in a theater space, and that Macbeth is, like other villains in Shakespeare, a masterful deceiver and manipulator of theatrical illusion. An important difference is that here the deceiver is also the title figure and protagonist of the play in whose psychic and moral conflicts we become deeply involved.

Lady Macbeth is concerned lest her husband prove inadequate to the assignment of acting out the great role of regicide that she and the Weird Sisters have scripted for him (see fig. 7.3). "Your face, my thane, is as a book where men / May read strange matters," she cautions him as the moment of Duncan's arrival at Inverness approaches. "To beguile the time, / Look like the time; bear welcome in your eye, / Your hand, your tongue. Look like th'innocent flower, / But be the serpent under't" (1.5.62–66). She coaches him in the art of appearances as if he were a neophyte actor. She herself is superb at the very skill she exhorts her husband to study. Her welcome to King Duncan, on the occasion of his royal visit to Inverness, is replete with fulsome compliment. "All our service, / In every point twice done, and then done double, / Were poor and single business to contend / Against those honors deep and broad wherewith / Your Majesty loads our house," she declares, in language that sounds conventional enough in its hyperbolic courtly flattery and yet also hypocritical to our ears, forewarned as we are by her homicidal intent (1.6.14–18). Duncan is hoodwinked, despite his understanding that appearances can be deceiving. "There's no art / To find the mind's construction in the face," he has observed only a short time earlier about the treasonous Thane of Cawdor. "He was a gentleman on whom I built / An absolute trust" (1.4.11–14). Duncan's warm faith in his thanes, however endearing, is fatally dangerous to him. *Macbeth* poses the dilemma of how to survive with decency and charity in a world where evil can assume the guise of a grateful nobleman and his graciously hospitable wife.

Macbeth's tragic conflict is that of a man who does not relish the part he seems destined to play in the killing of a king. Duncan has showered

7.3. Macbeth and Banquo encounter the three Weird Sisters in *Macbeth* (1.3). A woodcut in Raphael Holinshed's *Chronicles of England, Scotland, and Ireland*, 2nd ed. (1587). By permission of the Folger Shakespeare Library.

kindnesses on Macbeth for his loyal service, promoting him from being Thane of Glamis to Thane of Cawdor in place of the executed traitor previously bearing that title. Macbeth would prefer to think of himself as a nobleman who, as host, "should against the murderer shut the door, / Not bear the knife myself." He pictures himself instead as one who has no spur to prick the sides of his intent "but only / Vaulting ambition, which o'erleaps itself / And falls on th'other" (1.7.15–28). This image portrays him ingloriously as an inept rider attempting to mount the steed of his ambition only to push himself too far and fall over on the horse's opposite side, making of himself a laughingstock. In another soliloquy, he imagines a dagger set before him, beckoning him to commit murder: is it "palpable," or "A dagger of the mind, a false creation, / Proceeding from the heat-oppressèd brain?" (2.1.39–41). He cannot be sure; the act he is about to commit seems to him a kind of bad dream, a phantasmagoria, a scene in which he will walk through his part as though controlled by forces that are not a part of him.

Macbeth's agony of indecision lends itself theatrically to a sequence in which the physical stage of the Jacobean theater (alternatively the Globe, the indoor Blackfriars theater, and the royal court) reflects his perturbed state of mind. As Duncan prepares to enter Macbeth's castle

(1.6), he invites his hearers (and us as audience) to admire the handsome architectural appearance of the theater's tiring-house facade: castle-like, it features many a "jutty, frieze, / Buttress," and "coign of vantage" where martlets build their nests (3–9). The tiring-house wall is thus, for the moment, the exterior of the castle, as in many a history play; Duncan calls attention to its handsome carvings and architectural detail. When Duncan and his entourage "*Exeunt*" at the scene's end, they do so by means of a stage door representing the main gates. Immediately thereafter (1.7), servants enter "*with dishes and service*" and pass "*over the stage,*" indicating that we are now within the castle in some room adjacent to the great dining hall; exterior is now converted to interior, without break or scenic alteration, with the help of the audience's imaginative acquiescence, as in *Romeo and Juliet.* Duncan, we understand, is being feasted within, beyond the stage door through which the servants exit. Perhaps we hear the sounds of merriment issuing forth from the banqueting hall as the door opens and closes. Macbeth then enters from that same stage door to consider his options in soliloquy. We gather that he is standing in some antechamber, for soon his wife joins him to chide at him for having left the banqueting festivities over which he was presiding.

When they "*Exeunt,*" having resolved on the murder, the scene immediately changes (without any shift of stage scenery) to the inner courtyard of the castle. We learn where we are from the entrance of Banquo "*with a torch before him*" and his son Fleance. It is late that night; the torch is a theatrical signal of an utter and ominous darkness (as in *Romeo and Juliet,* for example, or *Othello*). Here Banquo and Fleance are encountered by "*Macbeth and a Servant with a torch*" (2.1.1–9) and then make their way to bed, leaving the stage to Macbeth. "*A bell rings*" as a signal from his wife that he is to go ahead with the murder. He exits through a door on his mission. Lady Macbeth enters (2.2), hearing offstage muffled cries signifying that Macbeth is about his work. He soon joins her with bloody daggers in his hands. As they prepare to retire and give some plausibility to their planned alibi of having been asleep, they hear knocking at "the south entry" (70). This knocking continues as they exit and are followed onstage by the inebriated Porter (2.3), who, after a comic soliloquy filled with ironic foreshadowings of infernal damnation and the gates of hell, opens his gates to Macduff and Lennox so that they may awaken the King. The action is made continuous by the knocking, even though we are to imagine a shift in location to the south entry. The murder itself takes place behind the scenes. The dramatist insists on our picturing the murder in our imaginations as we hear cries and then the terse reactions of Macbeth and his wife. The focus is on the psychological states of the chief actors as they ponder what it is that they have done. Throughout this taut sequence, the theater space becomes the sphere of Macbeth's intense soul-struggle.

Macbeth's theatrical role shifts, after the murder, from that of poetically insightful commentator on his own moral dilemma to that of the cunning deceiver that his wife has wished him to become. The irony is that his secret deceptions now exclude her from his conversation. "Be innocent of the knowledge, dearest chuck, / Till thou applaud the deed," he says to her, not letting her know that he is arranging the murder of Banquo (3.2.48–49). He enlists "seeling night" to assist him in his purposes by scarfing up "the tender eye of pitiful day" (49–50). He presides at the banquet that is nominally in honor of Banquo with hypocrisies that immediately return to haunt him in the most devastatingly literal way. No sooner has he declared his wish for "the graced presence of our Banquo" (3.4.41) than Banquo obligingly appears, sitting in Macbeth's own place at the banqueting table. The table itself is plainly required onstage, arranged with chairs in such a way that the sudden appearances and disappearances of Banquo can be effected by a convincing theatrical sleight of hand. Macbeth learns to his cost that one must be careful not to ask for things that one does not really want.

Macbeth learns too that his specious self-dramatizations of innocence and bountifulness increasingly ring hollow among his hard-pressed subjects and soon engender a rebellion against him. That rebellion has to be secretive itself and wary of appearances; Macduff has to test Malcolm at length to determine if he is a true royal prince or another pretender. Scotland has become a land of secret whispers and savage, unexpected reprisals. Yet eventually prevarication brings about its own undoing in the riddling prophecies of the Weird Sisters and the diabolical apparitions who ascend from the trapdoor and then descend, leaving Macbeth beguiled by the half-truths and "honest trifles" through which the "instruments of darkness" betray him "In deepest consequence" (1.3.123–26). Macbeth is deceived by a stage trick: what has appeared to be so impossible, the movement of Birnam Wood to high Dunsinane Hill ("Who can impress the forest, bid the tree / Unfix his earthbound root?" he exults, 4.1.95–96), turns out to be a simple matter of Malcolm's ordering every soldier to "hew him down a bough / And bear't before him" (5.4.4–5) like a prop in a stage play. In production, all that the attacking soldiers need do is to come onstage with boughs in hand.

Macbeth's ultimate sad fate is to become the ranting stage tyrant who tears a passion to tatters, as he curses the servants who bring him news of an approaching army, boasts of his castle's strength able to "laugh a siege to scorn," and proclaims himself to "bear a charmèd life, which must not yield / To one of woman born" (5.5.3, 5.8.12–13). This is the role that the earlier, thoughtful Macbeth most wished to avoid (as does Hamlet), but it is, in Shakespeare's theatrical world, the role that he inherits by undertaking to be something that his better self abhorred. He sees at last that he is indeed a poor, strutting player in a tale told by an idiot. He sees that all those things that old age should cherish — "honor, love, obedience, troops of friends" — are things that he cannot now have. His life has truly "fall'n into the sere, the yellow leaf" (5.3.22–28). He has known from the start that acts have their consequences, and that his wife is wrong to suppose that "a little water clears us of this deed" once their hands are covered in blood (2.2.64–71). At the last he is diminished from thoughtful tragic protagonist to stereotypical blusterer. The memory of the sensitive man remains, but chiefly as a mock to the stage villain he has become.

Performance history of *Macbeth* has often devoted more attention to spectacular theatrical effects than to subtleties of role-playing. "Here we saw *Macbeth*," writes Samuel Pepys in his diary on April 19, 1667, "which, though I have seen it often, yet it is one the best plays for a stage, and variety of dancing and music, that ever I saw." His special delight in the "divertissement," i.e., the song and dance, suggests the pervasive presence of operatic and scenic effects. At the Dorset Garden Theatre in 1664 and afterward, under the guidance of William Davenant, the play was "dressed in all its finery, as new clothes, new scenes, machines, as flyings for the witches, with all the singing and dancing in it." Flying witches continued well on into the eighteenth century. Such magical effects, which even in Shakespeare's own day had been augmented with songs and other material by Thomas Middleton, were an irresistible feature. David Garrick, attempting to restore something resembling Shakespeare's text in 1744, had to back down in the face of his audiences' demands for more spectacle and song. Late eighteenth- and nineteenth-century actor-managers tended to augment this tendency with visibly impressive sets and decor, as in Charles Macklin's Scottish historical rendition at Covent Garden in 1773, or John Philip Kemble's production at Drury Lane in 1794, in which the "mittens, plaited caps, laced aprons, red stomachers, ruffs," and so on of the Weird Sisters in Garrick's day were replaced by as many as fifty witches singing and dancing in a grotesquely comic style.

Edmund Kean, in 1814, outfitted his stage with a rocky pass and a bridge, an elaborate interior of Macbeth's castle, a cavern and "car of clouds," Hecate's cave, and still more, with Kean as Macbeth wearing kilts and an armored breastplate. For William Charles Macready's production at Drury Lane in 1837, a mist rose slowly in act 1 to reveal a barren heath and highland landscape towered over by a rustic bridge. In the opulent interior of Dunsinane Castle, Banquo's ghost entered unbidden to Macbeth's feast by means of a trapdoor hidden from the audience by servants. At Birnam Wood, the spectacle of soldiers carrying branches was so elaborate that it indeed resembled a forest, receding into the distance in the form of a painted diorama rear-stage. Charles Kean, at the Princess's Theatre in 1853, chose as his *mise en scène* a presumed eleventh-century Scotland under Danish invasion. *Lloyd's Weekly* complained that "now we have the costume without Macbeth." Herbert Beerbohm Tree, at His Majesty's Theatre in 1911, staged Lady Macbeth's sleepwalking scene on a grand staircase.

More recently, the trend has been to less elaborate sets and presentational staging. At the Old Vic in 1930, Harcourt Williams cleared away such trappings in favor of simple sets and swift-moving action that provided instead an intense psychological focus on John Gielgud as a morally isolated protagonist. Theodore Komisarjevsky, at Stratford-upon-Avon in 1933, employed modern dress and a World War I setting, with the Weird Sisters as old hags rifling the corpses of fallen soldiers and telling the fortunes of Macbeth and Banquo by means of palmistry. Tyrone Guthrie deleted the witches from scenes 1 and 3 in his Old Vic production of 1934 so that they would not dominate the play. Orson Welles's *Macbeth*, performed by an all-black cast at New York's Lafayette Theatre in 1936, substituted voodoo doctors for the Weird Sisters. John Gielgud's set at Stratford-upon-Avon in 1952 was a cluster of menacingly dark masses lit only by torchlight. Laurence Olivier and Vivien Leigh played Macbeth and Lady Macbeth in Glen Byam Shaw's production at Stratford-upon-Avon in 1955 with unsparing cruelty, as was especially evident in the slaughter of Lady Macduff and her son. Trevor Nunn's unsuccessful 1974–1975 RSC production at Stratford-upon-Avon and London featured Helen Mirren as Lady Macbeth and Nicol Williamson as a brooding, secretive Macbeth who, in the words of drama critic Irving Wardle, "becomes more and more unreachable until by the end events are happening only in his head." In some productions the Weird Sisters have been in control throughout, as at Stratford, Ontario in 1983, when one of them took the part of the Third Murderer at the killing of Banquo in order to make sure that Banquo's son Fleance would escape as determined by destiny. Similarly, in a Kabuki *Macbeth* at Wisdom Bridge Theatre in Chicago in the same year, the Weird Sisters were puppet masters, frequently onstage and coordinating their movements to those of Macbeth and Lady Macbeth, giving the illusion that the play's great tragic events were controlled by spirits as though through invisible wires.

Some film and video versions have managed to show us, in intense close-ups interspersed with heart-stirring violence, the unsettling potential of *Macbeth* as a tragedy about role-playing in which the parts chosen by the protagonists are like "strange garments" that "cleave not to their mold" (1.3.147). In Akira Kurosawa's *Throne of Blood* (1957), Washizu (Toshiro Mifune) and his Banquo-like friend Miki (Minoru Chiaki) encounter, in a nightmarishly storm-lashed forest, a spirit prophesying to them that Washizu will be promoted to great political and military power but that Miki's son will eventually inherit. Washizu's wife (Isuzu Yamada), like Lady Macbeth, translates her husband's hopes into a plot of assassination, seeking vicarious power through her husband's career that restrictive samurai custom will not grant to a woman. Her terrifying understated resolve leads her and Washizu into a conspiratorial murder sequence that is entirely wordless for seven spellbinding minutes. Roman Polanski's *Macbeth* (1971) is unrelentingly dark in its vision of a cycle of political violence that is not resolved at the film's end; in an epilogue, Donalbain visits the Weird Sisters in search of their malevolent prophesying. In a highly acclaimed version by Trevor Nunn, first onstage in 1976 at the experimental Other Place in Stratford-upon-Avon and then adapted for television in 1979, Ian McKellen and Judi Dench as Macbeth and Lady Macbeth are grouped in a simple circle of light surrounded by other members of the cast sitting on chairs and stools as though at a studio rehearsal. As they come forward in turn into the center of the arena to act out their scenes, the performers are the focus of an intensely metatheatrical atmosphere (fig. 7.4). Yukio Ninagawa's film adaptation, available in the West since 1985, centers the play on a Buddhist family altar and the pervasive visual image of the cherry blossom as a symbol of transitory beauty desecrated by human folly. In productions such as these, *Macbeth* displays its fascination as a play about theater of imagination.

7.4. Ian McKellen as Macbeth being shown apparitions by the Weird Sisters in 4.1 of Trevor Nunn's 1976 production of *Macbeth* for the Royal Shakespeare Company. Photo credit: Joe Cocks Studio Collection. Copyright Shakespeare Birthplace Trust.

III

Cleopatra in *Antony and Cleopatra* (1606–1607) is both fully aware of the role-playing demanded of great persons in history and entirely comfortable with her theatrical identity. Like Hamlet, she places a high premium on the quality of the performance: one must act one's role superbly, not cheaply. Hamlet deplores ham acting (an irony, since "ham" in this sense derives from the stage tradition of innumerable overacted Hamlets); Cleopatra fears that she will be lampooned as some sort of stage freak. Cornered at last by Octavius Caesar in her Egyptian monument, Cleopatra imagines the worst that might befall her: being taken to Rome in Caesar's triumph and put on display as his captive prize. "Mechanic slaves / With greasy aprons, rules, and hammers shall / Uplift us to the view," she warns Iras. "The quick comedians / Extemporally will stage us and present / Our Alexandrian revels; Antony / Shall be brought drunken forth; and I shall see / Some squeaking Cleopatra boy my greatness / I'th' posture of a whore" (5.2.209–21). Shakespeare dares to call his spectators' attention to the fact that Cleopatra and her women are being portrayed by boy actors on an open stage without the scenic aid of opulent sets. Cleopatra and her women are not even *"above"* in this final long scene of the play: they did appear *"aloft"* earlier when the dying Antony was lifted up to Cleopatra (4.15.0.1), but now the main stage has become the interior of her monument in order to provide adequate room for a busy and majestic death scene. Here she has been "surprised" and captured by Proculeius and other Roman soldiers, who come at her from behind, through a stage door, visually suggesting that they have gained access through the gates of the monument. Here she receives Octavius Caesar and his train, learns privately from Dolabella that she is right in fearing a public humiliation in Rome, and is brought the asps in a countryman's basket of figs with which she will end her life "after the high Roman fashion" (4.15.92) in suicide.

Cleopatra has long prepared for her final scene of theatrical greatness. Her first meeting with Antony on the river of Cydnus in Asia Minor, as reported by Enobarbus to his Roman counterparts (and as derived by Shakespeare from Thomas North's vigorous English translation of Plutarch's Life of Mark Antony), is filled with piquant details of a staged setting: the barge that is like a "burnished throne" for Cleopatra, the poop of beaten gold, the purple sails, the silver oars, the "pretty dimpled boys, like smiling Cupids, / With divers-colored fans," the waiting-gentlewoman "like the Nereides, / So many mermaids," and all the rest (2.2.201–19). Cleopatra resourcefully surrounds herself with luxurious props that assault all the five senses: the silken tackle swells to the touch, a "strange invisible perfume hits the sense / Of the adjacent wharfs," and so on. The very fact that this momentous meeting is described rather than presented onstage is a theatrical way of enhancing the scene by appealing to the auditors' imaginations. Cleopatra herself, says Enobarbus, "beggared all description." Her mystique is conveyed by her surroundings, by cloth-of-gold of tissue and all the rest. She is a theatrical event unto herself.

Cleopatra is proud of her acting. She changes mood with mercurial suddenness, crossing Antony's disposition by being merry when he is sad, and sullen when he is mirthful. When Charmian questions this strategy, urging instead that Cleopatra "Cross him in nothing," Cleopatra is almost contemptuous in her pity for such innocent advice: "Thou teachest like a fool: the way to lose him" (1.3.2–10). As holder of the PhD in seduction of men, and with an impressive list of triumphs to her credit (Pompey the Great, Julius Caesar, and now Antony), Cleopatra is not about to take advice from a subaltern. Her bravura performances during Antony's absence are dazzling and self-aware of the roles that she is playing: languid and raunchy one moment as she fantasizes about bearing the weight of Antony, like Antony's horse (1.5.19–23), homicidally violent on a next occasion when a messenger has the misfortune to bring her news of Antony's marriage to Octavia (2.5), and positively catty a short time later when she coaxes the messenger into assuring her that Octavia is a woman of low voice and short stature ("Dull of tongue, and dwarfish," she mockingly observes, 3.3.14–17). She laughs amusedly when Charmian recalls for her the practical joke she once played on Antony as a way of twitting him for his macho pride in his prowess as a fisherman: she had one of her servants tie a salt fish to his fishing line, "which he / With fervency drew up" (2.5.10–18). Cleopatra likes to think of herself as one who "betrays" men in this playful fashion.

Her playacting in the role of admiral of the fleet at the battle of Actium, on the other hand, is not so amusing. Indeed, her reputation for playing any part at will puts her in serious trouble with the men who find her untrustworthy, including, finally, Antony. She becomes, in his eyes, a "Triple-turned whore" and a "right gypsy" who has "at fast and loose" betrayed him to "the very heart of loss," or so he believes (4.12.13–29). Her tactic of evasion at this point, sending word to Antony that she is dead, is understandable in that he appears to be both mad and dangerous, but it becomes one more way in which her constant shifting of roles makes for fatal misunderstanding.

Cleopatra stages her final scene with a theatrical instinct that never deserts her. "Show me, my women, like a queen," she instructs Charmian and Iras. "Go fetch / My best attires. I am again for Cydnus, / To meet Mark Antony" (5.2.227–29). Her finale is thus to be a deliberate reprise of her *coup de théâtre* on the river of Cydnus so admiringly described by Enobarbus. She will once again "make defect perfection" and demonstrate that "Age cannot wither her, nor custom stale / Her infinite variety" (2.2.241–46). "Give me my robe," she commands as Iras returns with her royal attire. "Put on my crown. I have / Immortal longings in me" (5.2.280–81). The ceremony of dressing her is a vital display of restored greatness. This is how Cleopatra will go about to "call great Caesar ass / Unpolicied" (307–8). She will deny him his coveted triumph in Rome by substituting a scene of noble dying in place of the ignominious and circus-like public humiliation that Octavius Caesar has planned for her. She sees with utter clarity that his intent to insult her in this fashion is not simply his way of maximizing the political advantage of his military triumph in Egypt; it is also his attempt to contain her threatening sexuality by branding her as a whore. Cleopatra wins in this contest, and it is a contest that means far more to her than her own life. Like Hamlet, she insists on acting out her great role in a high and noble style. Caesar, having lost her as his prize exhibit, graciously accedes to her wish that she be honored as a queen of heroic stature. "She shall be buried by her Antony," he announces. "No grave upon the earth shall clip in it / A pair so famous" (358–60). Cleopatra has fought for, and achieved, the right to share with Antony the status of tragic protagonist. She, not Octavius Caesar, is the deviser and star player of the play's final moments.

Directors in the theater and on screen have understandably been tempted to substitute visual splendor for the magic of imagination through which Shakespeare's script invites actors to conjure up images in the hearers' and viewers' minds. John Philip Kemble, at Covent Garden in 1813 with Helen Faucit as Cleopatra, entertained his audiences with a spectacular sea fight at Actium and an equally grandiose funeral procession at the end. Nineteenth-century actor-managers, faced with a play written in forty-two scenes, some of them brief vignettes of battles designed originally for quick entrances and exits on an open presentational stage, inevitably cut down this seeming welter of episodes to allow the use of massive sets. Neoclassical dismay at the play's flagrant violation the so-called unities of time, place, and action by transporting its scene back and forth between Rome and Egypt (not to mention Messina in Sicily, Misenum in southern Italy, Athens, Actium on the coast of northwest Greece, and some indeterminate location in the Middle East) and over a span of some eleven eventful years of Roman history offered actor-managers another incentive to curtail changes of scenery. John Dryden's adaptation called *All for Love, or The World Well Lost* had shown, in 1678, that the story could be confined to Egypt and the last forty-eight or so hours of the protagonists' lives.

William Charles Macready, in 1833, ambitiously filled his stage with "a splendid hall in Cleopatra's palace," the "garden of Cleopatra's palace," a "portico attached to the house of Octavius Caesar, with the Capitol in the distance," "a hall in the house of Lepidus," a locale "near the promontory of Misenum," the "promontory of Actium with a view of the fleets of Antony and Caesar," and still more. With as many sets as these, the number of scenes had to be markedly reduced. The Egyptian scenes in Samuel Phelps's production in 1849 were reported to be "exceedingly *vraisemblable*"; so were the banqueting scenes on board Pompey's galley. Frank Benson's production at Stratford-upon-Avon in 1898 was the costliest yet seen there, owing to the huge expense of costumes, properties, and sets.

The famous meeting of the lovers has loomed large in a number of productions, literalizing in the theater what Enobarbus describes to his Roman counterparts when they meet in Rome (2.2.201–51). A production at Drury Lane in 1873 transported the Cydnus River from its historical location in southeast Asia Minor to Egypt, so that the first meeting of Antony and Cleopatra could be displayed in full pictorial detail. Herbert Beerbohm Tree, at His Majesty's Theatre in 1906, employed a large cast of extras, costumed as in the days of the old Pharaohs, to lend a maximum impact to the event. Obviously, this rich display of spectacle had its own charm and rationale. The shift from pageantry in the nineteenth century to metatheater in numerous recent productions is not a matter of wrong and right, but of a response in the theater to seismic shifts in cultural attitudes and preferences.

At all events, more theatrically self-aware productions have preferred to capture the magic of the play in its poetic invocation of what cannot be seen and can only be imagined. Peter Brook's *Antony and Cleopatra* at Stratford-upon-Avon in 1978 was, in the director's own words, "a small, intimate, personal play," staged on a single set in the form of a semicircular pavilion made out of six translucent panels. The business of "lifting" the dying Antony (Alan Howard) up to Cleopatra (Glenda Jackson) was accomplished all on one level, as Cleopatra and her women mimed the effort of tugging at long cloth banners wrapped around Antony's body (fig. 7.5). Barrie Rutter, in his production for Northern Broadsides in Halifax, Yorkshire, 1995–1997, costumed his actors as working-class roustabouts in tee shirts and slacks and encouraged them to use their natural North of England voices. Audiences were vibrantly aware that they were watching a series of performances. Michael Bogdanov located his English Shakespeare Company version, Hackney Empire Theatre, 1998, in a contemporary world of tabloid news reporters, walkie-talkies, guerilla terrorists, and large wall clocks set to the varying time zones of Rome and Egypt. Mark Rylance's all-male casting at the Southwark Globe in 1999 successfully called attention to the production's theatrical artifice, and that of Shakespeare, by assigning women's roles to male actors and then daring the audience to

7.5. Iras (Juliet Stevenson), Cleopatra (Glenda Jackson), and Charmian (Paola Dionisotti) "haul up" Antony (Alan Howard) to Cleopatra's monument by means of cloth banners, all on a flat level, in Peter Brook's 1978 production of *Antony and Cleopatra* for the Royal Shakespeare Company, Stratford-upon-Avon. Photo credit: Joe Cocks Studio Collection. Copyright Shakespeare Birthplace Trust.

savor the illusion. Modern ideas of gender as a kind of performance merge brilliantly with the larger sense in which *Antony and Cleopatra* is about showmanship in the enactment of history.

IV

Something needs to be said briefly here about the tragedies that have been omitted till now. *Titus Andronicus* (c. 1589–1592) is, like Shakespeare's early history plays, muscular in its use of theatrical space. The long opening scene (fig. 7.6), in which the imperial crown is refused by the military hero Titus and taken instead by the dead emperor's son Saturninus, begins with tribunes and senators entering *"aloft"* while the

7.6. An early modern illustration of 1.1 of *Titus Andronicus*, the so-called Longleat drawing, showing the spear-carrying Titus with his sons on the left and Queen Tamora with her two sons and Aaron the Moor on the right. Reproduced by permission of the Marquess of Bath, Longleat House, Warminster, Wiltshire, Great Britain. Courtesy the Photographic Survey Department of the Courtauld Institute of Art.

competitors enter below at two doors until Saturninus and his brother Bassianus *"go up into the Senate house."* The Gothic Queen Tamora also enters *"aloft"* with her two sons and Aaron the Moor. Later, in a forest scene of hunting, a trapdoor proves necessary when Tamora's sons come upon the eloped Bassianus and Titus's daughter Lavinia near a tree under which the villainous Aaron has hidden a bag of gold as a ruse to ensnare Titus's sons (2.3.1). Tamora's sons stab Bassianus to death before Lavinia's eyes, throw the body into a "loathsome pit" or "hole" (176, 186), and drag Lavinia off to be raped and mutilated. And, even though the rape itself takes place offstage, the play revels in onstage gore and violence: Lavinia is subsequently seen with stumps instead of hands; Titus cuts off one of his hands in an ineffectual attempt to ransom one of his imprisoned sons; Titus cuts the throats of Tamora's wicked sons while Lavinia obligingly holds a basin with her stumps to receive the blood (5.2.165–96); and, in the finale, Titus outfits himself as a cook in order that he may serve up Tamora's sons to her in a dish before stabbing Lavinia and then Tamora to death. Saturninus thereupon stabs Titus and is killed in his turn by Titus's son Lucius.

Performance history has tended to exploit this violence as sensationalism, as for example in Edward Ravenscroft's *Titus Andronicus, or The Rape of Lavinia* at the Theatre Royal, Drury Lane, in 1687. As its subtitle implies, this version played up the horrors of the tale by enhancing the role of Aaron and the unspeakable cannibalism of the grisly banqueting scene in act 5. At one point a drawn curtain revealed the corpses of Tamora's sons Demetrius and Chiron "in chains, in bloody linen," beheaded and with severed hands. Peter Brook's production (starring Laurence Olivier as Titus) at Stratford-upon-Avon in 1955, on the other hand, though plainly speaking to the terrors of hatred and cruelty in the world of the twentieth century, transmuted the image of the raped Lavinia (Vivien Leigh) into that of a desolated young woman with scarlet ribbons trailing from her wrists and mouth to betoken her loss of hands and tongue. Julie Taymor's 1999 film version (starring Anthony Hopkins) has had a notable success, in part because it imagines the violence of its ancient tale from the perspective of a youngster of today playing furiously with his war-game toys that are then reified and embodied in a legend of horror.

Julius Caesar's self-awareness as theater in 1599 manifests itself in a series of ironic contrasts. Bursts of *"Thunder and lightning"* orchestrate a taut sequence (1.3 and following) in which the Romans of this play reveal what they are like by their varied responses to the ominous storm taking place on the very night before Caesar is assassinated: Casca is terrified, Cassius defiant, Brutus self-absorbed and nearly oblivious of the night's events, Cicero philosophically impartial and skeptical. Most of all, the play centers on a comparison of Brutus and Caesar. In adjoining scenes (2.1 and 2.2), these great, proud men betray a surprising similarity to each other, despite their political differences, by their refusal to heed the warnings of their wives and by their fatal susceptibility to flattery. Brutus is vulnerable to Cassius's appealing to him as the savior of Republican Rome. He overrides the advice of his co-conspirators that they recruit Cicero and kill Mark Antony, and is so confident of his own speaking ability that he allows Antony to follow him in the marketplace after the assassination of Caesar, with results that are disastrous to the conspiracy. Later, he vetoes Cassius's urging that they avoid a pitched battle at Philippi, and once again is fatally wrong in his inflexible self-certainty. Caesar, meanwhile, shows how his supreme self-confidence is at once his strength and his greatest weakness, for it allows him to be flattered into proceeding to the capitol on the fatal Ides of March in disregard of prophetic warnings. The greatest men of Rome are ironically the victims of being who they are.

Production history has viewed these ironies from an increasingly disillusioning and political point of view, as in Orson Welles's version at New York's Mercury Theatre in 1937 subtitled *Death of a Dictator,* by way of drawing analogies between Caesar and Benito Mussolini. In the film version of 1953 by John Houseman and Joseph L. Mankiewicz, the crowd scenes bore an uncomfortable resemblance to Nazi rallies, with omnipresent images of Caesar (Louis Calhern) as the Great Leader and arms raised in fascist salutes. At Stratford-upon-Avon, in 1972, under the directorship of Trevor Nunn, Evan Smith, and Buzz Goodbody, a colossal statue of Caesar loomed over the proceedings through much of the play, dominating the lives of those who presumed to conspire against him. Terry Hands's Caesar, in a 1987 production for the RSC, was so monolithically fascist that reviewers wondered why Brutus should hesitate in joining the conspiracy against him. David Thacker's modern-dress production at the Other Place in Stratford-upon-Avon (1993) prompted analogies to the civil war in Bosnia. With an actress in the role of Caesar, a production at the Baron's Court Theatre, London, in 1993 suggested liberal chafing at the conservative program of prime minister Margaret Thatcher. Of course not all modern productions adopt strategies like these. Invitingly clever as such analogies may be, they may also lose sight of the sustained ironies of the play, as it repeatedly juxtaposes images of Brutus and Caesar only to find that they are more like each other than either of them realizes.

The title figure of *Timon of Athens* (c. 1605–1608) shares with other protagonists in Shakespeare's classical plays an inflexibility and unsuitability for the role he must play that determines his fate. Staging patterns visualize the sudden change in his fortunes as he goes from being the wealthiest and most courted aristocrat of Athens to becoming an embittered and self-willed outcast. The opulent banquet and masking scene with which he lavishly entertains his guests (1.2) serves to define what is sybaritic and even decadent about Timon's oversized generosity, as Apemantus points out. A second banquet, fitted out with a table, seats, handsome place settings, music, and servants in attendance is a conscious echo of that earlier feast, but is so for the purpose of a savagely satirical inversion. The dishes, when uncovered, turn out to contain nothing but warm water and stones. The enraged Timon throws water in the faces of his dismayed guests and drives them off (3.6). Once he has taken up residence in a cave, his fortunes are visibly opposite to those he enjoyed in Athens.

Some productions of this seldom-staged play have found inventive means to underscore the contrast between the wealthy Timon and the embittered outcast. Peter Brook, in a strikingly metatheatrical production in Paris in 1974, located the action in the orchestra of an abandoned Victorian theater, with the audience on all sides and the decayed backstage wall of what had once been the stage constantly on view as a symbolic reminder of the decline of Western culture. Jerry Turner, at Ashland, Oregon, in 1978, outfitted Timon and his fair-weather friends in Texas ten-gallon hats and three-piece white suits amid a scene of gargantuan and competitive display of new wealth; then, as Timon's fortunes declined, Turner revolved his stage set to reveal a guerilla jungle of camouflage outfits and submachine guns. The dramatic effect in the theater was to show chaos and violence as the soft underbelly of a decadent civilization haunted by its own tortured memories of Vietnam. Ron Daniels, at the Other Place, Stratford-upon-Avon, 1981, began in that experimental and nonscenic theater space with a geometrically neat set and Japanese-style costumes that gave way increasingly to a space chaotically hung about with nets and strewn with debris. The televised *Timon* directed by Jonathan Miller in the same year for the BBC shifted from posh interiors at the start to a ruined seaside hovel for Timon (Jonathan Pryce) that was strewn about with doleful reminders of a collapsing civilization, including the half-buried statue of a horse.

The climax of *Coriolanus* (c. 1608), the protagonist's aborted assault on his native city of Rome, is also the moment of most intense awareness of theater and role-playing. Forced to confront the impossibility of saving the lives of his mother, wife, and son without also betraying his allegiance to his former enemy, Aufidius, Coriolanus sees that he has been somehow chosen for a role he does not know how to enact. "Like a dull actor now, / I have forgot my part, and I am out, / Even to a dull disgrace," he wryly concedes (5.3.40–42). To be "out" is to have forgotten one's lines — the ultimate loss of face for any professional actor. Small wonder that Coriolanus's career as politician is so ill-starred; he is hugely miscast. To his credit be it said, he never desired the part thrust on him by his mother and his supporters of running for the office of consul. His own political ideology seemed to point to him as the potential savior of patrician Rome from what he and his allies have fearfully regarded as mob rule, but his distaste for political theater means that he is decisively unqualified. The impasse has led to his banishment. He is astute enough to see the absurdity of it all: "The heavens do ope, / The gods look down, and this unnatural scene / They laugh at," he mordantly observes (183–84). Coriolanus's utter inability to enact any other role than that of the person he has become is at once his strongest point and his fatal weakness. He would rather "play / The man I am" (3.2.16–17) than be otherwise. He is too absolute for the theater of the world in which he finds himself.

As in the case of *Julius Caesar,* performance history of *Coriolanus* has often provided directors with a means of grinding some particular political ax. Nahum Tate named his 1682 Drury Lane adaptation *The Ingratitude of a Commonwealth, or The Fall of Caius Martius Coriolanus,* in order to emphasize the folly of mob rule and the meddlesomeness of the tribunes. Tate's Coriolanus was by implication a Tory and royalist, loyal to the Stuart monarchs, who were mired in constitutional conflict when this version was produced. John Dennis's *The Invader of His Country, or The Fatal Resentment,* at Drury Lane in 1719, took the side of George I's Hanoverian monarchy in the wake of the failed Jacobite attempt in 1715 to restore the Stuart pretender, son of James II, to the British throne. James Thompson produced his version of the play at Covent Garden in 1749 in response to a second Jacobite rebellion (1745) on behalf of the so-called Young Pretender, Charles Edward. Conversely, William Charles Macready's sympathy for the Roman plebeians in his 1838 production at Covent Garden signaled a shift toward the political left. Samuel Phelps, at Sadler's Wells Theatre in 1848, similarly portrayed Coriolanus as achieving the "sublimity of disdain" in his contemptuous abuse of Rome's aroused citizenry.

The twentieth century has seen interpretations on both sides. A staging at the Comédie Française in Paris, 1933–1934, resulted in violent confrontations when radical leftists saw the production as an unfriendly critique of social democracy, whereupon the Maly Theater in Moscow produced its own avowedly leftist interpretation in the following year. It was followed in 1951 by Bertolt Brecht's adaptation, with its Marxist sympathy for Rome's proletariat. Peter Hall's 1974 production at London's National Theatre connected the play to the British miners' strike of that year by depicting the plebeians as angry mine workers aroused to action by spray-painted slogans and the exhortations of their shop-steward tribunes. More balanced performances include that of Ian McKellen at the Nottingham Playhouse in 1963, under the direction of Tyrone Guthrie, in which McKellen brilliantly caught the sense of Coriolanus's ironic failure to perform what is demanded of him in a way that was at once tragic and wryly amusing. Richard Burton, too, in a performance preserved only in a sound recording, manages to be both sympathetic in his brusque candor and troublesomely fanatical in his old-guard ideology. Multiplicities of ambiguity do especially well in capturing what is so theatrically self-aware in Shakespeare's depiction of civil conflict. In its mordant self-reflexiveness, this last Shakespearean tragedy persuasively captures the unstable spirit of skepticism that is so characteristic of Shakespeare's self-destructive protagonists in *Titus Andronicus, Julius Caesar, Othello, King Lear, Macbeth, Antony and Cleopatra,* and *Timon of Athens.*

$\mathscr{L}\,8\,\mathscr{L}$

Insubstantial Pageant

SHAKESPEARE'S FAREWELL
TO THE STAGE

Prominent among Shakespeare's late plays are a group variously known in criticism as the romances or tragicomedies. The categorical names suggest both a continuity and a new development in Shakespeare's writing of comedy. These plays — *Pericles, Cymbeline, The Winter's Tale,* and *The Tempest* — resemble earlier comedies in their love plots ending in marriage and reconciliation. At the same time, the late plays dwell on hazards of jealousy, hatred, separation, and unhappy states of mind in ways that seem newly emphasized. As "romances" they recount the wanderings, separations, and distressful misunderstandings of romantic adventure; as "tragicomedies" they begin in tragedy and death but eventually find their way to a happiness that is all the more precious for having been recovered at such cost. The earlier comedies often traverse dangerous hazards as well, like the threatening of Antonio with death in *The Merchant of Venice* or the slandering of Hero in *Much Ado about Nothing,* so that the differences between early and late are more a matter of emphasis than of clear distinction. It is as though Shakespeare's experience as a writer of harrowing tragedies had brought him to a darker view of the human condition. *Cymbeline* is in fact grouped with the tragedies in the First Folio of 1623; *The Winter's Tale* and *The Tempest* are grouped with the comedies. (*Pericles* was excluded.) Shakespeare's last history play, *Henry VIII* (1613), written seemingly in collaboration with John Fletcher some fourteen years after Shakespeare had set aside the genre of English history, is similarly suffused with the spirit of tragicomedy;

so too is *The Two Noble Kinsmen,* another Fletcher collaboration. We will look briefly at *Henry VIII* in chapter 9.

What sorts of staging challenges did these late plays present to Shakespeare and his company, and in what ways do they investigate Shakespeare's self-aware fascination with theater and acting as he approaches the end of his career as a dramatist? How have these issues been addressed in performance history? These late plays do indeed offer a coherence of theatrical method and effect, defining their purpose as one of new exploration combined with summation and closure. The story begins with *Pericles.*

I

Whether *Pericles* (c. 1606–1608) is entirely Shakespeare's is very much to be doubted, but for our present purposes the question of multiple authorship doesn't much matter. As a theatrical entity, *Pericles* revels in opportunities for presenting to the spectators' eyes a sequential narrative of separation and wandering. Whereas *A Comedy of Errors* relates its saga of separation at sea by the classical expedient of an onstage narrator telling us what happened years ago, *Pericles* shows us its happenings to the best of its ability. In doing so, it repeatedly calls upon staging devices and dialogue as a way of establishing a series of locations and happenings. "*Enter Pericles, wet,*" reads a stage direction (2.1.0.1), telling us at once that we are on a seacoast in the wake of a shipwreck. "*Enter Pericles a-shipboard,*" reads another stage direction (3.1.0.1), inviting the acting company to devise appropriate costuming and other effects (perhaps as at the beginning of *The Tempest,* where "*A tempestuous noise of thunder and lightning*" signals the onset of a storm). Props take on an important role in establishing setting. "*Enter two or three with a chest,*" and then "*Enter one with napkins and fire*" (3.2.50.1, 88.1) as Lord Cerimon receives and resuscitates the body of the seemingly dead Queen Thaisa that had been cast into the sea.

Old Gower, the medieval poet acting as narrator and chorus for the play, is essential to the business of establishing, in the absence of conventional scenery, a series of imagined stage locations. He first introduces us to Antioch by pointing to a row of severed heads impaled on the fortifications of that town, presumably backstage on the tiring-house wall. Many a suitor to the King's daughter has died because he could not answer the riddle of incest, Gower tells us, "As yon grim looks do testify" (1 Chorus 40). Presumably he gestures in the direction of the heads, and then steps aside to let the scene do its business. This is his usual way. Repeatedly his appearances as chorus are interspersed with dumb shows. He acts as a kind of stage manager and master of ceremonies, appealing constantly to our imaginations to fill out the scene. "In your imagination hold / This stage the ship, upon whose deck / The sea-tossed Pericles appears to speak" (3 Chorus 58–60). "Imagine Pericles arrived at Tyre" (4 Chorus 1). In order to transport the hero to Tarsus, we are to "think his pilot thought" (4.4.18), and then "think" that we "are all in Mytilene" (51). At Mytilene harbor, Gower bids us, "In your supposing once more put your sight; / Of heavy Pericles think this his bark" (5 Chorus 21–22). As in *Henry V* and often elsewhere, Shakespeare apologizes for the crude limitations of a theater that cannot hope to reproduce the real object, and yet also seems to revel in that limitation since it invites us to participate in an active and collaborative enterprise of metonymy.

Not infrequently, the characters tell us where they are. "So, this is Tyre, and this the court," declares Thaliard, as he arrives at the palace of Tyre with his commission to assassinate Pericles (1.3.1). In the next scene, Cleon, the governor of Tarsus, lets us know that "This Tarsus, o'er which I have the government" (1.4.21). When Pericles, dripping wet, admits to the fishermen he encounters that he does not know on what coast he has been shipwrecked, the First Fishermen obligingly tells him (and us): "This is called Pentapolis, and our king the good Simonides" (2.1.100–101). In the first of several bordello scenes, Pander orders his servant to "Search the market narrowly. Mytilene is full of gallants," thereby informing us that we are in Mytilene (4.2.3–4). The play is unusually conscious of the need for such expository devices in dramatizing a narrative of such varied locations.

Despite its textual inadequacies, then, *Pericles* is a thoroughly pragmatic piece of work for theatrical performance, with unusually close attention to how its staging effects and illusions are to be created. Theater directors have responded to the challenge essentially in two ways. Some have endeavored to provide, through stage magic, what the original production could not manage. Samuel Phelps, at the Sadler's Wells Theatre in 1854, created the effect of a storm at sea, in which the deck of Pericles' ship actually pitched and rolled. Rowers manned the oars to carry Pericles from one location to another while a panorama moved behind them to create the illusion of travel. In her visionary appearance to Pericles and Marina, the goddess Diana entered in a chariot amidst the clouds. Other directors have preferred an unadorned presentational staging that makes possible a rapid movement from scene to scene, aided by continued appeals to the audience's imagination. David Ultz, at the Theatre Royal Stratford East in 1983, employed large crates on a virtually bare stage and considerable doubling of roles to promote an atmosphere of self-aware theatricality. Various translations of locale have added to the imaginative journey. New York's Shakespeare Festival production of 1974, directed by Edward Berkeley, conceived of the play as a traveling show, with actors climbing down from their wagons to clown for the audience before the play itself began. Tony Richardson, at Stratford-upon-Avon in 1958, cast the West Indian actor Edric Connor as Gower in the guise of a seafaring calypso singer (fig. 8.1). In 1986, at Stratford, Ontario, Gower was played by a black female gospel singer of extraordinary vocal range. The Gower in Barbara Gaines's production for the Chicago Shakespeare Theatre in 1991–1992 was a Chicago Transit Authority bus driver who had become a local legend for singing to his passengers from the driver's seat.

II

Cymbeline (c. 1608–1610) proclaims its genre in a virtuoso display of theatrical effects typically found in tragicomic romance, though seldom in such profusion, and resembling also the devices of earlier romantic comedies and other plays: an exchanged ring and a bracelet that are wagered upon and eventually restored to their rightful owners (as in *All's Well That Ends Well* and *The Merchant of Venice*), a mantle and a birthmark used to identify long-lost children (as in *The Comedy of Errors, Twelfth Night,* and *The Winter's Tale*), a magical sleeping potion that induces temporarily the appearance of death (*Romeo and Juliet*), the use of disguise by a young woman dressed as a young man and of men disguising themselves in the garments of other men or of other nations (*As You Like It* and many others), misdirected and feigned letters (*The Two Gentlemen of Verona* and others), ghostly visitations (*Richard III*), a riddling prophecy (*All's Well, Macbeth*), a divine epiphany (Diana in *Pericles*), and still more. These plot devices rely heavily on stage props and costumes, along with some electrifying special effects including a bed thrust onstage with its occupant (2.2.0.1, as in *Othello*), a trunk brought onstage with a man in it who emerges and disappears into the trunk (2.2.10–51), a headless corpse and a corpseless head (4.2), and the opening and closing of the "heavens" above the stage to facilitate the descent and reascent of the god Jupiter (5.4.92–113).

These devices give theatrical form to an essentially romantic plot, as

8.1. Edric Connor as a calypso singer playing Gower, in Tony Richardson's 1958 production of *Pericles* for the Royal Shakespeare Company, Stratford-upon-Avon. Photo credit: Angus McBean. Copyright Royal Shakespeare Company.

the play moves from the court of King Cymbeline of England to Italy and back and then to the mountains of Wales, where magical things can happen. The bracelet and the ring belong originally to Posthumus Leonatus, a "poor but worthy gentleman" (1.1.7), and Imogen, the King's daughter. Their secret marriage has led to Posthumus's being banished by the wrathful King, who intended Imogen for Cloten, the churlish son of the scheming woman whom the recently widowered Cymbeline has made his queen. As Imogen and Posthumus tearfully part, she puts on his finger a diamond ring once belonging to her mother as a pledge of eternal fidelity, and she accepts a bracelet from him with the same intent. We in the audience assume, if we are at all knowledgeable in the ways of romantic plotting, that these love tokens will play a key role in the play's denouement. In the meantime, these props must also figure importantly in the plot complications that necessarily precede the happy conclusion. Accordingly, Posthumus's vows, and his faith in Imogen, are severely put to the test when he wagers his ring on her chastity in a quarrel with the Italian Iachimo. This villain thereupon journeys to England, is received by Imogen with his letter of introduction from Posthumus, assails her virtue without success, and is accordingly driven to the expedient of asking her to provide safekeeping for a valuable trunk that he has brought with him. She readily accedes to the request and offers her own bedroom as the place of security.

The ring and the bracelet thus join with Iachimo's trunk and Imogen's bed as the essential props around which Shakespeare constructs his scene of great peril threatening the heroine. "*Enter Imogen in her bed,*" the scene begins (2.2). As in *Othello* and *Romeo and Juliet,* this direction means that Imogen lies on a bed which is thrust onstage through one of the stage doors or the discovery space. The main stage is thereby understood to be her bedroom for the duration of the scene. A trunk is brought onstage, presumably by stagehands. Iachimo is in it, unless it is set up at a trapdoor or other doorway in such a way as to allow him to slip into it unobtrusively. When Imogen is asleep, Iachimo emerges "*from the trunk.*" He intently observes the furnishings of the room and certain details about her person, especially "A mole cinque-spotted" (38), to enable him to convince Posthumus, when Iachimo has returned to Italy, that he has enjoyed sexual intimacy with Posthumus's wife. He slips the bracelet from the arm of the sleeping Imogen to provide an even more graphic "proof." As the "*Clock strikes,*" he vanishes into the trunk, and Imogen's bed is removed from the stage with her in it. A simple "*Exeunt*" covers both exits, with Iachimo presumably carried off inside the trunk. These maneuvers are quietly performed without curtains or other means of concealment, in the full light of day in the Elizabethan theater; the audience understands the conventions of stage illusion, as it does in today's presentational theater. The ruse works as planned: Iachimo, back in Italy, wins the ring from Posthumus and keeps the bracelet until the play's final scene of clarification in which Imogen spies the ring on Iachimo's finger, demands in the presence of the King to know how he obtained it, and extracts from Iachimo a confession that restores Imogen to her rightful place as Posthumus's loyal and long-suffering wife.

The sleep-inducing drug is another stage prop by which the tragicomic shape of the play's plot is delineated. Indeed, to tell the story of this drug is to relate a narrative through which the play achieves its linear and yet logically causal sense of form. The saga begins as the wicked Queen orders from her physician, Cornelius, a small box containing what she believes to be a poisonous compound by means of which she can practice on the lives of Posthumus and Imogen. She does not admit to Cornelius that she has any such murderous intent; he, for his part, so mistrusts her that he gives her instead (as he confides to us in soliloquy) a substance that "Will stupefy and dull the sense awhile" (1.5.37). The Queen, thus deceived by Cornelius, leaves the box where it is found and picked up by Pisanio, loyal servant of Posthumus and Imogen. He, being told by the Queen that it is a miraculous restorative, gives it to Imogen after he has conducted her to Wales and has provided her with a protective male disguise (3.4.189), assuring her that it is a remedy for sickness. When she feels unwell in her new forest home with Belarius, Guiderius, and Arviragus, she swallows some of the drug and is found apparently dead by her new companions (4.2.38, 197). Laid out for burial beside the body of her stepbrother Cloten, who has been beheaded by Guiderius, she awakens alone, mistakes the headless body for her husband Posthumus whose garments Cloten had misappropriated, and is found in her inconsolable grief by the Roman general Lucius, who takes a fancy to the seeming young man and welcomes "Fidele" into his service. In the final long recognition scene, Cornelius and Pisanio relate the strange history of the Queen's drug and the part it has played in a story of estrangement and eventual reunion (fig. 8.2). *Cymbeline*'s extensive reliance on such an elaborate prop-driven narrative is characteristic of the play's fascination with the genre of tragicomedy.

Seldom does Shakespeare make such extensive use of disguise as in *Cymbeline*. Once again, the result is a linear and narrative structure in which the elements are linked by a causal connection that becomes evident to the characters only in the play's denouement. Imogen, in Wales, is given a cloak bag by Pisanio that enables her to pass herself off as a young man, Fidele. In this guise she is welcomed by Belarius, Guiderius, and Arviragus, and cherished as one of their family. Her stepbrother Cloten, discovering her sudden absence from court and resolving to take his vengeance on her and Posthumus for having disappointed his

8.2. David Bradley as Cymbeline, Nicholas Farrell as Posthumus Leonatus, and Harriet Walter as Imogen in the final scene of *Cymbeline,* directed by Bill Alexander in 1987 at Stratford-upon-Avon. Photo credit: Ivan Kyncl. By permission of the Ivan Kyncl estate.

amorous hopes, worms out of Pisanio their place of rendezvous in Wales and dragoons Pisanio into providing Cloten with a suit of Posthumus's garments. Thus attired, he encounters Guiderius, is beheaded by this seeming mountaineer, and is laid out for burial beside "Fidele," with the result that she believes the headless corpse to be that of her husband. Belarius, meantime, has adopted the name of Morgan to conceal the fact that he stole the King's two sons many years ago and took them with him into banishment in the mountains of Wales, giving them the names of Polydore and Cadwal; they are in fact Guiderius and Arviragus. They are identified in the final scene by the typical romance device of birthmarks and accouterments: Belarius assures the King that the child Arviragus was "lapped / In a most curious mantle, wrought by th' hand / Of his queen mother," which Belarius can produce, while Guiderius bears on his neck "a mole, a sanguine star" (5.5.364–68).

Posthumus's story is similarly one in which repeated shifting of disguise provides the narrative structure of misunderstanding, separation, and eventual reunion. Returning to his native country in the outfit of an Italian soldier serving under Lucius, he determines to disrobe himself "Of these Italian weeds" and outfit himself "As does a Briton peasant" (5.1.22–24) in order that he may fight against the Romans with whom he came and thereby die in battle by way of expiation for having ordered the death of his wife for her supposed adultery. Dressed as a British peasant, he performs valiant deeds in the battle and helps to rescue no less a person than King Cymbeline. Still inconsolable over the imagined death of his wife, he reverts once more to his Italian outfit so that he may be captured by the victorious British and executed by them. In the climactic finale, he recognizes and challenges Iachimo as the villain who misled him into turning against Imogen, proclaims himself publicly as the slayer of the king's daughter, and strikes "Fidele" for interfering with his self-denunciation, until he is eventually reconciled to the young page who is now revealed to be his wife. Disguise costuming is a major staging vehicle of plot complication and reconciliation.

Cymbeline has no single character who acts as stage manager, scripting the lives of the other characters as does the Duke in *Measure for Measure,* for example, or Iago in *Othello.* Nor does *Cymbeline* have a choric narrator like Gower in *Pericles* to lead us step by step and provide a homiletic interpretation. Instead, events are under the control of a providential force epitomized in the god Jupiter. Although his single appearance is belated, it is theatrically stunning, with thunder and lightning as the "heavens" open to permit Jupiter to be lowered by means of rope and pulley, *"sitting upon an eagle"* (5.4.92.1–3). Shakespeare uses this technique of descent from the heavens only sparingly, and only in his late plays (*Cymbeline* and *The Tempest*); it may not have been available to him earlier in his career. Jupiter is at all events a *deus ex machina,* in both a literal and a thematic sense. He serves a crucial function in a play of so many journeys, disguises, and surprising plot developments to suggest that all the seeming vicissitudes of the story are in fact under the control of a benign overseeing deity. Jupiter's own interpretation of what we as spectators have seen is explicitly providential in these terms. "Be not with mortal accidents oppressed," he counsels the ghosts of the Leonati and implicitly us as well. Addressing himself to the "petty spirits of region low," Jupiter offers metaphysical comfort. "Whom best I love I cross, to make my gift, / The more delayed, delighted," he assures us. "Be content" (93–102).

Jupiter's is a classical name well suited to a play about pre-Christian Britain, as in *King Lear.* His pronouncements are not theological. Indeed, Jupiter is more of a theatrical figure than a stand-in for any deity, Christian or non-Christian. He is the spirit of a dramatic shape vested in the play itself and in the theater space where the play is to be performed. The staging is deliberately spectacular, even exaggerated, to make the point that Jupiter's appearance is a theatrical event. The prophecy that he leaves with the Leonati is manifestly quaint, with its talk of a "lion's whelp" or "lion-born" as signifying "Leo-natus," and "tender air" or *mollis aer* as signifying *mulier,* that is, woman, wife, Imogen (5.4.138–44, 5.5.447–62). Such childlike wordplay invites genial laughter rather than devotional belief. Modern audiences often find the whole ending funny, encouraging actors to send it up as a sort of campy joke. More plausibly, the effect is to focus our attention as audience on a theatrical playfulness that is also serious about the nature of tragicomic drama. The intent of a play like this is to do for us exactly what Jupiter promises: we are asked to see the reward of patient waiting and suffering as all the more precious because the happy ending is so long delayed. The contentedness that Jupiter asks us to seek is the satisfaction of beholding a well-shaped story that ends suitably in reconciliation. As a metaphor for life, it also urges us to be patient and then grateful for a world that is ultimately well-ordered, even though we mortals cannot guess where the story is going until it is finished. What appear to us as our misfortunes and mistakes may turn out in the long run to be essential to some intricate design. As Lucius expresses it, "Some falls are means the happier to arise" (4.2.406). Pisanio formulates a closely related idea no less succinctly: "Fortune brings in some boats that are not steered" (4.3.46).

In production, directors have tended to go in two divergent directions, as in the staging of *Pericles.* John Philip Kemble, at Drury Lane in 1785 and again in 1801, finding the play's ancient British setting and romantic saga of wandering in the Welsh highlands well suited to dawning Romantic sensibilities, provided expensively verisimilar surroundings for his actors. The bed for Imogen's bedchamber was of such massive proportions that (according to a contemporary account) the actor playing Iachimo, William Barrymore, though a tall man, "stood almost in need of a ladder to take a view of Imogen's person." Imogen was played by the great Sarah Siddons, the sister of Charles and John Philip Kemble.

Charles Kemble, at Covent Garden in 1827, strove for historical authenticity by gleaning as much information as possible from Tacitus's historical accounts about both the ancient Romans who invaded Britain and the Celts who resisted them, so that the stage could give an accurate picture. A production at the Queen's Theatre in 1872 featured a palace built in Anglo-Saxon architectural style, with Posthumus outfitted as a Viking. Henry Irving, in an especially opulent production at the Lyceum Theatre in 1896, provided elaborate Celtic sets for Cymbeline's palace gardens and interior rooms, a Roman banqueting hall for Posthumus's visit to Rome, a handsomely decorated bedchamber for Imogen, an impressive mountain cave for Belarius, a battlefield in which the British soldiers wore kilts, and a spectacular dream vision setting for the descent of Jupiter.

Contrastingly, Ben Greet at the Old Vic in 1918 and Nugent Monck at the Maddermarket Theatre in Norwich, 1923, chose to adorn the play with Elizabethan simplicity. Barry Jackson and H. K. Ayliff did a modern-dress production at the Birmingham Repertory in 1923. At the Cambridge Festival Theatre in 1934, Terence Gray set his action on a giant checkerboard. Theodore Komisarjevsky began his 1950 production in Montreal with a cocktail party in which some characters sang "We're off to see the Wizard, the wonderful Wizard of Oz." For A. J. Antoon, at New York's Delacorte Theatre in 1971, the play was a grotesque fairy tale, with Cloten's severed head as a bouncing ball, King Cymbeline as an ancient clown, and the final battle a contest between papier-mâché animals and birds. Robin Phillips, at Stratford, Ontario, in 1986, chose three contrastive period styles to differentiate the action: prehistoric Britain for the sequences in Wales, the trenches of World War I for the battle in act 5, and the fashionable Europe of the gay 1920s for scenes at court. Jupiter was a World War I ace in goggles.

III

The Winter's Tale (c. 1609–1611) delights, as does *Cymbeline,* in big theatrical moments that call attention to their very theatricality, notably the exit of Antigonus *"pursued by a bear"* (3.3.57) and the coming to life onstage of a seeming statue of a woman we have been assured is dead (5.3.102). The play is amply furnished with the stigmata of tragicomic romance: a babe abandoned on a desert shore where she is found by shepherds in a baptismal mantle rich enough "for a squire's child" (3.3.112) and furnished with a chest full of gold, this same child coming of age in the course of sixteen years as the Chorus unabashedly leaps over that interval of time, a rustic countryside with shepherds and shepherdesses, sea voyages, long separations leading eventually to reunion, and throughout a sense of wondrous improbability. The play's very title suggests a venerable folktale: its story is "so like an old tale that the verity of it is in strong suspicion" (5.2.29–30).

At times, indeed, *The Winter's Tale* deals in wonders that seem to go beyond the power of speech to utter or of theater to present them. Shakespeare chooses not to stage the scene of revelation in which Perdita is discovered to be the long-lost daughter of King Leontes and in which Leontes is reunited after years of sorrowful separation with his dear friend Polixenes and his cherished counselor Camillo. The dramatist adopts this strategy in part not to upstage the climactic action in which the "statue" of Queen Hermione comes to life, but also as a way of conveying a sense of wonderment so inexpressibly moving that we as audience are asked to imagine rather than actually see what it must have been like. As a gentleman puts it, talking to one who was not present at the reunion, "Then have you lost a sight which was to be seen, cannot be spoken of" (5.2.43–44). The participants were themselves wordless in their joy: "There was speech in their dumbness, language in their gesture. They looked as they had heard of a world ransomed, or one destroyed" (14–16). As for the unfortunate Antigonus, pursued to his death by a bear after he had left the infant Perdita in the deserts of Bohemia, the gentleman narrator can only say that the matter is "Like an old tale still, which will have matter to rehearse though credit be asleep and not an ear open" (62–64). Then, having asked us to ponder the limits of theater and of language, Shakespeare shows us onstage the greatest miracle of all: the restoration to life of one whom we have supposed dead.

In order to bring off this *coup de théâtre*, Shakespeare does something he never does elsewhere: he assures us that Queen Hermione is dead and then keeps us in this ignorance until the final scene of her apparent coming to life. Her death seems not only undeniable but an integral part of what is so tragic about the play's first half. Leontes' irrational jealousy of his wife is so unshakable that he overrides the advice of all his counselors and presses forward with her judicial trial. Their only son, Mamillius, dies of anxious concern for his mother, and is indeed irrevocably gone. Upon hearing this terrible news, the King realizes that he has erred in not heeding the clear pronouncement of the oracle of Delphi that "Hermione is chaste, Polixenes blameless, Camillo a true subject, Leontes a jealous tyrant, his innocent babe truly begotten" (3.2.132–34). His remorse is too late; he learns that the news of Mamillius's death "is mortal to the Queen" (148). The terrible justice of this tragic event seems entirely appropriate to the insane wrath with which he has pursued Hermione.

Moreover, her spirit then appears to Antigonus in a dream, urging that unfortunate courtier to carry out his mission of abandoning Hermione's newborn infant to "some remote and desert place quite out / Of our dominions" (2.3.176–77). "And so, with shrieks, / She melted into air," reports Antigonus of this vision, adding that although he places little faith in dreams ordinarily, this one was so extraordinary that he feels he must obey the Queen's wish. "I do believe / Hermione hath suffered death," he declares, adding his utter conviction that Apollo himself wishes to have the child laid on the desert shore of Bohemia "Either for life or death" (3.3.35–44). The seeming certitude of Hermione's death is thus the turning point in the play; she is reportedly dead, but Apollo and his oracle are in control of the story that will eventually unfold. The oracle has specified that "the King shall live without an heir if that which is lost be not found" (3.2.134–36). This riddle, and the circumstance of the infant being placed on a desert shore in accordance with the wishes of the dead Queen, offer a potential for an eventual happy ending; but the Queen and her son, we are told, are dead.

The climactic event of Hermione's statue coming to life is suffused with a sense of theatrical magic. Paulina is the mistress of ceremonies, the stand-in here for the dramatist as controller of the action and deviser of stage illusion. She insists that she is not "assisted / By wicked powers" (5.3.90–91); her magic is lawful. Leontes gratefully agrees: "If this be magic, let it be an art / Lawful as eating" (110–11). Such a magic, Paulina insists, requires imaginative participation by its viewers: "It is required / You do awake your faith" (94–95). What she has accomplished, indeed, asks two contradictory interpretations. On a rational level, it appears that Paulina has sequestered the Queen for sixteen years in her own residence to give time for Leontes' remorse to do its painful but healing work and for the conditions of Apollo's oracle to be completed; before Hermione can be restored to her husband, that which is lost (i.e., Perdita, grown to womanhood) must be found. Yet this explanation seems improbable and inadequate as a complete answer. The restoration to life of Hermione is a miracle. It is so in the theater: the coming to life of the statue never fails to move audiences to tears of joy and sorrow. Yet audiences know that this magnificent staging effect is a theatrical contrivance. Audiences must awaken their faith, as Paulina asks of Leontes' courtiers. They must experience a "belief" in the power and veracity of theatrical illusion.

Along with Paulina as stage manager, the moving forces behind this miracle are said to be the gods themselves. "You gods, look down / And from your sacred vials pour your graces / Upon my daughter's head!" prays Hermione, in her first and only speech of awakening from seeming death (5.3.122–24). Apollo's oracle has been fulfilled. Paulina is Apollo's minister and agent; her theater magic serves that higher purpose. Time, as chorus figure, fulfills a similar function. His single appearance, as the play makes its transition from tragedy to romance, depicts Time as the controller of a theatrical event. "It is in my power," boasts Time, "To o'erthrow law and in one self-born hour / To plant and o'erwhelm custom" (4.1.7–9). That is to say, the theater itself has at its disposal the means to represent sixteen or more years in the passage of a single afternoon. When Time turns his hourglass, thereby marking the interval required for a theatrical performance, he can "give my scene such growing / As you had slept between" (16–17). As in *A Midsummer Night's Dream,* the experience of watching a play is compared with a dreaming sleep, both real and unreal, truthful and illusory. The gods who preside over this paradoxical experience are the gods of tragicomedy, ensuring that a play like *The Winter's Tale* will develop and unfold according to a plan in which individual humans become, both wittingly and unwittingly, the agents and ministers of that great theatrical truth.

The play's insistence on theater's privileged right to "o'erthrow law" and "o'erwhelm custom" did not sit well with the neoclassical tastes of the Restoration and eighteenth century. As a result, *The Winter's Tale* was extensively rewritten. Mcnamara Morgan's *The Sheep-Shearing, or Florizel and Perdita* (Covent Garden, 1754) eliminated the first half entirely. Heeding Ben Jonson's barbed criticism of Shakespeare for having provided Bohemia with a seacoast, this production adopted the suggestion of Shakespeare editor Thomas Hanmer that "Bohemia" be changed into "Bithynia," in northwest Asia Minor not far from modern-day Istanbul, where a coastline could be safely assumed. David Garrick followed suit at Drury Lane in 1756 by commencing the play's action after the "wide gap of time" separating the play's two halves and by locating all the action in Bithynia (later changed to "Bohemia").

Nineteenth-century productions, while restoring the text to something like its original scope, explored ways to give graphic and visual form to Shakespeare's theatrical fantasy. William Burton, at his Chambers Street Theater in New York in 1851, provided a cutout of Mount

Etna backstage as part of the scenic effect for Sicily, from which color-ful eruptions periodically issued forth in token of Leontes' fiery jealousy. Bohemia, contrastingly, featured a pastoral cottage swathed in flowers and vines, amid a landscape of streams, meadows, and distant moun-tains. To one awed spectator, the stage spectacle recalled Wordsworth's image of a heaven that "lies about us in our infancy." Charles Kean, at the Princess's Theatre in 1856, located the play's Sicilian action in ancient Syracuse (c. 300 BC), with an architectural splendor rivaling that of Athens itself. On display were the fountains of Arethusa, the temple of Minerva, and a banqueting hall in which the guests could recline as they watched thirty-six handsome young women dancing in warlike garb. Hermione's dungeon in act 2 was modeled on the infamous "Ear of Dionysius" where the tyrants of Syracuse were fabled to have tortured their prisoners. The interval between the play's two halves was taken up with an allegorical pageant of Time in which the chariot of the Moon sank into the ocean while that of Phoebus Apollo arose in a blaze of light. The *mise en scène* of the second half, located in the countryside of Bithynia with that country's capital, Nicaea, handsomely visible in the distance, made much of a Bacchic celebration of the sheepshearing by some three hundred or more cavorting satyrs. Such sets were of course hard to move, so that the text was cut and freely rearranged in order that the stage picture be allowed to give a full literalization of Shakespeare's imaginings.

In conscious rebellion against this stage tradition, and with the avowed purpose of recovering something like the original intent of Shakespeare's script, Harley Granville-Barker, at the Savoy Theatre in 1912, staged *The Winter's Tale* in nearly continuous action on a large apron stage extending out into the main floor of the theater. Peter Brook, in-defatigable iconoclast, extended Granville-Barker's idea in 1951, at the Phoenix Theatre, by using a permanent single set throughout in which to explore the psychological dimensions of the insane jealousy of Leontes (John Gielgud). Trevor Nunn's set, at Stratford-upon-Avon in 1969, was a three-sided white box in which, as one reviewer noted, "nothing is ever literally represented." The doubling of the roles of Hermione and Perdita by Judi Dench underscored the sense in which the production was aware of its own theatrical artifice. More thematic doubling occurred in 1976, in a version directed by Nunn and John Bar-ton: John Nettles was both Time and the famous bear. This animal has become a plaything of the modern theater, as in Terry Hands's produc-tion at Stratford-upon-Avon in 1986, where the huge bearskin rug of the play's first half, gracing the cool marble floor of a Regency-style palace, raised itself up to become the nemesis of Antigonus on the coast of Bohemia. Hermione's coming to life as a statue remains in today's theater what it appears to have been for Shakespeare: a demonstration of the power of the theatrical imagination.

IV

Among the many ways in which *The Tempest* (c. 1611) reads like a summation of Shakespeare's career as dramatist, none has more relevance to theater than the characterization of Prospero as master deviser and showman. The island of *The Tempest* is his stage. In its theatrical space he arranges his dramatis personae in accordance with his master plan, creating a storm to separate his characters into groups. Ferdinand lands on one part of the island, while his father Alonso and the members of his entourage land elsewhere. Prospero thus creates in them the illusion of loss: Ferdinand of his father, Alonso of his son. Ferdinand meets Miranda according to the script that Prospero has written for them. Stephano and Trinculo, a drunken butler and a jester in the Italian party, are shipwrecked in still another part of the island, where they encounter Caliban and plot the overthrow of Prospero; throughout this action, Ariel acts as Prospero's agent in overhearing and forestalling the conspiracy. Ariel similarly foils the scheme of Alonso's brother Sebastian and Prospero's brother Antonio to murder Alonso and seize control of the island. Meanwhile, Prospero (through Ariel) has stowed the Italians' ship and its crew safely in the harbor so that they will be able to journey back to Italy after the play is successfully concluded. Every action in *The Tempest* takes place under Prospero's watchful eye and as a result of his direction.

Like the Duke in *Measure for Measure,* Prospero devises various plots for his characters with a view to testing them. He offers temptations and deceives with deliberate misrepresentations in order to see how persons will react. Such controlling devices are heavily intrusive into the lives of the characters. Both Prospero and Duke Vincentio have taken a great deal of heat in recent criticism for being manipulative, authoritarian, and patriarchal; Prospero suffers the further reproach of being colonialist. All of these charges are accurate enough, but in making such accusations we must take care not to confuse theatrical art with real life. Prospero and Duke Vincentio do what dramatists do, moving characters around as on a chess board, devising stratagems and tests. To be a dramatist is to be manipulative, even arrogant, and insufferably all-wise. Prospero is impossibly bossy, but that is an inescapable component of his role as theater magician. Prospero is quite aware that he labors under a heavy burden of officious responsibility; it is one that he is anxious to lay aside once he has completed his tasks of chastisement, correction, and reform. He is more than ready to break his magic staff and drown the books from which he has learned his magical skills (5.1.54–57). He is even ready to bid farewell to Ariel, that eternal spirit of poetic inspiration that has enabled him as a mere mortal to perform godlike and daunting accomplishments.

As one who acts with an unseen power, testing the intents of various humans, Prospero functions like the power of conscience. Alonso, deliberately misled into believing that his son has drowned, is both grief-stricken and burdened with a terrible sense of guilt. He is forced to consider that his active involvement in the ousting of Prospero from the dukedom of Milan some twelve years ago is now being paid for by the death of his son (just as Leontes in *The Winter's Tale* blames himself for the death of his son Mamillius). As Ariel, in the guise of a harpy, declares, it is for this "foul deed" of supplanting Prospero from Milan that "The powers, delaying, not forgetting, have / Incensed the seas and shores," with the result that "Thee of thy son, Alonso, / They have bereft" (3.3.73–76). Alonso is wholly ready to acknowledge his terrible blameworthiness. The name of "Prospero" pronounced by Ariel, says Alonso, "did bass my trespass," that is, did proclaim the offense as loudly and as insistently as a bass note on an organ. "Therefor my son i'th'ooze is bedded" (100). Because he sees the drowning of his son as the just consequence of his own guilt, Alonso's only wish is to be joined with Ferdinand in death: "I'll seek him deeper than e'er plummet sounded, / And with him there lie mudded" (101–2). Yet since Ferdinand is not in fact dead, Alonso can be led through a health-giving remorse to a penitent reconciliation, much as Angelo in *Measure for Measure* can be forgiven because his intended acts of forceful seduction and murder have not taken place. Like the Duke of that play, Prospero acts as the spirit of tragicomedy, leading Alonso through the illusion of guilt while controlling the plot in such a way that the offense does not actually occur. The "ministers of Fate" (61) who have chastised Alonso in a terrifying vision are also part of this theatrical illusion, since the harpy is in fact Ariel.

Antonio and Sebastian must be dealt with more harshly by Prospero. Antonio is, after all, the younger brother of Prospero whose itch for power led not only to the ouster of Prospero from Milan but to the abandonment of Prospero and his infant daughter to what was supposed to have been a certain and agonizing death, in a rotten sea vessel lacking tackle, sail, and mast, and so unseaworthy that "the very rats / Instinctively have quit it" (1.2.147–48); only the ministrations of the kind Gonzalo supplied them with enough food to enable them to reach the island still alive. Accordingly, Prospero's devices for Antonio and Sebastian are aimed more at uncovering an ingrained iniquity than at reform. Again, the scenario is carefully scripted by Prospero and carried out by Ariel. Alonso, Gonzalo, and their followers are put into a sudden sleep in order to see what knavery Antonio and Sebastian will attempt. As if on cue, since Prospero as master dramatist knows what his characters will do, the two villains proceed to plot the murder of Alonso and the rest. The prospect seems irresistibly logical: Ferdinand can be assumed to have drowned, and then the next heir of Naples, his sister Claribel, is married to the King of Tunis and thus too distant from Italy to control events, so that the murder of Alonso will deliver Naples into the hands of Alonso's brother Sebastian, while Antonio will maintain and strengthen his hold on the dukedom that he has stolen from his brother Prospero. As for conscience, says Antonio, it is a mere figment of conventional morality and can be entirely ignored (2.1.277–82).

The only flaw in this astute conspiracy is the villains' assumption that they are unwatched and thus free to act as they choose. Ariel is not only there, invisible and listening; he has engineered the temptation according to Prospero's plan, and of course reports back to his master the predictable result. Ariel is "invisible" because he says so; we as audience see him onstage, walking among the sleeping figures and the would-be murderers. This theatrical effect augments our awareness of Ariel's manipulations as stage trickery to which we, as omniscient spectators, are made partners. We understand too that Antonio and Sebastian are the most incorrigible of the persons with whom Prospero has to deal and toward whom he is most justly angry. With Ariel's counseling he is able to forgive his enemies at last, but it is a forgiveness that does not erase Prospero's disapproval for what they have done. Their last speeches in the play suggest that they have learned little and that the threat they represent will not go away simply with the ending of the play.

The stratagem that Prospero devises to deal with Stephano, Trinculo, and Caliban is theatrically appropriate to a plot of lower-class buffoonish comedy. Theirs are the most amusing scenes of the play, especially when Ariel, again "invisible" to the clowns but entirely visible to us as spectators, mimics the voice of Trinculo in such a way as to mislead the drunken Stephano into thinking that Trinculo is calling him a liar (3.2.41–80). Once again, the invisibility has a thematic point to make: the clowns, in their plotting to overthrow Prospero, think they are unobserved and free to act as they wish but are in fact overseen by an invisible power. That power is godlike in its ability to know all and to forestall mischance by timely intervention. Yet it is not the power of the gods in any theological sense; instead, the power of conscience and control lies in Prospero and his agent. It is a theatrical power of shaping a plot, and thus represents the spirit of the play itself in creating complications and testings while ensuring that permanent harm will be avoided.

Prospero's ways of creating theatrical illusions for his daughter and prospective son-in-law are manifestly benign, since he loves both Miranda and Ferdinand and vests his own future happiness in their romantic union. Yet Prospero is just as manipulative and intrusive here as he is elsewhere. Indeed, he invents for himself the role of the stern and forbidding father. When Ferdinand attempts to draw his sword to resist the constraint that Prospero threatens to use, Ferdinand "*is charmed from moving*" (1.2.470). Miranda is truly alarmed; she has never seen her father so angry. Prospero proceeds to do as he has threatened, constraining Ferdinand to carry firewood and other menial tasks normally assigned to Caliban. At the same time, Prospero repeatedly confides to his theater audience that he is only playacting. He is delighted at the success of the match he has arranged, and yet he knows as a wise and experienced person that matters must not be allowed to proceed too quickly. "This swift business / I must uneasy make, lest too light winning / Make the prize light," he tells us (454–56). Because the young people might assume that they can proceed to sex without harmful consequences, since they are apparently all alone on a desert island with no social proprieties to worry about, Prospero will enact the role of conscience. Moreover, he knows as theater artist that a story of young lovers needs plot complication in the form of some opposition from parents and society; hence, Prospero will play the part of the disapproving father, like Egeus in *A Midsummer Night's Dream*. And lest we be misled by his anger into thinking him in earnest, he reassures us that all is going according to his plan. "It works," he says (498). "Fair encounter / Of two most rare affections! Heavens rain grace / On that which breeds between 'em!" (3.1.74–76). "My rejoicing / At nothing can be more" (3.1.94–95).

Prospero is thus like a god on his island, dispensing justice, correcting, nurturing. He is not a god, however. He is mortal, acutely aware in his advancing years that he must lay aside his art and prepare for death.

He is a theater artist, able to work his spells in the theatrical space that is his little kingdom but aware also that he has no control outside the bounds of his island. In mainland Naples, years ago, his artistic and intellectual proclivities proved his undoing as a political leader, for his studies so absorbed his attention that he allowed power to be gathered into the hands of his Machiavellian younger brother. Marooned on the island, he knows that he can exert temporary control over his Italian visitors only because "By accident most strange, bountiful Fortune, / Now my dear lady, hath mine enemies / Brought to this shore." The time at his disposal is limited: "I find my zenith doth depend upon / A most auspicious star, whose influence / If now I court not, but omit, my fortunes / Will ever after droop" (1.2.179–85). He is aware, further, that "Providence divine" had a role in his reaching the island safely with his infant daughter, even if that Providence took the form of a kindly old Gonzalo willing to supply their boat with food and other necessities (160–65). Thus Prospero knows that he is no god. Yet as theater artist he playacts a godlike role in the world of artifice given to him as his realm. The fallen world outside the island will continue to go its ways. Persons from that world will visit Prospero's island for a time, much as audiences come to the theater and then return to their daily lives. Those visitors will be moved to varying degrees by what they have seen and experienced in the artificial world presided over by the theater artist. Such is at once the potential and the limit of the artist's efforts to make some difference in the ways that people live.

The Tempest does bring gods onstage, as do As You Like It and The Two Noble Kinsmen (Hymen appears in both plays), Timon of Athens (Cupid), Pericles (Diana), and Cymbeline (Jupiter). These are the only divine epiphanies in all of Shakespeare's plays; we encounter plenty of ghosts, fairies, witches, and the like, and humans often pray to deities, but no other gods materialize in the usual sense of that term. Moreover, in all but one of these comparatively rare instances the gods are theatrically contrived. The Hymen who joins the happy festivities at the end of As You Like It to bless the various weddings is so puzzling an entity that some editions of the play label him as an actor playing Hymen. More accurately, the character can best be described as embodying the spirit of comedy whose function it is to "make conclusion / Of these most strange events" by joining the hands of various lovers in marriage (5.4.125–26). A similarly ambivalent Hymen appears in the first scene of The Two Noble Kinsmen, without being given any lines. Cupid in Timon of Athens is nothing more than one of the masquers providing Timon's feast with lavish entertainment (1.2.120–26). Jupiter in *Cymbeline,* as we have seen, is presented in such theatrically self-aware language and action as to suggest the embodiment of tragicomedy, delaying and then finally bestowing happiness on those mortals who have patiently submitted to destiny. Diana in *Pericles* may be a sole exception to this pattern: her brief single appearance to Pericles in a dream (5.1.243–52) could perhaps be interpreted as an illusion, but the dream is in fact a true one in that it does direct Pericles to a happy reunion with his wife at the play's end.

Certainly the gods of *The Tempest* are theatrically contrived. Iris, Ceres, and Juno, appearing in a masque to honor the forthcoming marriage of Ferdinand and Miranda, are enacted by Ariel and his fellow spirits at Prospero's behest. As Prospero says to Ariel, "I must / Bestow upon the eyes of this young couple / Some vanity of mine art" (4.1.39–41). Prospero carefully manages the entire performance. "Do not approach / Till thou dost hear me call," he warns Ariel. Then, at the appropriate moment, he orders, "Now come, my Ariel! Bring a corollary / Rather than want a spirit. Appear, and pertly!" (49–58). Prospero will tolerate no shortfalls in the company roster; the "corollary" he insists on is a surplus of actors to guarantee sufficiency. He is no less dictatorial in admonishing the onstage audience (and perhaps the theater audience as well) as to how to behave. "No tongue! All eyes! Be silent!" (59). No dramatist wants to have his play interrupted by inattentive auditors, and Prospero is plainly the author as well as stage manager of this masque. He knows what will come next at any given moment. He speaks of the show as a piece of magic: "Hush and be mute, / Or else our spell is marred," he cautions (126–27). The illusion is indeed compellingly persuasive. Ferdinand is so enraptured by the "majestic vision" that he needs to ask if the actors are spirits or indeed gods. Prospero assures him that they are "Spirits, which by mine art / I have from their confines called to enact / My present fancies" (118–22). Thus *The Tempest*'s most overtly magical moment, involving spells and spirits, is Prospero's metatheatrical play-within-the-play, demonstrating what the theater of stage imagination can achieve.

Prospero is the maker of the gods in *The Tempest,* much as Edgar in *King Lear* invents a mythology of gods and devils for his credulous and brokenhearted father. Providence may operate at an abstract distance, but within the purlieus of the island Prospero is indeed the embodiment of artistic and moral control. As such, he brings down the curtain on his own artistic career in a way that seems irresistibly relevant to Shakespeare's own impending retirement from the theater. Declaring that "Our revels now are ended," he notes that the actors he has employed "were all spirits and / Are melted into air, into thin air." The masque just witnessed, and by extension *The Tempest* itself, become an "insubstantial pageant faded," a "baseless fabric," a mere "vision" of "cloud-capped towers" and "gorgeous palaces" that must eventually dissolve, just as any theatrical performance must end and as the "great globe itself" will eventually disappear and "Leave not a rack behind." Both theater and life itself are like a dreaming sleep, as in *A Midsummer Night's Dream* and in old Time's chorus of *The Winter's Tale*. "We are such stuff / As dreams are made on, and our little life / Is rounded with a sleep," says Prospero (4.1.148–58). This visionary view of his art has stayed with Shakespeare from first to last.

Prospero is both proud of his achievement and abashed at his hubris in daring to play with character's lives in such theatrical fashion. Prospero has requisitioned the aid of airy spirits in devising his pageants. He has commanded the elements of sea and sky for his settings. He claims to have opened graves to bring forth persons of former times to enact his fantasies. All these bold achievements are the very things that dramatists like Shakespeare must do. They are also dangerous; indeed, Shakespeare invokes these wonders by borrowing from Ovid's representation of that formidable black magician, Medea. Small wonder, then, that Prospero is ready to "abjure" the "rough magic" of this so "potent art" by breaking his magic staff and drowning his book (5.1.33–57). What he must do instead, as an aging male and parent, is to learn to forgive his enemies, retire into the comfort of his daughter's family, and ponder his own mortality.

Prospero's last gesture, indeed, is to address the audience in an epilogue that is intensely self-aware of the speaker's theatrical setting and role. He begs his auditors to show their approval of his art by their applause, for he is now an ordinary mortal. As one who is indistinguishable from the dramatist who wrote the play, Prospero acknowledges that the spell of performance is broken. He no longer can command "Spirits to enforce, art to enchant." His fate is in the hands of his audience, for they are his patrons. They will determine whether his art will live or die.

The Tempest presents an interesting challenge for directors and actors because it does indeed call for spectacular effects and yet continually challenges us as audience to imagine what cannot be shown. The play begins with a storm: "*A tempestuous noise of thunder and lightning heard*" (fig. 8.3). The mariners enter and exit in a frenzied attempt to save their ship,

8.3. The frontispiece to Nicholas Rowe's 1709 edition of *The Tempest,* visualizing Alonso's ship caught in a furious storm, with Ariel and other spirits hovering overhead and Prospero directing the storm from a place ashore. Special Collections, Regenstein Library, University of Chicago.

while their aristocratic Italian passengers mill unhappily about, refusing the Boatswain's order that they "keep below." A short time later, "*Enter Mariners, wet.*" Surely, modern directors are justified in filling the theater with sailors hauling on ropes or climbing up into windswept rigging suspended from above, while sheets of real water cascade down from the flies to be collected and drained away in scuppers artfully concealed in the theater's deck.

Yet Shakespeare's script also calls for mimetic effects in which small gestures stand synecdotally for a grand design. In the original production, the sailors evidently poured water over their nautical costumes as they started onstage. The rest was evoked through gesture and speech. "Down with the topmast!" bawls the Boatswain. "Yare! Lower, lower!" The dialogue makes plain that the actors are on the main deck of a ship. "Keep your cabins!" the Boatswain orders his rebellious passengers. Stage directions like "*A cry within*" and "*A confused noise within*" are cues for actors and stagehands behind the scenes to howl "Mercy on us!" and "We split, we split!" Even the lightning of the opening stage direction is "*heard*" from within; lacking suitable means of setting off bright flashes of illumination, Shakespeare and his company created the effect of thunder and lightning by rolling cannon balls and agitating sheets of thin metal. Shakespeare's big storm at the Globe in 1611 or thereabouts took place in the full light of the afternoon in an open-roofed theater. (It was also performed at the royal court and presumably in the second Blackfriars Theatre, where similar staging effects were possible.)

From its earliest days as an enduringly popular staple in the Shakespeare canon, *The Tempest* has invited actors and directors to visualize the spectacle in ways that Shakespeare's theater could not achieve. Thomas Shadwell, in 1673, added to the popular adaptation by William Davenant and John Dryden (Lincoln's Inn Fields, 1667) by providing a number of new musical settings. As the overture played, a rising curtain discovered an arched frontispiece supported by Corinthian columns and festooned with roses, around which flew winged Cupids. The sky darkened as the storm began, revealing a coastline of menacing rocks and a wind-whipped sea in continual motion. When the ship began to sink, "the whole house" was darkened, while "a shower of fire" fell upon the actors. Presently the storm cleared away, leaving in its wake a beautiful island with three cypress-tree-lined walks. Ariel and Milcha (an added spirit), when they were not busy "flying away with a table furnished out with fruits, sweetmeats, and all sorts of viands," sang duets and danced a sarabande. Allegorical figures of Pride, Fraud, Rapine, and Murder took part in a masque of Furies. Another masque showed Neptune and Amphitrite rising "in a chariot drawn with sea-horses," attended by Tritons and Nereides. At the end, when Prospero set free Ariel and Milcha, they both flew up and crossed "in the air," soaring with other spirits from the rising sun toward the spectators and hovering in the air as the play's last lines were spoken. This production was often revived in the eighteenth century under the title *The Enchanted Island,* with music by Henry Purcell. David Garrick called his 1756 production at Drury Lane *The Tempest: An Opera, Taken from Shakespeare.*

The storm-tossed ship of scene I never ceased to fascinate the actor-managers of the late eighteenth and nineteenth centuries. John Philip Kemble, in 1789, began with the following stage picture: "The sea. A ship in a tempest. Spirits of the wind dancing. Chorus by spirits of the storm. The ship seems to founder. Ariel and all the other spirits disappear." William Charles Macready's 1842 revival at Covent Garden featured a huge sea vessel, fully rigged and manned, that was hurled about on an angry sea, "now rising so as to discover the keel and then dipping to the level of the stage, seeming to sink into the mimic waters," as a reviewer marvelingly wrote. A huge fireball struck the mast of another full-scale ship that was similarly tossed about by the opening storm in Samuel Phelps's production at the Sadler's Wells Theatre in 1847. A version at the Surrey Theatre in 1853 used dioramas and pictorial illustrations to convey the impression of a storm and shipwreck. In 1857 at the Princess's Theatre, as directed by Charles Kean, the stage deck actually tossed and pitched during the storm scene and appeared to founder with all on board. The final tableau in Herbert Beerbohm Tree's production at His Majesty's Theatre in 1904 was of Caliban standing on the shore of the island, reaching out "in mute despair" toward the ship as it sailed off into the distance toward Italy (see fig. 8.4). "Of all of Shakespeare's works," wrote Tree, "*The Tempest* is probably the one which most demands the aid of modern stagecraft." Nor has this spectacular tradition lost its appeal in today's theater, as seen for example in Robert Falls's production for the Chicago's Goodman Theatre in 1987, where the opening scene was of a modern-day cruise ship, with tourist passengers in deck chairs or playing shuffleboard until disaster struck.

Some modern directors, to be sure, have interrogated the need for images of a literalizing sort. Peter Greenaway's striking and often obsessive images in his film, *Prospero's Books* (1991), along with his seeing the

8.4. Herbert Beerbohm Tree as a hairy Caliban, in Tree's production of *The Tempest* at His Majesty's Theatre (1904), as painted by Charles A. Buchel. By permission of the Folger Shakespeare Library.

entire play as a figment of Prospero's imagination, is calculated to enforce the point that film and drama alike should be self-reflexive and multiple in perspective. Peter Brook explored the very nature of theater in his avant-garde *The Tempest* at London's Roundhouse Theatre in 1968, with an international cast of French, Japanese, English, and American actors in turtleneck sweaters and kimonos. Abandoning Shakespeare's text almost entirely, Brook unfolded a story in which Caliban, born violently from between the legs of an enormous Sycorax, took over the island with his wild followers and assaulted Prospero in a way suggestive of homosexual rape until Ariel engineered a rescue. At the end, having forgiven his enemies, Prospero joined the rest of the cast in reciting the epilogue, after which the audience was left with an empty, curtainless theatrical space.

Giorgio Strehler, in his long-running production of *The Tempest* (first shown at the Piccolo Theater, Milan, in 1978), created a bare theatrical space in which Ariel hung suspended over Prospero on a wire, gossamer and phantomlike, landing at times as though on his fingertip. Their contest for control became a metaphor for the relationship of director and actor. When at last Ariel was released, he stumbled on shaky legs through the audience and so out of the theater. As Prospero approached the audience to pronounce his epilogue, the simple set behind him suddenly disassembled, revealing the bare interior of the theater building. Yet when the audience applauded, the set reconstructed itself and Ariel returned to stand by Prospero's side. Strehler wrote of his memorable production: "we have felt the fallible, desperate, triumphant grandeur and responsibility of our profession."

Derek Jarman's 1979 film version is no less intentionally transgressive and postmodern. The young and romantic-looking Prospero (Heathcote Williams) of this film is a reclusive and brooding student of the occult, living in a medieval fortress of winding staircases and gloomy interiors. The storm scene turns out to be a figment of his restless imagination. His relation to Ariel (Karl Johnson) is sexually ambiguous and marked by a tug-of-war as to who can dominate the other. In Jarman's view, Ariel is "a projection of Prospero's mind" struggling "to free itself and escape." Miranda (Toyah Wilcox) is stridently contemporary in her adolescent rebelliousness and awakening sexual desire. Caliban (Jack Birkett, known as "The Incredible Orlando") is huge and ungainly, grimacing, drooling, gargoyle-like. Miranda seems annoyed but not frightened by his voyeuristic gazing at her. A flashback shows us this Caliban as a mammoth infant, nursing at the breast of his grotesquely naked mother, Sycorax, while a tied-up Ariel looks on. Trinculo is a drag queen whose capering elicits admiring whistles from the sailors. The goddess who blesses the marriage of Ferdinand and Miranda in the fourth-act masque turns out to be the African American singer Elisabeth Welch, doing a show-stopping blues rendition of "Stormy Weather." Through such compelling and disturbing images, Jarman takes aim at racial prejudice, homophobia, and every sort of reactionary social attitude. As is true also of *Pericles, Cymbeline,* and *The Winter's Tale,* Shakespeare's *The Tempest* shows its remarkable appeal to the imagination in the extraordinary range of interpretations it has inspired.

This Falls Out Better
Than I Could Devise

AN AFTERWORD

If, as seems likely, Shakespeare wrote *The Tempest* as his retirement piece in about 1611, at the age of forty-seven, he did not stop writing entirely. He seems to have collaborated with John Fletcher, his successor as chief dramatist for the King's Men, on *Henry VIII* in 1613 and *The Two Noble Kinsmen* in 1613–1614. *Henry VIII* was included by Shakespeare's colleagues and editors, John Heminges and Henry Condell, in the First Folio of 1623, whereas *The Two Noble Kinsmen* was not; perhaps the editors felt that *Henry VIII* was more dominantly his.

At all events, a brief look at *Henry VIII* can help bring our story to an end in two ways: its theatrical self-awareness can be used to epitomize and summarize Shakespeare's use of his theater space throughout his writing career, while at the same time it plentifully illustrates a trend toward the metatheatrical sophistication that is characteristic of his late work (and that we could find in *The Two Noble Kinsmen* as well). The collaboration with Fletcher is symptomatic, for it too points in the self-reflexive direction that the Jacobean London theater was already taking at the time of Shakespeare's retirement.

I

Henry VIII is an English history play adapted to the form of romance and tragicomedy. Its historical materials are of profound interest to an Elizabethan audience, for they tell of King Henry's divorce of Katharine of Aragon and his break with Rome in order that he might marry Anne Bullen (or Boleyn) and father a male heir. The early part of the play is dominated by a succession of tragic falls from power, as first the Duke of Buckingham, then Queen Katharine, and finally Cardinal Wolsey topple from their high state to misfortune. At the same time, another and still more momentous story is unfolding: the birth to Henry and Anne not of a son but of a daughter, Elizabeth, who is to become Elizabeth I. The actors in this mix of tragedy and romance are not aware of the part they are playing in England's future greatness. An all-seeing providence is at work in ways that most human beings, blindly caught up in their own parochial concerns, cannot fathom. As the Protestant Archbishop Cranmer prophesies in the closing moments of the play, speaking of the infant Elizabeth: "She shall be, to the happiness of England, / An agèd princess; many days shall see her, / And yet no day without a deed to crown it" (5.5.57–59). The King joins Cranmer in thanking their Maker (69) for an unforeseen miracle.

To accompany and orchestrate this saga of political struggle and mistaken intentions leading ultimately to reconciliation and forgiveness in a typically tragicomic pattern, *Henry VIII* exploits the Globe Theatre stage in a way that is typical of the late Shakespeare. (We know that the play was acted in the Globe because the building burned to the ground on June 29, 1613, during a performance, when the firing of cannon unintentionally set the thatched roof on fire.) Stately processions mark the entrances of Cardinal Wolsey, King Henry, Queen Katharine, and Buckingham. When the Cardinal puts on a lavish entertainment for honored guests, including the King and Anne Bullen, the stage must provide "*A small table under a state for the Cardinal; a longer table for the guests*" (1.4.0.1–2). The "*state*" is a richly canopied throne, elevated above its surroundings. Music sounds repeatedly. The guests are seated according to their rank. King Henry and others then enter "*as masquers, habited like shepherds*" (64.1–2). They "*pass directly before the Cardinal and gracefully salute him.*" Wolsey comes down from his chair of state, identifies one of the masquers as King Henry, and offers him obeisance. Henry dances with Anne Bullen and is captivated by her beauty, whereupon the history of England takes a radical change of course. The subsequent judicial inquiry into the legitimacy of the King's marriage to Katharine commences with an extraordinarily elaborate stage direction, calling for musicians, vergers (attendants to church dignitaries), scribes, bishops, gentlemen bearing the insignia of Wolsey's great office, noblemen, cardinals, and finally the King, who "*takes place under the cloth of state*"

(2.4.0.1–21). The coronation procession for Anne Bullen is, if anything, more elaborate still, with musicians, judges, the Lord Chancellor, and an array of great noblemen and ladies, "*passing over the stage in order and state*" (4.1.36.1–27). Queen Katharine's last moments on earth are celebrated by an elaborate vision of dancing figures in white robes and golden vizards, bearing branches of bay or laurel (4.2.82.1–17).

Perhaps the most inventive piece of staging is the sequence involving the attempt of Cranmer's Catholic enemies to arraign him for heresy. In the late years of his reign, King Henry has seemed to give Bishop Gardiner and others the scope they desire to halt the spread of Protestantism in England. Cranmer, as archbishop of Canterbury and an ardent reformer, is their chief target. Called before a meeting of the Privy Council to answer the charge of filling the whole realm "with new opinions, / Divers and dangerous, which are heresies / And, not reformed, may prove pernicious" (5.3.17–19), he comes onstage and approaches a door representing the entrance to the council chamber, where he is curtly informed that he must wait till called for. This business is observed by the King's physician, Doctor Butts, who is so alarmed at this "piece of malice" that he resolves to let the King know of it at once (5.2.8–10). He exits and then reenters with the King a few lines later "*at a window above*" (19.1). From this vantage he is able to show Henry how Cranmer is being demeaningly treated, obliged to wait at the door "'mongst pursuivants, / Pages, and footboys" (24–25). The King and Butts are to be imagined at some window that looks down into the antechamber where Cranmer attends his summons. The King quickly agrees with Butts that "there's knavery" afoot and orders his physician to "draw the curtain close. / We shall hear more anon" (33–35). The curtain is drawn at the window. Cranmer remains onstage below, waiting at the door.

The scene then shifts to the interior of the council chamber, but does so without a break in the staging. "*A council table brought in with chairs and stools, and placed under the state,*" reads the stage direction at what is conventionally marked as a new scene (5.3) though it is not so marked in the First Folio. The table and chairs are presumably brought on unobtrusively by stagehands, as in the earlier scene of Wolsey's lavish banquet. The council members file in and take their places. When the Duke of Norfolk asks the Keeper at the door "Who waits there?" the Keeper replies with a request for clarification: "Without, my noble lords?" That is, are you asking who is waiting outside the door? Assured that he understands the request aright, the Keeper replies that the person waiting is "My lord Archbishop" (5.3.4–5). Yet it appears that Cranmer is still onstage. The door at which he has been waiting is the same door to the council chamber, but it is now seen from the inside; we are in the council chamber itself. The stage has reversed outside to inside by this theatrical sleight of hand, much as it does repeatedly in *Romeo and Juliet* when Romeo and his friends enter from the street to the Capulets' feast and when Juliet descends from her room "*above*" to act out the scene of confrontation with her parents on the main stage. When the Keeper informs Cranmer that "Your Grace may enter now," the stage direction reads, "*Cranmer approaches the council table*" (7.1). He is not directed to "*enter,*" since he is already onstage. The inquisition that follows is severe and deeply threatening to Cranmer, but at length he shows them a ring that the King has given him as a token of royal protection. The King himself enters "*frowning on them*" and "*takes his seat,*" and Cranmer is saved. So is the English Reformation, and with it the future of England under the newborn Elizabeth.

The staging thus pictorializes, in the theater, the way in which Providence works its will through human agency. The plotters against Cranmer think they are unobserved and may do as they wish, much like Angelo in *Measure for Measure* or like Antonio, Sebastian, Trinculo, and Stephano in *The Tempest*. Yet Gardiner and his associates are truly being observed. The King is there, "invisible" by means of a curtained window, looking down at his subjects and intervening when necessary to make sure that the story of England will end happily as the form of tragicomic romance requires. Henry is thus, for all his quirkish ways, a figure of dramatic control, not unlike Helena in *All's Well That Ends Well,* the Duke in *Measure for Measure,* Jupiter in *Cymbeline,* Paulina and old Father Time in *The Winter's Tale,* and Prospero in *The Tempest.* Indeed, Henry's very slowness to act, in his complacent allowing of Wolsey's earlier maneuvers aimed at Queen Katharine, serves the purposes of tragicomic romance by delaying the happy providential ending. Quirkishness and ambiguity are vital components in all these figures of dramatic control, since the working out of human destiny will accordingly be unpredictable and wondrous. Hamlet understands the architectonic beauty of this view of human life and of dramatic construction when he observes that "There's a divinity that shapes our ends, / Rough-hew them how we will" (*Hamlet,* 5.2.10–11). Macbeth acknowledges a similar truth when he sees in his own catastrophic failure the story of "a poor player / That struts and frets his hour upon the stage / And then is heard no more" (*Macbeth,* 5.5.24–26).

Staging traditions of *Henry VIII* have generally been true to the spirit

9.1. The scene of Queen Katharine's trial (2.4) in Herbert Beerbohm Tree's 1910 production of *Henry VIII* at His Majesty's Theatre. V&A Images/Victoria and Albert Museum.

of the text, chiefly perhaps because the solemnly public nature of the script is perfectly receptive to grand effects in the theater or on screen. *Henry VIII* enjoyed a steady popularity in the Restoration period and long afterward; Samuel Pepys in 1668 professed to be "mightily pleased with the history and shows of it." Barton Booth played the role of King Henry in 1727 in a spectacular production mounted to celebrate the coronation of King George II. William Charles Macready revived the play in a command performance for Queen Victoria and Prince Albert at Drury Lane in 1848. More than a century later, the Old Vic revived *Henry VIII* in honor of the coronation of Queen Elizabeth II in 1953. Henry Irving lavished unprecedented expense on his production at London's Lyceum Theatre in 1892, with an elegant banquet for the meeting of Henry and Anne Bullen at Wolsey's Hampton Court, a beautifully detailed set of "the King's Stairs, Westminster" for the scene in which Buckingham is led to his execution, a magnificent "hall of Blackfriars" in which an enthroned Henry heard the case against Queen Katharine, "a street in Westminster" done up in Tudor three-storied wooden-beamed houses for the coronation of Anne, and a church interior with stained-glass windows and timeworn stairs for the play's finale. This was a big play for the nineteenth century: it had opera-sized roles for the leading participants, and it invited splendor (fig. 9.1).

II

Many of Shakespeare's plays, as we have seen, center on a dramatist-figure who moves the plot forward, manages the lives of the other characters, and shapes the design of the story: Puck and Oberon in *A Midsummer Night's Dream* ("This falls out better than I could devise," says Puck, 3.2.35), Helena in *All's Well That Ends Well,* the Duke in *Measure for Measure,* Richard III in the play named for him, Iago in *Othello,* Edmund and Edgar in *King Lear,* Cleopatra in the final act of *Antony and Cleopatra,* Jupiter in *Cymbeline,* Paulina in *The Winter's Tale,* and Prospero in *The Tempest,* among others. Some plays depict an anarchic world of internecine warfare where no one is in charge, as in *Troilus and Cressida,* the *Henry VI* plays, *Julius Caesar,* and *Coriolanus,* where civil conflict moves forward in its relentless and dispiriting course. Still another option is to see a providential force at work of whose mysterious operations the human characters are only dimly and belatedly aware. What these patterns have in common is that they provide a structural scheme for each play as a whole.

These patterns invite us to see each play in its theatrical environment, where we as audience must follow the dramatist's lead in imagining the scene in its fullest dimension. The theatrical experience is dreamlike in that it is "unreal" and yet more vitally true than the ordinariness of our own lives. We enter the magical world created by the dramatist and his actors, be it the island of *The Tempest* or the forests of *As You Like It* and *A Midsummer Night's Dream,* and we are somehow transformed, even though the daily lives to which we return go on as before. Throughout, we have encountered dramatic characters who are intensely aware of their theatrical existence, and who act out the parts assigned them in ways that are shaped for them by the theatrical world to which they belong and where they eternally dwell.

Further Reading

The following reading suggestions aim at two purposes: to indicate where one can find further information on the topics taken up in the various chapters of this book, and to acknowledge, in the absence of formal footnotes, my indebtednesses to critics and scholars. That indebtedness is indeed extensive; it represents, in part, a lifetime of reading and teaching. The first section lists books and articles that are applicable to many parts of this present book; other items are listed by chapters.

Throughout this book, act-scene-and-line references to the plays of Shakespeare are to David Bevington, ed., *The Complete Works of Shakespeare,* 5th ed. (New York: Pearson Longman, 2003). The line numberings may differ from those of other editions owing chiefly to different column widths in the printing of prose and to differing editorial views of where line breaks occur in verse, but generally one ought to be able to find a particular passage close to where it is cited in this book.

Of General Interest:

Beckerman, Bernard. *Shakespeare at the Globe, 1599–1609.* New York: Macmillan, 1962.

Bevington, David. *Action Is Eloquence: Shakespeare's Language of Gesture.* Cambridge, MA: Harvard University Press, 1984.

Bulman, J. C., and H. R. Coursen, eds. *Shakespeare on Television.* Hanover, NH: University Press of New England, 1988.

Dessen, Alan C. *Recovering Shakespeare's Theatrical Vocabulary.* Cambridge: Cambridge University Press, 1995.

Gurr, Andrew. *Playgoing in Shakespeare's London.* 2nd ed. Cambridge: Cambridge University Press, 1996.

———. *The Shakespearean Playing Companies.* Oxford: Oxford University Press, 1996.

——. *The Shakespearean Stage, 1574–1642.* 2nd ed. Cambridge: Cambridge University Press, 1980.

Hodges, C. Walter. *The Globe Restored.* 2nd ed. New York: Coward-McCann, 1968.

Linthicum, Marie C. *Costume in the Drama of Shakespeare and His Contemporaries.* Oxford: Oxford University Press, 1936.

Odell, George C. D. *Shakespeare from Betterton to Irving.* 2 vols. New York: C. Scribner's, 1920.

Rosenthal, Daniel. *Shakespeare on Screen.* London: Hamlyn, 2000.

Rothwell, Kenneth S. *A History of Shakespeare on Screen: A Century of Film and Television.* Cambridge: Cambridge University Press, 1999.

Rothwell, Kenneth S., and Annabelle Henkin Melzer. *Shakespeare on Screen: An International Filmography and Videography.* New York: Neal-Schuman, 1990.

Rutter, Carol, et al. *Clamorous Voices: Shakespeare's Women Today.* New York: Routledge, 1989.

See also the new critical editions of individual plays in The Arden Shakespeare, 3rd series, the New Cambridge Shakespeares, the new Oxford Shakespeares, and the new Pelican Shakespeares.

Chapter 1: Actions That a Man Might Play: An Introduction

See the list *Of General Interest,* above.

Chapter 2: There Lies the Scene: Actors and Theaters in Late Elizabethan England

See, in the list *Of General Interest* above, works by Bernard Beckerman, Alan Dessen, Andrew Gurr, C. Walter Hodges, and Marie Linthicum.
Also:

Chambers, E. K. *The Elizabethan Stage.* 4 vols. Oxford: Clarendon Press, 1923; rev. 1945.

——. *William Shakespeare: A Study of Facts and Problems.* 2 vols. Oxford: Clarendon Press, 1930.

Foakes, R. A., and R. T. Rickert, eds. *Henslowe's Diary.* Cambridge: Cambridge University Press, 1961.

McMillin, Scott, and Sally-Beth Maclean. *The Queen's Men and Their Plays.* Cambridge: Cambridge University Press, 1998.

Chapter 3: A Local Habitation and a Name: Stage Business in the Comedies

Barber, C. L. *Shakespeare's Festive Comedy.* Princeton: Princeton University Press, 1959.

Hunter, Robert Grams. *Shakespeare and the Comedy of Forgiveness.* New York: Columbia University Press, 1965.

Frye, Northrop. "The Argument of Comedy." *English Institute Essays 1948.* New York: Columbia University Press, 1949.

Kahn, Coppélia. *Man's Estate: Masculine Identity in Shakespeare.* Berkeley: University of California Press, 1981.

Hattaway, Michael, ed. *As You Like It,* The New Cambridge Shakespeare. Cambridge: Cambridge University Press, 2000.

Leggatt, Alexander. *Shakespeare's Comedy of Love.* London: Methuen, 1974.

Potter, Lois. *Twelfth Night.* Text and Performance. London: Humanities Press International, 1985.

Rose, Mary Beth. *The Expense of Spirit: Love and Sexuality in English Renaissance Drama.* Ithaca: Cornell University Press, 1988.

Thompson, Ann, ed. *The Taming of the Shrew.* The New Cambridge Shakespeare. Cambridge: Cambridge University Press, 1984.

Young, David P. *Something of Great Constancy: The Art of "A Midsummer Night's Dream."* New Haven: Yale University Press, 1966.

Chapter 4: Thus Play I in One Person Many People: Performing the Histories

Calderwood, James L. *Metadrama in Shakespeare's Henriad: "Richard II" to "Henry V."* Berkeley: University of California Press, 1979.

Colley, Scott. *"Richard's Himself Again": A Stage History of "Richard III."* New York: Greenwood, 1992.

Craik, T. W., ed. *King Henry V.* The Arden Shakespeare, 3rd ser. London: Routledge, 1995.

Bevington, David. *Action Is Eloquence: Shakespeare's Language of Gesture.* Cambridge, MA: Harvard University Press, 1984.

Edelman, Charles. *Brawl Ridiculous: Swordfighting in Shakespeare's Plays.* Manchester: Manchester University Press, 1992.

Hodgdon, Barbara. *The End Crowns All: Closure and Contradiction in Shakespeare's History.* Princeton: Princeton University Press, 1991.

Howard, Jean E., and Phyllis Rackin. *Engendering a Nation: A Feminist Account of Shakespeare's English Histories.* London: Routledge, 1997.

Kastan, David Scott. *Shakespeare and the Shapes of Time.* Hanover, NH: University Press of New England, 1982.

———, ed. *King Henry IV, Part I.* The Arden Shakespeare, 3rd ser. London: Thompson Learning, 2002.

McMillin, Scott. *Shakespeare in Performance: "Henry IV, Part One."* Manchester: Manchester University Press, 1991.

Rackin, Phyllis. *Stages of History: Shakespeare's English Chronicles.* Ithaca, NY: Cornell University Press, 1990.

Watson, Robert N. *Shakespeare and the Hazards of Ambition.* Cambridge, MA: Harvard University Press, 1984.

Chapter 5: *Like a Strutting Player: Staging Moral Ambiguity in* Measure for Measure *and* Troilus and Cressida

Bevington, David, ed. *Troilus and Cressida.* The Arden Shakespeare, 3rd ser. Walton-on-Thames: Thomas Nelson, 1998.

Kirsch, Arthur. *Shakespeare and the Experience of Love.* Cambridge: Cambridge University Press, 1981.

Rutter, Carol Chillington. "Shakespeare, His Designers, and the Politics of Costume: Handing Over Cressida's Glove." *Essays in Theatre/Études théâtrales* 12 (1993–1994): 107–28.

Taylor, Gary. *Reinventing Shakespeare: A Cultural History, from the Restoration to the Present.* New York: Weidenfeld and Nicolson, 1989.

Wheeler, Richard P. *Shakespeare's Development and the Problem Comedies: Turn and Counter-Turn.* Berkeley: University of California Press, 1981.

Chapter 6: *The Motive and the Cue for Passion:* Romeo and Juliet, Hamlet, *and* Othello *in Performance*

See, in the list "Of General Interest" above, the work by David Bevington. Also:

Bednarz, James P. *Shakespeare and the Poets' War.* New York: Columbia University Press, 2001.

Bradley, A. C. *Shakespearean Tragedy.* London: Macmillan, 1904.

Charney, Maurice. *Style in "Hamlet."* Princeton: Princeton University Press, 1969.

Danson, Lawrence. *Tragic Alphabet: Shakespeare's Drama of Language.* New Haven: Yale University Press, 1974.

Dickey, Franklin. *Not Wisely But Too Well: Shakespeare's Love Tragedies.* San Marino, CA: Huntington Library Publications, 1957.

Ferguson, Frances. *The Idea of a Theater.* Princeton: Princeton University Press, 1949.

Goldman, Michael. *Acting and Action in Shakespearean Tragedy.* Princeton: Princeton University Press, 1985.

Halio, Jay. *"Romeo and Juliet": Texts, Contexts, and Interpretation.* Newark: University of Delaware Press, 1995.

Hankey, Julie. *Plays in Performance: "Othello."* Bristol: Bristol Classical Press, 1987.

Honigmann, E. A. J., ed. *Othello.* The Arden Shakespeare, 3rd ser. Walton-on-Thames: Thomas Nelson, 1997.

Jenkins, Harold, ed. *Hamlet.* The Arden Shakespeare, 2nd ser. London: Methuen, 1982.

Mack, Maynard. "The World of *Hamlet.*" *Yale Review* 41 (1952): 502–23.

Rose, Mark. "*Hamlet* and the Shape of Revenge." *English Literary Renaissance* 1 (1971): 132–43.

Rosenberg, Marvin. *The Masks of "Hamlet."* Newark: University of Delaware Press, 1992.

———. *The Masks of "Othello."* Berkeley: University of California Press, 1961.

Spivack, Bernard. *Shakespeare and the Allegory of Evil.* New York: Columbia University Press, 1958.

Chapter 7: *A Poor Player That Struts and Frets His Hour upon the Stage: Role-playing in* King Lear, Macbeth, *and* Antony and Cleopatra

Bevington, David, ed. *Antony and Cleopatra.* The New Cambridge Shakespeare. 2nd ed. Cambridge: Cambridge University Press, 2004.

Bradley, A. C. *Shakespearean Tragedy.* London: Macmillan, 1904.

Braunmuller, A. R., ed. *Macbeth.* The New Cambridge Shakespeare. Cambridge: Cambridge University Press, 1997.

Calderwood, James L. *If It Were Done: "Macbeth" and Tragic Action.* Amherst: University of Massachusetts Press, 1986.

Cavell, Stanley. *Disowning Knowledge in Six Plays of Shakespeare.* Cambridge: Cambridge University Press, 1987.

Colie, Rosalie L., and F. T. Flahiff, eds. *Some Facets of "King Lear."* Toronto: University of Toronto Press, 1974.

Elton, William R. *King Lear and the Gods.* San Marino, CA: Huntington Library, 1966.

Foakes, R. A. *"Hamlet" Versus "Lear": Cultural Politics and Shakespeare's Art.* Cambridge: Cambridge University Press, 1993.

———, ed. *King Lear.* The Arden Shakespeare, 3rd ser. Walton-on-Thames: Thomas Nelson, 1997.

Kirsch, Arthur. *The Passions of Shakespeare's Tragic Heroes.* Charlottesville: University Press of Virginia, 1990.

Kliman, Bernice. *Macbeth.* Shakespeare in Performance. Manchester: Manchester University Press, 1992.

Kott, Jan. *Shakespeare Our Contemporary.* Trans. Boreslaw Taborski. New York: Doubleday, 1964.

Lamb, Margaret. *"Antony and Cleopatra" on the English Stage.* Rutherford, NJ: Farleigh Dickinson University Press, 1980.

Leggatt, Alexander. *King Lear.* Shakespeare in Performance. Manchester: Manchester University Press, 1991.

Levine, Laura. *Men in Women's Clothing: Anti-Theatricality and Effeminization, 1579–1642.* Cambridge: Cambridge University Press, 1994.

Mack, Maynard. *King Lear in Our Time.* Berkeley: University of California Press, 1965.

Madelaine, Richard, ed. *Antony and Cleopatra.* Shakespeare in Production. Cambridge: Cambridge University Press, 1998.

Matchett, William H. "Some Dramatic Techniques in *King Lear.*" In *Shakespeare: The Theatrical Dimension,* ed. David A. Samuelson, 185–208. New York: AMS, 1959.

Rabkin, Norman. *Shakespeare and the Common Understanding.* Chicago: University of Chicago Press, 1984.

Rosenberg, Marvin. *The Masks of "King Lear."* Berkeley: University of California Press, 1972.

Scott, Michael. *Antony and Cleopatra.* Text and Performance. London: Humanities Press International, 1983.

Spivack, Bernard. *Shakespeare and the Allegory of Evil.* New York: Columbia University Press, 1958.

Chapter 8: Insubstantial Pageant: Shakespeare's Farewell to the Stage

Bartholomeusz, Dennis. *"The Winter's Tale" in Performance in England and America, 1611–1976.* Cambridge: Cambridge University Press, 1982.

Bishop, T. G. *Shakespeare and the Theatre of Wonder.* Cambridge: Cambridge University Press, 1996.

Draper, R. P. *The Winter's Tale.* Text and Performance. London: Macmillan, 1985.

Kernan, Alvin B. *The Playwright as Magician: Shakespeare's Image of the Poet in the English Theater.* New Haven: Yale University Press, 1979.

Kirsch, Arthur. "*Cymbeline* and Coterie Dramaturgy." *ELH* 34 (1967): 285–306.

Matchett, William. "Some Dramatic Techniques in *The Winter's Tale.*" *Shakespeare Survey* 22 (1969): 93–107.

Mowat, Barbara. *The Dramaturgy of Shakespeare's Romances.* Athens: University of Georgia Press, 1976.

Vaughan, Virginia Mason, and Alden T. Vaughan, eds. *The Tempest.* The Arden Shakespeare, 3rd ser. Walton-on-Thames: Thomas Nelson, 1999.

William, David. "*The Tempest* on the Stage." In *Jacobean Theatre,* ed. John Russell Brown and Bernard Harris, 133–57. Stratford-upon-Avon Studies 1. London: Edward Arnold, 1960.

Chapter 9: This Falls Out Better Than I Could Devise: An Afterword

Berry, Edward I. "*Henry VIII* and the Dynamics of Spectacle." *Shakespeare Studies* 12 (1979): 229–46.

Index